MEXICO AND THE SPANISH CONQUEST

MODERN WARS IN PERSPECTIVE
General Editors: *H.M. Scott and B.W. Collins*

ALREADY PUBLISHED

Mexico and the Spanish Conquest
Ross Hassig

MEXICO AND THE SPANISH CONQUEST

ROSS HASSIG

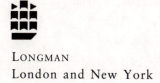

LONGMAN
London and New York

Longman Group UK Limited
Longman House, Burnt Mill,
Harlow, Essex CM20 2JE, England
and Associated Companies throughout the world

Published in the United States of America
by Longman Publishing, New York

First published 1994

ISBN 0 582 06828 2 CSD
ISBN 0 582 06829 0 PPR

British Library Cataloguing-in-Publication Data
A catalogue record for this book is
available from the British Library

Library of Congress Cataloging in Publication Data
Hassig, Ross, 1945–
    Mexico and the Spanish conquest / Ross Hassig.
        p. cm. -- (Wars in context)
    Includes bibliographical references and index.
    ISBN 0–582–06828–2. -- ISBN 0–582–06829–0 (pbk.)
    1. Mexico--History--Conquest, 1519–1540. I. Title. II. Series.
F1230.H37 1993
972'.02--dc20   92-46022
                                                                  CIP

Set by 7BB in 10/12 pt Sabon Roman

Produced by Longman Singapore Publishers (Pte) Ltd.
Printed in Singapore

CONTENTS

LIST OF MAPS

ACKNOWLEDGEMENTS

I have been helped by many people in writing this book but I owe particular thanks to Professors J. Richard Andrews of Vanderbilt University, Claudio Lomnitz of New York University and Samuel M. Wilson of the University of Texas for their invaluable assistance. I am also greatly indebted to my wife, Debra Hassig, for reading and commenting on the entire manuscript. This work was funded by a grant from the Harry Frank Guggenheim Foundation, whose support was invaluable to the completion of this book.

NAHUATL PRONUNCIATION GUIDE

I have generally followed the standardized Nahuatl orthography in J. Richard Andrews's *Introduction to Classical Nahuatl*, with the exception of not marking vowel length or showing glottal stops, as these would unduly burden the general reader. I have minimized the number of Nahuatl personal names mentioned and all have been standardized but the honorific *-tzin* has been omitted. This would typically, although not invariably, have been added to the names of kings and nobles, but it also obscures them so I have omitted it for the sake of clarity.

PRONUNCIATION GUIDE

Letter	Pronunciation
c + a/o	as in *can*
qu + e/i	like *k* in *kit*
c + e/i	as in *cease*
z + a/o	like *s* in *sod*
ch	as in *church*
chu	like *ckw* in *backward*
cu/uc	like *qu* in *quick*
hu	like *w* in *wake*
uh	like *wh* in *wheel*
tl	similar to *tl* in *settler*, but a single sound
tz	like *ts* in *hats*
x	like *sh* in *ship*

All other letters are pronounced with standard Latin values. Except in the rare case of the vocative noun-final *é*, meaning 'oh' (which does not occur in this book), Nahuatl words do *not* have accent marks as the penultimate syllable is stressed.

The names of gods are also standardized, as are those of towns because the names of their inhabitants derive from these. Thus, a person from Tlaxcallan is a Tlaxcaltecatl (singular) and more are

Tlaxcalteca (plural), which I have Anglicized to Tlaxcaltec and Tlaxcaltecs. However, I have chosen to refer to Moteuczoma's subjects as Aztecs, rather than Mexica, in keeping with common usage. Similarly, a person from Tetzcoco or Chalco is a Tetzcoca or a Chalca (from Tetzcocatl and Tetzcoca or Chalcatl and Chalca), pluralized by adding an s. This approach also permits the singular form to serve as an adjective: 'Tetzcoca town', 'Chalca town'. I have used standardized names for towns, such as Ixtlapalapan, but have used the modern terms for geographical areas, such as the Ixtapalapa peninsula where the ancient town was located. Similarly, I have used early spellings for places with Spanish names, such as Vera Cruz, reserving Veracruz for the modern state.

To make the book as accessible as possible, where English-language translations of the Spanish documents are available, I have included parallel citations. Not all have English translations, or readily accessible ones, so some materials are necessarily cited only in the original Spanish. Moreover, because of the focus of my analysis, many recorded incidents of the Conquest will be omitted: some are details, others are errors, and still others are contradicted in the sources themselves, but most are extraneous to the main thrust of this analysis. I invite readers to consult the original accounts for some fascinating details of this adventure, although I also warn against accepting any one source at face value.

For my brother, Logan, who has supported my work
for many years and in many ways

INTRODUCTION

I doubt that there is a more trodden trail than that of Cortés. The conquest of Mexico has captured the interest of historians for centuries and the expedition has been subjected to relentless investigation. However, there are only a limited number of first-hand accounts by Spanish participants in the Conquest – Cortés, Díaz del Castillo, Aguilar, Tápia and the Anonymous Conquistador* – supplemented by various shorter claims and legal testimony. There are also a number of histories written by non-participants such as Peter Martyr and López de Gómara, who had access to conquistadors. Indian accounts were written decades after the Conquest but throw light on those events that are often otherwise unreflected in the Spanish histories.

Unfortunately, these accounts frequently conflict even in such apparently objective facts as numbers, dates and sequence of events and I have found no satisfactory way to reconcile them. Moreover, they were all written for political purposes – to justify actions, to gain political and religious legitimacy, and to seek favours – and all are patently self-serving. Nevertheless, I draw on all the first-hand accounts and many second-hand ones, but I emphasize the former and, at least for numbers and event sequences, I have put somewhat greater trust in Cortés's account simply because he wrote it closer to the time of the events described and is probably more trustworthy, at least as to these more mechanical aspects. Nevertheless, I see no convincing basis for choice in many cases other than general preference for one author over another. Consequently, I am not focusing on disputed events, at least where the specifics are not pivotal to the interpretation. For instance, in a major battle, an attack by two thousand Indians is as plausible as one by five thousand, and though the fact of the battle is important, the exact number of participants is less so. I have left the debate over such matters to others, focusing instead on what I consider to be the

---

* For brief sketches of the participants see pp. 161–5

1

major elements of the Conquest, about which there is considerable agreement among the sources.

The divergences between the various accounts permit enough latitude to reconstruct the conquest of Mexico in many different versions. Most histories of the Conquest are taken largely at face value from the Spanish records.[1] Even those that give the Aztecs a voice depart little from the general script in terms of new analyses.[2] The reasons given for the defeat of the Aztec empire include the Aztec belief that the Spaniards were returning gods,[3] the psychological and ideological collapse of the Aztecs,[4] Cortés's and the Spaniards' personal characteristics,[5] the Spaniards' cultural, religious or psychological superiority,[6] the Indians' poor or misguided war-making ability,[7] the Spaniards' superior weapons and tactics,[8] flaws in the Aztec political system,[9] the impact of smallpox,[10] and the Spaniards' superior grasp of the symbolic system.[11]

Often, these various explanations are posited because only by such non-material factors can the seemingly astonishing defeat of the Aztecs be explained. But believing in this apparently miraculous feat depends on accepting the Spaniards' account of it. Once an Indian view of events is presented, the Spaniards' role is less impressive and the campaign's outcome is more understandable. The relative

1 For example, see the works of Brundage 1972:252–90; Collis 1972; Davies 1974:233–83; Gibson 1966:24–8; Innes 1969; Johnson 1987; Kirkpatrick 1967:66–100; McHenry 1962:35–46; MacLachlan and Rodríguez 1980:68–76; Madariaga 1969; Merriman 1962, 3:458–502; Miller 1985:66–93; Moreno Toscano 1981; Parkes 1969:39–58; White 1971:159–262.

2 E.g. Leon-Portilla 1966; Sahagún 1975; 1978.

3 Brundage 1972:252; Collis 1972:55–60; Davies 1974:239, 258–60; Elliott 1984:181; Innes 1969:116; Kirkpatrick 1967:71–2; Leon-Portilla 1966:13; McHenry 1962:35, 40, 41; MacLachlan and Rodríguez 1980:69; Madariaga 1969:16, 118–19; Merriman 1962, 3:475, 478; Miller 1985:78; Moreno Toscano 1981:313; Padden 1967:118, 122–5; Parkes 1969:50; Todorov 1984:118–19.

4 Carrasco 1982:150–1, 200–3; Elliott 1984a:181–2; MacLachlan and Rodríguez 1980:72; Padden 1967:205–7; Vaillant 1966:238.

5 Elliott 1984a:175; Madariaga 1969:185–6; Merriman 1962, 3:479; Vaillant 1966:238.

6 Davies 1974:252; Elliott 1966:65; 1984a:175, 180; Parry 1970:85.

7 Davies 1974:251; Madariaga 1969:177; Merriman 1962, 3:478.

8 Collis 1972:91; Davies 1974:250–1; Elliott 1966:65; 1984a:175; Gardiner 1959; Kirkpatrick 1967:67; MacLachlan and Rodríguez 1980:70; Merriman 1962, 3:478; Padden 1967:156; Todorov 1984:61; Vaillant 1966:238–9; White 1971:169, 171; Wolf 1970:154.

9 Elliott 1984a:183; Wolf 1970:154–5.

10 Baxby 1981:13; Elliott 1984a:182; Hopkins 1983:205–6; Innes 1969:179; McNeill 1977:183; Padden 1967:206; Todorov 1984:61.

11 Todorov 1984:118–19.

importance of the factors suggested as pivotal depends on how the authors saw them. Many were not as important as most writers made them out to be, as will be seen from the discussion of various causal elements in the body of this text. But most importantly, the various forms of psychological and ideological explanations offered by modern authors do not fare well when examined against the actual events of the Conquest. The Aztecs of Tenochtitlan fought to the end – bitterly, effectively and valiantly. Conquest accounts show no sign of the various forms of ideological or psychological undermining to which the Aztec defeat is often attributed. Instead, by focusing on the military and political aspects, including such mundane yet crucial issues as logistics and march rates, I hope to present a fuller and more accurate interpretation of these events.

Most past interpretations have explicitly or implicitly accepted Spanish accounts of the events of the Conquest, largely as an artifact of the data available. But accepting a Spanish-centred interpretation assumes that Cortés must have fully understood native politics and manipulated them unerringly, which is highly unlikely. In fact, virtually everything that had to be 'manipulated' was firmly in Indian control. The Indians already understood their political system and the personalities involved and it is much likelier that they – not the Spaniards – were the primary manipulators of Conquest events. Only Cortés's perfidy at the end undercut Indian goals, and this may well have been part of his plan as he was doubtlessly seeing the end game and going along with Indian manipulation, and it *was* Indian manipulation because only they knew their political system so well and could act on it effectively. That is, it is much likelier that the Indians understood how the Spaniards could be exploited than that Cortés saw how he could use the Indians in a political system he clearly did not understand. An Indian-centred analysis does not support the notion that the Aztecs were defeated through a series of fortunate events for the Spaniards, as a Spanish-centred analysis demands. Rather, it makes the actions understandable in terms of both Spanish and Indian political interests, without recourse to chance as an explanation.

I attempt to present both sides of the conflict in my analysis, even though the sources of information are a major obstacle to this endeavour. All first-hand accounts are Spanish and the relatively few Indian accounts were written long after the events in question, often not by participants, and in much sketchier fashion than in Spanish sources. Thus, whatever flaws the Spanish accounts may conceal, they do treat matters ignored in the Indian accounts, as the latter are very heavily skewed toward events in the Valley of Mexico. Spanish records offer the best itinerary of Cortés's party. They also offer the best dates: although the Aztec calendar is largely understood, its correlation with the Christian calendar is still debated and, in any case, when Aztec dates are given, they are usually only for months, not days. Thus, for these reasons alone, Spanish accounts remain the backbone of the Conquest saga. I do not give Spanish accounts priority over Indian, but using the former allows me to present a fuller picture first and then weave in the less complete Indian accounts in a way not possible if the procedure were reversed.

In many ways, the conquest of Mexico is familiar: everyone knows what happened so the outcome is no surprise. The focus of analysis must be on the how and why, and it is this that makes the Conquest intriguing.

1 THE SPANISH BACKGROUND TO THE CONQUEST OF MEXICO

Spanish expansion into Mexico grew out of Spain's earlier success in expelling the Moors from the Iberian Peninsula that, in turn, was part of a broader pattern of general expansion by Christian Europe. The Moors had invaded and conquered much of Spain from North Africa in the early eighth century as part of a general expansion of Islam. There they remained for over three centuries with little effort by the Christian kingdoms to expel them. And even when it finally started, the *Reconquista* (Reconquest) of Spain (al-Andalus) began gradually. By the beginning of the eleventh century, wider and more sustained ties had been established between Spain and the rest of Europe, largely through the emergence of the cult of relics centred around the pilgrimage church of Santiago (St James) at Compostela and the gradual resettlement of much of Iberian lands by Christian populations. After the early, largely peaceful resettlement of Spain, the *Reconquista* became more militarized, with forced attempts to seize and hold territory, although this was as much a power struggle among Christian states as against the Moors. With the appearance of Moroccan warriors supporting the Muslim states in Spain toward the end of the eleventh century, the *Reconquista* became more religiously and culturally defined, taking on the character of a crusade.[1]

The *Reconquista* was also aided by the internal disputes within the Moorish states. What had been a united caliphate since 711 disintegrated into many small states after 1008 and no longer presented a unified front to Christian expansion. At this time, there was also a major increase in commerce in Spain, as in the rest of Europe, and crusading knights and financial aid from other Christian countries and the papacy helped fuel the reconquest. In the early thirteenth century, King Alfonso IX received a pledge of fealty from the Moorish ruler of Valencia, who hoped to secure Christian help against royal contenders in Morocco. With Castilian support,

1 Chaunu 1979:85–9; Elliott 1966:44–5; 1984b:152–3; Gibson 1966:4; MacKay 1977:55, 60–3; O'Callaghan 1975:91–2; Ramsey 1973:51–78; Rowdon 1974:35–6; Wright 1969:39–40.

this ruler conquered other Moorish states in Spain, including Córdoba, which Castile occupied on the king's assassination. Events in North Africa also refocused much Moorish attention away from Iberia. Internal struggles over rule in Morocco led many Moorish leaders in Spain to raise armies and leave for battle across the Mediterranean, effectively ceding control of their Iberian territories to Christian rulers. Thus, the *Reconquista* increased in momentum, fuelled as much by Moorish distractions elsewhere as by Christian successes. Moorish populations were increasingly incorporated into Spanish kingdoms and where Moorish rulers remained in power, they now did so as tributaries of Christian kings. Most of Spain was reconquered and in Christian hands by the end of the thirteenth century, with the major exception of Granada, which remained under Moorish rule. When Granada fell in 1492, the reconquest was finally completed, at least within the boundary of the Iberian Peninsula. This did not mark the end of all Spanish expansion, however, which continued elsewhere into Europe, the Mediterranean and, ultimately, the New World.[2]

The reconquest of Spain was part of a general European expansion that arose, in part, from the economic and social dislocation that followed the massive depopulation caused by the Black Death in the fourteenth century. But Europe also felt threatened by Moors to the south and Ottoman Turks to the east, and much of its expansion was dictated conceptually and guided geographically by these concerns, which technological advances in seafaring made possible. Along with other Europeans, Spaniards expanded into other lands, not only driven by the zealotry of the Church Militant, but also encouraged by the lure of greater trade, new lands and subject populations. Thus, when the Spaniards moved into the New World, their expansionary experience left a powerful legacy that was to colour relations with the Indians.[3]

The men who reached Mexico were already participants in the Spanish expansion into the New World and built on their experiences of conquering and colonizing Arab Spain and the Canary Islands. The Spanish expansion beyond Iberia was primarily economic in nature, especially the push into the Canary Islands which was undertaken in order to establish sugar cane plantations, and similar considerations undergird the settlement of the Indies.[4]

2 MacKay 1977:15, 50, 66.
3 Chaunu 1979:85–9; Cipolla 1965:78–81; Elliott 1984b:152–3; O'Callaghan 1975:338–9, 343–5.
4 Chaunu 1979:98; Parry and Sherlock 1971:14–17.

A crusade-like religious fervour marked much of the expansion into Mexico, as it had the *Reconquista*, and this purpose is repeated throughout the accounts of the conquistadors, which describe among other things the appearance of Santiago on a white horse leading the Spaniards to victory, the same apparition credited with leading them during the *Reconquista*. The Spaniards used essentially the same ideology in their conquest of native populations as they had against the Moors during the *Reconquista*. Primarily, however, the conquest of Mexico was a military affair.[5]

During the *Reconquista*, settlements throughout the Iberian Peninsula organized town militias. These militias were used defensively, but they also took offensive actions against the Moors as needed and feasible. The militias produced a large pool of skilled and seasoned fighters, all free men and all required to bear arms, regardless of class. However, the success of Spanish forces was the result not only of larger armies, but also of better organization.[6]

The Spaniards were the beneficiaries of a long tradition of European military organizational development. Medieval warfare, at least up to AD 1200, largely reflected the politically fragmented state of Europe after the fall of the Roman Empire in the West. Great emphasis was placed on the construction and defence of strongholds to control surrounding territories. Armies increasingly consisted of heavy (i.e. armoured) cavalry supported by archers and later crossbowmen, but these troops had to be constituted for specific campaigns rather being part of a permanent standing army. As a result, the armies rarely trained as units and, instead, they emphasized quality over quantity, but they did so at an individual level and armies rarely functioned as an integrated whole. Moreover, since the leadership came from the mounted knights, the role of the infantry was largely discouraged except in sieges, and armies were small – rarely more than ten thousand men.[7]

This situation began changing in the thirteenth century. Greater wealth enabled kings to employ professional soldiers and improved transportation significantly lessened logistical constraints. But most of the impending changes arose from technological innovations. Heavier armour had kept the knights immune to most weapons, especially those of the commoner infantry, but by the mid-fourteenth century, cannons had become common, followed by a

5 Alfonso el Sabio 1972, 2:228; Castro 1971:416–19; Elliott 1966:55, 57; Pagden 1990:13–36; Ramsey 1973:238, 266–7.
6 Powers 1988:16, 112; Quatrefages 1988:6–7; Ramsey 1973:56.
7 Jones 1987:93, 114–21, 141.

variety of hand guns, although they could not yet compete against the crossbow. All of these weapons could pierce armour and the role of mounted heavy cavalry diminished. Now, heavy infantry dominated European warfare. Fighting in organized, trained units, infantry formations broke the domination of heavy cavalry. In the Spanish army in particular, pikemen were added, often replacing swords and shields, armour was lighter, and cavalry declined. This evolution of warfare in Europe was driven by material and technological innovations that the Spaniards would not face in the New World, but their new organizational sophistication would serve them well in a way that the earlier system emphasizing heavy cavalry but little integrated unit combat would not.[8]

By the beginning of the sixteenth century, the Spaniards created the royal guards – heavy cavalry units of 2,500 lances divided into twenty-five captaincies of a hundred men each, entirely under the control of the monarchs. However, the Spaniards relied more heavily on infantry than did the French since the latter regarded commoner foot soldiers as incompetent whereas the Spaniards held them in high esteem and used them effectively. This reliance on infantry culminated in the famed *tercio* (corps) system begun in 1536, organized around a commander of ten 250-man companies, further divided into squads of twenty-five men, giving the reorganized Spanish forces enormous mobility and flexibility.[9]

Part of the emphasis on infantry was an adaptation to Spanish terrain. The hilly countryside was unfavourable to heavy cavalry so infantrymen, armed with pikes, swords and shields, dominated at least during the late phases of the *Reconquista*. Combat was largely between opposing individuals rather than opposing organized forces. Spanish combat in Italy at the end of the fifteenth and beginning of the sixteenth centuries marked a change, with the partial adoption of the Swiss square of densely packed, heavy infantrymen. Combining pikemen and harquebusiers (soldiers armed with harquebuses), the Spaniards decisively defeated the French and thereafter the Spanish army was remodelled to emphasize pikes and harquebuses – smoothbore matchlock guns somewhat smaller than muskets which replaced them in the mid-sixteenth century – in large infantry formations.[10]

Some of these developments were irrelevant to the Spaniards who came to the New World, as much of the ongoing development

8 Jones 1987:150–4, 175–8, 190.
9 Quatrefages 1988:3–4, 6, 12–13, 18; Rowdon 1974:58.
10 Jones 1987:173, 184–5, 190–1.

of military strategy in Europe did not reach them before the Conquest. But the conquistadors who reached Mexico did draw heavily on general European trends, relying very heavily on infantry armed with pikes and swords, wearing various degrees and types of armour, and augmenting the infantry with crossbowmen and harquebusiers. To this was added a small cavalry unit, but the bulk of the combatants were foot soldiers trained in the Iberian tradition of individual combat.

The idea of national armies and national wars was still alien to Europe and soldiers of many cities and countries fought for others on a financial basis, although entire populations could be raised for battle, as in Spain's *Reconquista*. Nevertheless, these wars often entailed huge losses of life and continual tactical, organizational and technological advances combined to make them more deadly yet.

European formations, tactics and arms were more than adequate defence against the first natives that the Spaniards encountered in the New World, those in the Indies (now the West Indies – the Europeans did not yet know about the East Indies). Native political organization was relatively simple in the Indies – loosely centralized chiefdoms at best – and warfare was largely a matter of raiding and of individual glory. It was not the organized clash of trained military formations. Spanish arms and tactics were decisive against the Caribbean Indians so, on the eve of the discovery of Mexico, the Spaniards had no reason to believe that anyone they were likely to encounter elsewhere in the New World would pose a more serious military threat.

Aside from the martial disparity between the Spaniards and the native peoples of the New World, there were also major differences in how wars were fought, how people were governed, and who the king was and what powers he could legitimately exercise. There was also a spiritual dimension to warfare as the Conquest was also a conflict waged by Christians against non-Christians. But the religious imperative was not always present in European conflicts and the Spaniards shared with the rest of Europe the idea that most war was a political exercise in the use of force. Religion provided a justification for war but, as we shall see, the Conquest found its cause in the more pragmatic matters of wealth, power and privilege.[11]

The Spaniards also brought to the New World broader European notions about what constituted legitimate and appropriate

11 Elliott 1966:62–5; Ramsey 1973:258–60.

government, which were undergoing ferment. During the fifteenth and sixteenth centuries, strong European monarchs consolidated their power and increasingly claimed rule based on divine right. But who should rule depended on legitimate succession and was not simply a matter of power. The monarchs of Castile and Aragon ruled by divine right derived from their predecessors in a known and predictable fashion. Moreover, they ruled by law rather than by whim, at least in theory, and their expansion into the occupied lands of the New World was done under the colour of law, although the legitimacy of the enterprise was the subject of long and acrimonious debate. Imperial expansion under such monarchs meant the domination – usually military – of other lands and the control of these territories under the laws of Spain. Thus, Spanish rulers exercised power by divine right, they could legally expand their holdings in the New World, and they held and dominated the territories they conquered, changing forever the lives of those they ruled.[12]

The Indies were the portion of the New World first reached by Christopher Columbus in October of 1492. Probably landing first in the Bahamas, Columbus also sailed to Cuba and then to the island of Hispaniola (present-day Haiti and the Dominican Republic). Columbus sought gold which he believed must be plentiful, based on the ancient idea that it was engendered by heat in these warm lands whereas silver arose from cold, and he immediately began searching for it. Although he failed to find any on the first islands, he was spurred on by seeing a native ornament of silver and, in Hispaniola, he saw a few natives wearing small gold ornaments and heard stories of large quantities of the metal. Ultimately, placer gold was discovered in the mountainous interior of Hispaniola.[13]

When Columbus arrived, the Indies were already densely populated, supporting almost six million people. These were largely divided between two separate language families. The northern islands – the Greater Antilles: Cuba, Haiti, Puerto Rico, Jamaica and the Bahamas – were occupied largely by Tainos (also called Arawaks). The southern islands – the Lesser Antilles – were mostly inhabited primarily by Caribs. Filled with luxurious vegetation, the Indies had been colonized as early as 5000 BC by groups from Central America – Honduras and Nicaragua. A second wave of migration around 3000 BC, however, brought the Tainos from

12 Elliott 1966:75–6; MacKay 1977:96; MacLachlan 1988:1–12; Pagden 1990:13–36.
13 Elliott 1984b:162–3; Sauer 1966:20–8; Wilson 1990: 43–52.

lowland South America who pushed the earlier settlers into the more marginal areas. A third wave of migrants, the Caribs, also from South America, entered the Indies during the last few centuries BC. The Caribs moved northward, pushing the earlier inhabitants out, but by 1492 they had reached no further north than Puerto Rico.[14]

The Tainos were organized into ranked societies in which there were rulers (*caciques*) and other social statuses that the Spaniards interpreted as classes, imposing the more rigid divisions of their homeland onto the more flexible Indian societies. The Tainos were agriculturalists and lived in large villages sustained by the cultivation of sweet potatoes, yams and other tubers that they had originally brought from South America. However, the Tainos also had a second, less-important, complex of seed crops, including maize, beans and squash, that had recently reached the islands from Mesoamerica, and it was this that introduced the Spaniards to the crop complexes that they were to encounter and exploit in Mesoamerica. Hunting and fishing supplemented this vegetable diet but, aside from ducks and dogs, the Indies held no domesticated animals.[15]

Columbus embarked on a second voyage in 1493, intent on settling the lands he had discovered. This effort was not aimed at settling unoccupied areas but rather at settling where population was densest so native labour could be readily exploited. Reaching Hispaniola in November, Columbus's expedition brought no women, but did bring fifteen hundred men, livestock, and various seeds and plants and, with this, the colonization of the New World began.[16]

During the early years, Hispaniola with its dense population was almost the sole focus of Spanish settlement. The inevitable clashes of the early years were eased by the tolerance of the Tainos who did not object to the Spaniards' presence, at least initially. In 1494, however, the first Indian rebellion broke out in response to the

14 Denevan 1976a:291; Lockhart and Schwartz 1983:36; Parry and Sherlock 1971:3; Sauer 1966:37, 48; Wilson 1990:17–20. I am using the six million figure as a reasonably accepted estimate of the West Indian population, but more focused and detailed analyses have cast doubt on it. For instance, Rosenblat (1954, 1:102) puts the Caribbean population significantly lower, at 300,000, although he is also consistently and, I believe, unacceptably low for the rest of Native America as well. Rosenblat (1976:44–5) puts the population of Hispaniola (now Haiti and the Dominican Republic) at 100,000 in 1492 whereas Cook and Borah (1971:408) estimate it to have been some eight million.

15 Sauer 1966:50–9; Wilson 1990:22, 32.

16 Lockhart and Schwartz 1983:62–3; Sauer 1966:71.

capture of a native ruler. Spanish retribution was harsh and, over the next two years, Columbus militarily subdued all the natives of the island and subjected them to Spanish control. There was little of direct material wealth for the Spaniards to seize, save the labour of the Indians themselves and this they did through the institution of the *encomienda*. The *encomienda* was a political-economic system in which rights to the labour of the Indians residing in the granted area were allocated. Their labour was managed through the cooperation of the local *caciques*, but enforced by the Spaniards.[17]

Spanish subjugation of the indigenous population was a blow to native society, but it was disease that was to prove the most devastating. New World populations had never been exposed to most of the major contagious diseases that had evolved in the Old World. As a consequence, the Indians lacked immunities to the diseases the Spaniards brought with them, leading to massive deaths and precipitous depopulation. In Hispaniola alone, the population dropped from perhaps one million in 1492 to under sixteen thousand by 1518: within thirty years of Columbus's landing, the native population of the island was virtually extinct. The same fate befell the natives elsewhere in the Caribbean somewhat later, matching the slower rate of colonization in those areas.[18]

In 1499 a fleet of thirty ships brought an additional 2,500 settlers from Spain, greatly increasing the Spanish presence on Hispaniola, which became the major settlement in the Indies. However, because of war and disease, the Spaniards were left with a labour shortage that encouraged slave raids to other islands, especially the Bahamas, where the indigenous people also quickly succumbed to European disease, maltreatment and war.[19]

Puerto Rico was first settled in 1508 and Jamaica in 1509, followed by Cuba in 1511, where the town of Santiago became the main settlement until it was eclipsed by Havana as Caribbean trade changed. The 1514 attempt to settle what is now Florida was unsuccessful. Despite the flourish of activity in the Caribbean and the Gulf of Mexico, the Spanish population in the New World remained relatively small: Hispaniola was the most populous, followed by Cuba, Darien (in present-day Panama), and Puerto Rico, which was a distant fourth. An identified total of 5,481 people are known to have come to the Indies prior to 1520, which is

17 Elliott 1984b:165–6; Lockhart and Schwartz 1983:68–72; Sauer 1966:89–90.
18 Cook and Borah 1971:401; Elliott 1984b:166.
19 Elliott 1984b:166; Lockhart and Schwartz 1983:79; Parry and Sherlock 1971:9–10.

probably some 20 per cent of the actual total; of these, only 308, or 5.6 per cent, were women. Thus, by 1519, the total European population of the Indies and Darien would have been some 27,000 less the rather significant number of deaths that this colonization entailed. The bulk of the Europeans settled in Hispaniola, from which all the subsequent exploration of the Caribbean and surrounding areas was staged until Governor Velásquez launched his expeditions to Mexico from Cuba.[20]

This expansion into the Caribbean followed and grew out of the *Reconquista* and the occupation of the Canary Islands, so it is not surprising that many of the same political, economic and religious institutions developed in these earlier enterprises were adopted for New World colonization as well. Spaniards settled the lands, but dominated local groups and relied on the legalized expropriation of their labour to generate wealth. And perhaps most importantly, conquerors were not merely soldiers, but partners earning shares in any lands conquered. Thus, they were well poised for the next move, into Mesoamerica.

20 Boyd-Bowman 1973:2–3, 6–8; Elliott 1984b:169; Parry and Sherlock 1971:11–12.

2 MESOAMERICA AND THE AZTECS

When the Spaniards first reached the Yucatan Peninsula in 1517, Mesoamerica had enjoyed almost three thousand years of high civilization, sophisticated cultural achievements, and a long history that had seen the successive rise and fall of many states and empires. Mesoamerica, the area of high indigenous civilization in Mexico and Central America, is enormously varied, bounded by the desert roughly 170 kilometres (100 miles) north of current-day Mexico City, and encompassing Guatemala, El Salvador, Belize and much of Mexico and Honduras. United by its sophisticated indigenous culture, this area encompassed everything from tropical lowlands to mountainous heights exceeding 5,000 metres (18,000 feet), giving rise to many different societies.

Agriculture served as the economic basis for the rise of civilization in Mesoamerica. Emerging slowly over thousands of years, the development of the basic complex of maize, beans and squash provided a more reliable and bountiful food supply than hunting and gathering, permitting more people to live together for longer periods. Thus, agriculture enabled the early Mesoamericans to shift from small nomadic hunting and gathering bands to larger sedentary agricultural villages by 1500 BC. Everywhere throughout Mesoamerica, societies were becoming more complex, but the first truly sophisticated culture was that of the Olmecs, who emerged on the Veracruz Gulf coast around 1200 BC.[1]

Their rise was greatly aided by the movement of maize from the Mesoamerican highlands down into the tropical lowlands where the greater rainfall and fertile soils permitted at least two crops a year. This agricultural surplus fuelled the development of a complex society, which included sophisticated gods and religious innovations, important ceremonial centres, a great art style, the emergence of classes and the rise of kings.

1 For a fuller discussion of the role of warfare in the development of Mesoamerica as a culture area, see Hassig (1988; 1992), on which this account is based.

By the sixteenth century, Mesoamerica was a single culture area united by its major shared, albeit varied, traditions. But at the beginning of the Olmec period, it was not. There was little interplay between various groups and local traditions remained quite diverse. The emergence of the Olmecs, and their subsequent expansion, signalled the beginning of the regional connections that would ultimately mark Mesoamerica as an area of common traditions.

The Olmecs were the first Mesoamerican military power, with the first professional soldiers, the first weapons designed specifically for warfare (notably clubs, maces and slings) rather than hunting tools turned to military purposes, and the first kings whose power depended on military success. But the Olmec expansion beyond the Gulf coast lowlands was not, in all likelihood, military. There were simply too few soldiers to dominate vast areas by force of arms. But even more telling, it was simply too far for the Olmecs to be able to send and sustain enough troops to control distant areas.

Except in toys, the wheel was never used in pre-Columbian Mesoamerica, perhaps because of the mountainous terrain and the lack of draught animals: even by the time of the Spanish conquest, the only domesticated animals in Mexico were turkeys, dogs and bees. There was also a notable lack of year-round navigable rivers, which restricted the use of canoes and rafts primarily to coasts and lakes. Except for largely ceremonial *palanquins* or sedan chairs for the nobility, everyone travelled by foot and all trade goods went by human porters (*tlamemes*). Each porter carried an average load of 23 kilograms (50 pounds) for 21–28 kilometres (13–18 miles) per day.[2] Compared to the considerably more efficient wagons of the Old World, Mesoamerican transport was seriously constrained in long distance and loads, so the cost of moving goods was significantly higher.

This transport constraint was to have a pronounced effect on patterns of warfare in Mesoamerica. Each adult male soldier in Mesoamerica consumed, on average, 0.95 kilograms (2 pounds) of maize and half a gallon of water per day. Although this is not much individually, for an entire army, the logistical difficulties are apparent. Food either had to be carried by the soldiers themselves, which only added to the burden of their arms and could not have amounted to much, or specialized porters had to accompany the army. At the most favourable ratio (which is recorded much later for the Aztecs) of one porter for every two soldiers, an army could

---

2 For a discussion of *tlamemes*, see Hassig 1985:32 and *passim*.

travel only for eight days on its own supplies since each porter carried only twenty-four man/days of food.

The time limit that logistics placed on marches meant that armies simply could not go very far. Moreover, armies do not march as fast as individuals because of the dynamics of mass movements, and there is little reason to believe that any Mesoamerican army marched faster than its preindustrial peers elsewhere, or 8–32 kilometres (5–20 miles) a day, a march rate that accords well with modern practice of 4 kilometres (2.5 miles) per hour on roads and 2.4 kilometres (1.5 miles) off. Mesoamerican societies did not build formal roads between cities, except for the Late Classic Maya in Yucatan. Instead, they used the dirt roads that sprang up between centres, so the march rate of their armies doubtless tended toward the lower figure – 19 kilometres (12 miles) per day. Coupled with their logistical constraints, an Olmec army could thus be expected to have a combat radius of no more than 58 kilometres (36 miles) – three days there, one of combat, another for recuperation, and three days return.

Despite the far-flung areas of Olmec influence, it is highly unlikely that their expansion was achieved militarily. Man-for-man, the Olmecs were doubtless the best soldiers of their day, but they could not project their force over such vast distances. Instead, the Olmecs tied together much of Mesoamerica in a trading network, spreading new religious ideas, new intellectual triumphs such as writing, mathematics and a calendar system, and new forms of social organization that began linking the vast area into a common cultural region. By 400 BC, however, their time had passed. The Olmecs withdrew back into the lowlands but, as with their expansion, there is little evidence that this was militarily inspired. Rather, as irrigation agriculture developed in the highlands, newly emergent local elites could now successfully compete with the Olmecs for valuable trade goods and they could do so without the tremendous burden of transporting them to the distant Gulf coast. Without their competitive advantage, the Olmecs lost their dominance and reverted to being one among many of the emerging local state systems.

After the Olmec decline, no single society dominated Mesoamerica for hundreds of years, but warfare increased among the newly emergent states. New arms and armour were developed, including large rectangular shields, whose added protection hastened the decline of clubs and maces, and the thrusting spear emerged as Mesoamerica's dominant weapon. This period was one of political instability. As a result, warfare by professionally armed soldiers was rife and the construction of the earliest permanent Mesoamerican fortifications was prevalent.

Following this period of regional balkanization and conflict, the city of Teotihuacan, in the northeastern Valley of Mexico, gradually emerged as the capital of Mesoamerica's first major empire. Teotihuacan marshalled large numbers of professional soldiers armed with either thrusting spears and bucklers or spearthrowers (*atlatls*), darts and rectangular shields, a standardization that indicates state control of the armoury. Thus equipped, Teotihuacan's armies could pour dart fire into their enemies' ranks and disrupt them before the two sides closed for hand-to-hand combat. This proved a devastating tactic when backed by the large body of soldiers that Teotihuacan could muster from its huge population.

Teotihuacan was a cosmopolitan, multi-ethnic city, attracting and assimilating foreign peoples. This enabled Teotihuacan to become the largest city in Mesoamerica with 60,000 inhabitants as early as AD 100 and reaching a peak population of some 200,000 in AD 500. Teotihuacan was apparently a theocracy and the city's religious significance is signalled by its enormous temple-pyramids. But the city owed much of its importance to its obsidian industry. Obsidian was the basic material for most tools and weapons in Mesoamerica, playing a role similar to that of iron in Europe, and Teotihuacan controlled the main deposits in central Mexico and engaged in large-scale manufacturing of obsidian products. This industry underlay much of Teotihuacan's expansion as it sought foreign markets for its wares and exotic goods for its own consumption.

Within the first three centuries AD, Teotihuacan had expanded over much of central Mexico, created mineral-producing settlements north well beyond the boundaries of civilization, penetrated the Maya lowlands of Guatemala, and established colonies as far south as the highland Maya city of Kaminaljuyu on the site of modern-day Guatemala City. Elite Teotihuacan goods were in high demand in many places throughout Mesoamerica, but the creation of settlements and colonies, as well as the protection of incessant merchant expeditions, demanded an active military. This Teotihuacan could easily provide: its army was the largest in Mesoamerica, was well trained and equipped, and, by AD 400, its soldiers were armoured as quilted cotton jerkins were adopted.

Teotihuacan's military-backed expansion was the second major wave integrating the various areas of Mesoamerica, and with expansion came the spread of many ideas, technologies and patterns of organization. But its dominance was not to last. Teotihuacan could maintain its far-flung operations only with difficulty. Even as an urban giant, it could not muster enough troops to provide garrisons everywhere and, even if it could marshal enough soldiers, the logistical constraints on doing so were enormous. At the same time that Teotihuacan grappled with the limits of its military power, the mere presence of its merchants, colonists and other functionaries stimulated local social development. With sustained contact, colonized and contacted groups grew more sophisticated and eventually became competitors themselves. No city or group of cities actually rivalled Teotihuacan or directly confronted it. But at the great distances involved and the cost of dispatching and maintaining even small forces, even modest cities with their emergent elites increasingly seeking the very wares that Teotihuacan itself sought could compete with the great city.

With the increased competition borne of its own expansion, Teotihuacan could no longer maintain its far-flung holdings and began withdrawing from its most distant enclaves shortly after AD 500. This contraction alleviated the colonial problems, but the city's internal development was based on the existence of colonial markets. Now without them, Teotihuacan was vastly overproducing: workers were dislocated, the wealth of the city declined, and by AD 750, Teotihuacan's ritual centre was burned and the city was largely abandoned.

Teotihuacan had not controlled and integrated all of Mesoamerica: many places were too undeveloped to merit attention and others were too far away. Instead, it dominated many, though not all, major urban areas, largely ignoring relatively unimportant intervening areas. Teotihuacan's legacy was an increased interdependence that was regional, though spotty, and a further cultural homogenization of the areas in contact. But with the city's demise, Mesoamerica again broke into a vast number of local cities and states. Some cities, such as El Tajín, Xochicalco and Cacaxtla, rose to local prominence. However, no city exercised control over a significant area until the rise of the Toltecs.

The end of the first millennium AD was a period of reintegration of much of Mesoamerica. The Toltecs emerged as the rulers of a mercantile empire, strongly supported by military innovation and might, that pushed out competing trader groups that had established themselves during the fragmentation of central Mexico after the demise of Teotihuacan. However, they did not dominate Mesoamerica in the same fashion or as extensively as had Teotihuacan and regionally competing polities emerged elsewhere. The capital of the Toltec empire was Tollan, which reached its height from AD 950 to 1150 with a resident population of 60,000, many of whom were craftsmen, and an equal number of farmers in its immediate hinterland. But it was an important obsidian source near Tollan that Teotihuacan had exploited earlier that was probably the reason that the Toltec capital was situated where it was.

A major portion of Tollan's multi-ethnic population was composed of Mesoamericans imbued with the religious beliefs and cultural traditions of the region. But the majority were relative newcomers, migrants from the north who had recently moved south into the sphere of civilization, and it was the merging of these two traditions that gave rise to Tollan. Though Tollan was, in many ways, a continuation of Teotihuacan traditions – the Toltecs were not major cultural innovators – it nevertheless signalled a major political shift. Rather than a theocracy, Tollan was ruled by more secular rulers. But like Teotihuacan, Tollan owed its dominance to its obsidian industry and commerce.

There is, however, ample evidence of warfare in Tollan, and conquest doubtless played a major role in the city's rise. Although not as populous as its predecessor imperial capital, Tollan was larger than any other city of its day and enjoyed the advantage of new military technology and organization. Its primary innovation was a sword 50 centimetres (20 inch) in length, a curved wooden handle with obsidian blades along each edge. This short sword provided a much larger cutting surface than previous weapons and it did so with very little extra weight. Most previous weapons used entire stones fashioned into points and were essentially crushers, but the short sword substituted small blades that could be glued into light wooden handles, relying on slashing for its effect.

Because of their lightness, short swords did not have to be chosen in lieu of other arms, but could be carried with *atlatls*, allowing each soldier to function in a dual role. Arming Toltec soldiers with both projectiles and slashers effectively doubled their strength compared with traditional Mesoamerican soldiers. Toltec soldiers could now provide their own covering fire with *atlatls* while they advanced and still engage in hand-to-hand combat with short swords once they closed with the enemy. As at Teotihuacan, Toltec arms and armour included standardized weapons indicative of state ownership and control, a large army, and complementary weapons and units.

Both the nature and size of Tollan's empire is debated, but Toltec trade clearly extended throughout most of Mesoamerica and beyond, linking Tollan to Chiapas, Guatemala, and Central America, central Veracruz, the Huaxtec area, north and west Mexico, and perhaps even the American Southwest. However, this expansion was intermittent and apparently avoided strong competing sites. Instead of an area of uniform control, the Toltec empire was probably a series of ill-defined and rapidly changing relationships with other centres, some subordinate in varying degrees and others virtual partners.

The Toltecs established a trading empire that operated through merchant enclaves and settlements rather than by militarily colonizing outlying areas. Military power was important in protecting merchants in hostile areas, but the Toltecs lacked the manpower and logistical capacity to create and maintain a major empire. The general increase in population throughout Mesoamerica by Toltec times made distant logistical support increasingly feasible but the Toltecs lacked a tributary network capable of providing support. Instead, they created colonial enclaves throughout much of Mesoamerica during a period in which there was no large competitor, and linked the region through their own people sent abroad to trade, produce, and colonize.

As with Teotihuacan, Tollan owed its economic position to a far-flung trade network that supplied the city's craftsmen with needed raw materials and sold the goods they produced. If control of this trade were left in the hands of others, Tollan would have been vulnerable; it therefore seized direct control of the trade. In spite of its military advantages, however, the Toltec empire ended around AD 1179 when Tollan met a violent end as the result of famine, rebellion and barbarian invasions. Much of this can be attributed to long-term desiccation of the areas to the north that forced many groups to abandon their homes and migrate south into Mesoamerica, disrupting Tollan's control of its trade routes. A break up into city-states and regional powers again overtook Mesoamerica in the wake of Tollan's abandonment and new groups migrated into central Mexico from the north, taking over existing cities and establishing others of their own. A few city-states became the centres of small empires, such as the Tepanec empire that dominated much of the Valley of Mexico. But no city controlled vast areas until the emergence of the Aztecs following their overthrow of the Tepanecs in 1428.

The Aztecs migrated into the Valley of Mexico at the end of the twelfth century AD and settled at Tenochtitlan in 1345. As outsiders and relative barbarians, they needed allies to achieve political legitimacy among the other cities. They thus selected Acamapichtli, a noble from the city of Colhuacan, as their first king and he exercised control over external matters, such as war. However, internal matters, such as land ownership and tribute collection, remained largely in the hands of the traditional Aztec leaders – the ward (*calpolli*) heads – who controlled the flow of tribute from the commoners, and on whom the king was dependent. In traditional Mesoamerican fashion, Acamapichtli consolidated his position through marriage with the daughters of these leaders. The offspring united Acamapichtli's noble heritage with the *de facto* authority of the *calpolli* leaders and became the nucleus of an emergent Aztec nobility, paving the way for the eventual consolidation of both internal and external power in the hands of the king.

Being new and relatively few, the Aztecs became tributaries of the Tepanec empire in the western Valley of Mexico. The power of the Aztec kings grew very slowly until the assassination of Chimalpopoca, Acamapichtli's grandson and the third Aztec king, which precipitated a major change in the Aztec system of selecting kings. Previously, sons had succeeded fathers, but since the king enjoyed little more than titular powers, exactly who ruled was not a crucial matter. However, Chimalpopoca died without a suitable heir so Itzcoatl, a skilled soldier, was elected king by the other nobles. With this election, political legitimacy within a larger pool of upper nobles no longer depended on strict hereditary succession but on ability, and having a skilful ruler became increasingly important as the kings' power grew.

Itzcoatl, the fourth Aztec ruler, became king during an especially turbulent period in the Valley of Mexico. King Tetzotzomoc, the founder of the Tepanec empire, had died and the son he had chosen as his successor was assassinated by another of his sons, Maxtla, who then seized the throne. This undermined relations among the Tepanec cities which were ruled by Tetzotzomoc's other sons, who had equal claims to the imperial throne, leaving Maxtla in control of little more than the capital city.

Seizing this opportunity, Itzcoatl allied with other rulers who were equally dissatisfied with the Tepanecs. Principal among these were the king of Tetzcoco, a long-time enemy of the Tepanecs, and the king of Tlacopan, one of Maxtla's disgruntled brothers and himself a pretender to the Tepanec throne. With their assistance, Itzcoatl struck, defeating the badly divided Tepanecs, and this

Aztec-led Triple Alliance became the dominant power in the Valley of Mexico.

The overthrow of the Tepanec empire freed Tenochtitlan from external domination: Itzcoatl now received tributary goods and lands from the defeated cities, providing income that did not depend on his own people. The king was now notably less dependent on the commoners for either goods or political support, which significantly lessened the political importance of the ward leaders. Some support for war may have been ideological since religion played a role in it, as it did for many wars worldwide. But religious beliefs encouraging warfare, such as having to nourish the gods with human blood, were common throughout central Mexico and do not explain Aztec expansion in particular. Rather, the commoners generally supported war because this was one of the few avenues of social advancement open to them. Whatever their personal beliefs about its religious purposes, excelling in combat offered commoners the possibility of rising to elite status and receiving material rewards.

The Aztec rise provided more economic stability to the nobility in the form of greater tributary wealth, but this also led to increased political instability because of the way the Aztecs organized their empire. The Aztecs were faced with two alternative ways to structure their expanding empire. One alternative was to conquer new areas and consolidate their hold by replacing local leaders and armies with Aztec governors and garrisons. This would allow the Aztecs to extract large quantities of goods in tribute, but at a high administrative cost in replacing local rulers and maintaining troops to enforce their mandates. If they chose the second alternative, the Aztecs could leave the conquered government intact. This would limit the amount they could extract as tribute since it relied on some degree of voluntary compliance, but it would also reduce the empire's political and administrative costs. The first approach – a territorial empire – provides greater political control and more tribute but it also limits expansion because exercising direct control quickly absorbs the available manpower in garrison duty. The second approach – a hegemonic empire – collects less tribute because it exerts less control, but it also frees more men for further expansion. Faced with this choice, the Aztecs adopted the second alternative.

There are both advantages and disadvantages to the hegemonic system, which had ramifications for Aztec expansion. The more a hegemonic empire relies on power (the perception that one can enforce one's desired goals) rather than force (direct physical action to compel one's goals), the more efficient it is because the subordinates police themselves. But the costs of compliance must not be perceived as outweighing the benefits: the more exploitative a political system is perceived to be, the more it must rely on force rather than on power, and the less efficient it becomes. The hegemonic system had a major weak point, however: it required a strong king. Because the Aztecs imposed few or no institutional changes in tributary areas, the empire was vulnerable to collapse if their king was perceived as weak or indecisive. The king's military prowess was not simply a matter of ideology or honour, but was an essential element in sustaining the empire and his death could disrupt the system if his successor did not guarantee continuity in policy or ability. Thus, for the Aztecs, military prowess was a major concern in selecting a king.

Much of the Aztecs' own support for the empire grew from their ability to amass ever more tribute which required continued imperial expansion and a militarily successful king. Sustained military failure could incite rebellion, shrink the empire, and reduce tribute goods and lands. Failure struck hardest at the interests of the nobles and if the king lost their support, his safety could be imperilled. For example, Tizoc, the seventh Aztec king, was assassinated after five years of weak rule. Consequently, both wealth and self-preservation compelled the king to succeed militarily. Yet despite this impetus, the Aztecs were not continuously at war. Mustering troops, negotiating mass movements and supplying logistical support were patterned by the May-to-September rainy season, which determined when troops could be successfully mobilized and where they could march.

The commoners who made up most of the army were also farmers and were occupied during the summer and early autumn. But even if they had been available year-round, food was not. Needed supplies were most readily available just after harvest. Autumn also marked the beginning of the dry season when troop movements were significantly easier: dirt roads dried out, permitting passage of large groups that would turn wet roads into muddy quagmires, and swollen rivers shrank to fordable streams. As a result of all these factors, Aztec warfare was concentrated in a campaign season running from early December to late April.

Whatever the Aztecs' battle skills, combat effectiveness was only one aspect of warfare: the ability to carry the fight to distant enemies meant that the Aztecs had to muster troops, gather supplies and coordinate mass movements, all of which required considerable advance planning. In this, the king exercised overall authority, determining the army's route, the number of days it would march, and the battle plan once the target was reached.

Simply moving large numbers of men posed enormous problems since there were no wheeled vehicles or draught animals in Mesoamerica. Like preindustrial armies elsewhere, the Aztec army moved slowly (no more than 2.4 kilometres or 1.5 miles per hour). But the rate of march was less important than the army's configuration. Since the Aztecs did not build roads for military purposes, they relied on roads that served local trade which restricted the army to double files. This stretched out the standard Aztec command of 8,000 men (a *xiquipilli*) over a distance of 12 kilometres (7.5 miles), without considering the accordion effect that further lengthens the line. This meant that the last men would not begin marching until five hours after the first men had started: in order to complete its march by nightfall, each *xiquipilli* marched one day apart – a necessary expedient, but one that greatly increased the time needed to assemble the entire force for the attack.

The Aztecs could have increased the number of files per column by going cross-country, but marching off roads is slower and, despite its directness, seldom offers significant time savings. However, Aztec armies frequently did march along several alternative routes simultaneously, shortening the time required for everyone to reach the battle site and preventing the defenders from bottling up the Aztecs in a vulnerable pass.

Food was another limiting factor in warfare. Speeding the army was crucial to Aztec success because of the enormous logistical difficulties in Mesoamerica: any delay helped the defenders. Although individual soldiers took some supplies, most food was brought by accompanying porters, although this still limited a self-sufficient army to a total of eight days in the field. With the great population growth in Mesoamerica since Teotihuacan times, the Aztecs were able to extend their range by adapting the tribute system to their imperial aims and demanding food supplies from subordinate towns en route. Messengers were sent along the designated route two days before the march to alert all major tributary towns, each of which then gathered foodstuffs from its surrounding dependencies and supplied them to the passing Aztecs. To do otherwise meant rebellion at a time when Aztec troops were already en route and when the tributary town was not prepared for war and did not have enough time to ready itself.

The slow rate of march, the time needed to assemble the entire army in camp, and the clouds of dust kicked up by tens of thousands of feet on dirt roads stripped the Aztecs of tactical surprise, as did spies, foreign merchants and even the advance warnings the Aztecs sent to their tributaries to ensure adequate supplies. But there was little that a target city-state could do to take advantage of this warning as its occupants could not flee without leaving their city, homes, goods and fields to the mercy of the Aztecs. Instead, most cities either surrendered or fought, but they were usually outnumbered by the Aztecs and certainly outperformed.

Aztec battlefield assaults involved an orderly sequence of weapons use and tactics, as did the battles of earlier empires. However, the weapons had changed, notably by the addition of bows and arrows, which had been brought into Mesoamerica from the north around AD 1100. Signalled by the commander's drum or trumpet, the Aztec attack typically started at dawn. Fighting began with a projectile barrage after the armies closed to around 60 metres (66 yards). Wearing only breechcloths and sandals and perhaps carrying shields, archers and slingers could strike well beyond 60 metres. However, the high rates of fire quickly exhausted the limited supply of arrows and slingstones, so archers and slingers held their fire until they were close enough to guarantee the accuracy and effect of their projectiles.

When the barrage began, soldiers advanced carrying stone-bladed wooden broadswords (*macuahuitl*) and thrusting spears (*tepoztopilli*). These were both relatively recent innovations. The thrusting spear was an elaboration on earlier versions, but now possessed an elongated wooden head inset with obsidian blades. The broadsword, however, was a more radical departure and probably emerged in the mid-fourteenth century. Perhaps an evolution from the Toltec short sword, the broadsword was made of oak inset with obsidian blades and, with its greater size (0.84 metres or 2 feet 8 inches), it displaced the former. The most experienced and accomplished warriors were well protected, wearing quilted cotton armour under suits of woven feathers or skins and usually helmets, and carrying shields, which were as much a badge of achievement as functional protection. Although the elite warriors were heavily armoured, the novices wore no armour at all, a reflection of their respective accomplishments in battle.

Both sides opened with a deadly barrage, particularly to the less protected, so the opposing armies closed quickly. As they advanced, the soldiers shot darts, or short spears, with their spearthrowers: these had a much shorter range than arrows or slingstones but had greater striking force at close range, could penetrate cotton armour, and were used to disrupt the opposing formations. Soldiers carried only a few *atlatl* darts because each side advanced only about 30 metres (33 yards) before the armies met. At that point, they dropped the *atlatls* in favour of the greater effectiveness of swords or thrusting spears and the combatants intermingled in combat, forcing a halt to the massed projectile fire.

The most experienced soldiers led the attack. First came the military orders (similar to those of medieval Europe), followed by veteran soldiers leading organized units. Last came novice warriors under the supervision of veterans who ensured that they were not unduly endangered during training. Slingers and archers were unarmoured and required both hands to shoot, so they were extremely vulnerable if the enemy got close enough for hand-to-hand combat. Thus they remained back from the battle but continued to fire at isolated targets, harassing enemy reinforcements, covering withdrawals and preventing encirclement by the enemy.

Aztec movements into and out of battle were orderly so as to maintain a coherent formation, allowing the soldiers to concentrate their fighting toward the front rather than on all sides. But once the army closed with the enemy, combat was inevitably an individual affair, although small skirmishing units remained cohesive. Otherwise, soldiers risked being separated and captured by the enemy. But oral commands could not be heard over the din of battle, so the soldiers followed the tall feather standards worn by their leaders. Strapped to the back, these standards towered above the combatants and allowed the soldiers to see where their comrades were going. If the standard bearer was killed, his unit was effectively blinded and thrown into disarray.

Battle was heaviest between the soldiers at the front of the armies, as only they could bring their weapons to bear. The Aztecs usually extended their front as much as possible, taking advantage of their numerical superiority to envelop the enemy troops and cut them off from reinforcements and resupply. However, ambushes were also used on occasion, typically at physically disabling times and locations, such as narrow passes, where the advantage lay with the attacker. The most spectacular ambushes, however, involved feigned retreats in battle. If executed convincingly, the enemy troops advanced to press their supposed advantage until they were drawn into a compromised position. Then the Aztecs turned on them while hidden troops attacked from behind, disrupting the enemy formations and cutting them off.

Defenders occasionally chose to wait behind city fortifications rather than meet the Aztecs in the open. Urban fortifications were not typical in late preconquest central Mexico, but some cities, such as Quetzaltepec, were completely encircled by high walls, often in concentric rings, although usually not free-standing. A more common type of fortification was the stronghold, detached from the city and usually atop an adjacent hill where the advantage of height and a difficult ascent augmented walls and battlements, as at Cuezcomaixtlahuacan. From there, simply throwing stones down on attackers provided an effective first line of defence. However, strongholds were most often used as refuges for dependants and political leaders and did not protect the city itself. Instead, they offered safety while the city's terms of surrender were negotiated.

Unless they gained entry by deceit or through treason, or simply withdrew, the Aztecs had to breach or scale any fortifications they encountered, or they could besiege the city. Breaching fortifications was difficult and time-consuming: scaling walls with ladders was a quicker alternative but was relatively uncommon, probably because the attackers needed so many more men than the defenders. The remaining option was to lay siege to the town. This was feasible within the Valley of Mexico where the besiegers could be resupplied by canoe, but extended sieges were difficult to sustain elsewhere.

Fortified defences could be very effective tactically, but they were seldom used for several reasons. First, they were not foolproof whereas, under favourable conditions, the Aztecs' siege tactics were effective. Second, even if the defenders built effective fortifications, they required many soldiers to man the entire perimeter. This was particularly true for sprawling agricultural towns where manning the entire wall could disperse the defenders and effectively weaken their forces. But third, and most important, the city could not be divorced from its wider social networks: even if the city itself were safe behind fortifications, its fields and stores beyond the walls remained vulnerable, as did its smaller unfortified dependencies, and their loss meant economic catastrophe even if the city remained intact. Thus, only an active defence in which the enemy was met and vanquished would guarantee the city's continuation as the hub of a viable social network.

In any case, the Aztecs' primary objective was to induce the people to submit, not to destroy them, although the conquered temples and associated buildings might be burned as the ultimate sign of Aztec victory. Beyond the symbolic significance of defeating the local gods, burning the temples was a devastating practical blow since they were usually the most heavily fortified sites within the city and their destruction meant that the strongest resistance had been overcome. Furthermore, the temple precincts contained the city's armouries, which meant that their destruction deprived the defenders of additional arms and war supplies. The entire town was burned only if the people continued to resist after their main temple was destroyed.

We have seen that climatic cycles dictated when campaigns were fought, and where they were fought depended on the earlier expansion of the empire, which established where logistical support would be available. But neither of these factors actually determined the strategic direction of the empire's expansion. Although there were doubtless strategic goals – probably related to economic and security concerns – Aztec imperial expansion had a course-of-least-resistance quality. They launched all-out attacks primarily on towns that they were sure they could defeat.

Much of Aztec expansion was determined by geography. Broken terrain channelled conquests through easily travelled territory which gave the Aztec empire a patch-quilt appearance. Independent towns were often bypassed because they were not important to a particular campaign. Only towns posing a military threat to the further expansion of the Aztecs or needed to supply logistical support were conquered. Other towns could be bypassed in comparative safety, to be conquered later, either by force or by intimidation.

Most conquests took place along valley floors where major towns were located near their agricultural lands. Only major towns had to be conquered because that meant the *de facto* submission of their surrounding dependencies as well. Comprehensive conquest was unnecessary: because control was exercised through the existing political structure, unconquered dependencies also became part of the Aztec empire when their capitals were conquered. Thus, Aztec expansion depended less on a strategic vision than on the practicalities of logistical support that dictated the immediate direction and sequence of conquests.

In other words, the Aztecs did not simply emerge from the Valley of Mexico in all directions, sweeping everyone before them. Rather, practical considerations fostered two general strategies for conquests – a relatively straightforward approach for easy targets and a more complicated approach for difficult ones. Because they were concerned with military success, the Aztecs concentrated on easier targets, maximizing their chance of victory and minimizing the risk of failure. The primary advantage of this strategy was that victories over weaker opponents exacted a smaller toll on Aztec manpower so further expansion was unhindered. But this approach also eased three other goals of Aztec expansion. First, this expansion enabled the Aztecs to build a far-flung logistical network to support their armies in transit. Second, success buttressed the reputation of the empire and discouraged rebellions by other tributaries. And third, it ensured the tribute that the king needed to guarantee the support of the nobles. The Aztecs were excellent soldiers and their emphasis on easy conquests and targets of opportunity reflected internal political considerations rather than military weakness.

An Aztec defeat meant only the loss of a battle: an Aztec victory, however, meant the subjugation of the city-state and all its dependencies. The same was not true for confederacies and empire: they controlled large hinterlands, so advance warning allowed them to marshal large armies and march to their borders to meet the Aztecs, profoundly altering the consequences of winning the battle. Under these circumstances, victory meant the conquest of only the area around the battlefield: defeated confederated or imperial armies could withdraw into their territorial interiors while the Aztecs, who were dependent on tributaries for logistical support, could not safely pursue these armies into hostile territory. For a city-state, losing a battle meant subjugation, but for confederacies or empires, it meant the loss of only a limited area of their peripheries. Mesoamerican logistical limitations offered large polities a protection that their armies could not. A single, decisive blow to the heart of an empire was usually beyond the Aztecs' ability: conquering them was a long-term project achieved only by gradually chipping away at the edges of the polity. Even if the Aztecs could conquer such large opponents, some were nevertheless so strong that even a victory would leave the Aztecs too weakened to maintain control elsewhere. The costs of such a conquest were too high for an empire that had to balance many strategic interests. To deal with this situation, the Aztecs fought flower wars (*xochiyaoyotl*), designed to pin down major opponents while their own expansion continued elsewhere. Because of their prolonged nature, early accounts claim that flower wars were fought for military training, to take captives for sacrifice to the gods, and to display individual military skill. This was all true, but the flower war was only a part of a larger military strategy for dealing with major powers.

A flower war began as a show of strength in which relatively few combatants fought to demonstrate individual military prowess. An impressive display of capability could lead to the enemy's capitulation without further conflict. But if the opponent remained unintimidated, additional flower wars would be fought – often over a period of years – gradually escalating in ferocity. In the initial flower war, injuries and deaths were not deliberate and prisoners were not sacrificed afterward. But as the war escalated, captives were sacrificed rather than returned, the number of combatants increased, bows and arrows introduced indiscriminate death rather than individual demonstrations of skill and bravery until, eventually, the flower war resembled a conventional war of conquest. Thus, a flower war began as a low-cost exercise in military intimidation, but both costs and consequences escalated until it became a war of attrition. And with that, the numerically superior Aztecs could not lose since even equal losses by both sides took a greater toll on the smaller polity, gradually undermining its ability to resist.

It could take considerably longer to defeat an enemy through a flower war than through a war of conquest, but flower wars had significant advantages. By engaging the enemy in limited but enervating warfare, the Aztecs could pin down strong opponents and reduce their offensive threat. They then conquered the surrounding groups and gradually encircled their opponents, cutting them off from external assistance and reducing their areas of logistical and manpower support. By escalating flower wars, the Aztecs slowly chipped away at their enemies' territory until they fell. Thus, the Aztecs' weak-opponent-first strategy generated tribute revenue and increased their logistical capability at low cost, while flower wars isolated and slowly reduced opponents too strong to be attacked directly.

But what exactly did it mean to be conquered by the Aztecs? The most obvious consequence was having to pay tribute, which was the typical economy of Mesoamerican city-states. Although the crown, nobility and temples frequently held their own lands and labourers, most of their income was in the form of goods and labour paid as tribute by the commoner classes. In the case of an independent city-state, the king was the highest level in the tribute system, but once conquered, Aztec tributary demands were added, requiring the payment of additional goods and labour but operating through the local tribute system. The Aztecs merely tapped into the existing system, positioning themselves at the top. This tribute payment was a net loss to the subject towns but conquest typically caused few other overt changes in the local society. Except in the case of recurrent rebellion, conquered rulers remained in place and exercised local control, which freed the Aztecs from local administration and allowed them to continue their military expansion.

Local economic relations were left largely intact because the Aztecs sought to maintain healthy local economies that were able to pay their new tributary obligations. Imperial tribute siphoned off wealth, which was a local net loss, but Aztec demands also stimulated local production and often expanded trade relationships to secure the goods required. Moreover, tributaries were now linked into an Aztec-dominated trade network dispersing rare and elite goods throughout the empire. As long as local rulers complied with Aztec wishes, leaving them in power was more efficient than replacing them. However, this system was constantly vulnerable to dissolution because it did not shift the loyalty of tributary populations from their traditional rulers to the Aztec kings.

Religious organizations solidly supported the Aztec state and its imperial aspirations, but religious conversion did not play a major role in Aztec imperial ideology. Wars were not primarily religiously motivated, although kings often manipulated religious mandates to further their aims. For example, the Aztec kings occasionally demanded labour and materials from both tributary and independent towns to help in the construction of temples to the gods; failure to comply meant war. The timing of these construction campaigns was decided by the king, not by priests or regular religious events, and the groups targeted tended to be in the direct line of existing Aztec expansion, strongly indicating the primarily political use of religious mandates rather than the opposite. Moreover, conquered towns did not suffer forced religious conversion and Aztec gods were not exported beyond the Valley of Mexico except by the occasional migration of the Aztecs themselves; even then, the local gods and their ceremonies were left intact.

However, not everything continued in conquered city-states because Aztec domination caused major, even if unintentional, changes in the local political system. In most central Mexican polities, rulership did not descend in a fixed fashion, such as from father to eldest son. Mexican kings typically had multiple wives, numerous children and thus many potential successors. The selection of a royal successor was an issue internal to the kingdom, but who was chosen was greatly influenced by external ties. External as well as internal political support for a royal contender was crucial and the single most important factor in terms of the formal requirements for eligibility was his mother.

Intermarriage among allied rulers was common, with rulers

giving their daughters as wives to other rulers, which added an important political dimension to the selection of a successor. Consequently, the successor was likely to be the son of the king by his most important wife – the daughter of the king's most powerful ally. The pool of potential successors was determined by that kingdom's rules of succession, but which among the various eligible candidates was actually chosen depended on the larger political context, and this was massively altered by Aztec conquest.

To be without political alliances left a city-state vulnerable to aggression, breach of trade, and so forth. The king of a conquered polity achieved and held his position in large part because of his alliances with other city-states. But the Aztecs inevitably altered these – first and foremost by inserting themselves as the most important ally, but also because not all of a given polity's original allies were likely to have been incorporated into the Aztec empire at the same time; even if they were, their own political situation was also drastically altered. Whatever the impact of this on succession, Aztec conquest altered the local political environment and shattered the reigning king's political base. There were still other political contenders who had different ties and many of these nobles might well have greater support under the altered circumstances. Thus many reigning kings cleaved closely to their new dominant ally – the Aztecs – to avert overthrow from within. Nevertheless, the potential for dethroning kings remained, and any major shift in political power in the region could easily lead to a change in rulers.

Although the Aztecs reigned supreme in Mesoamerica, they did not rule everywhere, nor did they preside over a group of homogenized societies fully integrated into the empire. Many areas of Mesoamerica remained independent and often hostile. Nevertheless, most posed little military challenge to Tenochtitlan, despite their access to the same military technology as the Aztecs.

Most central Mexican armies shared common weapons and adopted others as they were disseminated by, or in advance of, the Aztecs. Commoner soldiers typically wore loincloths and primarily relied on such weapons as bows and slings, whereas the nobles and military leaders wore more elaborate armour, carried shock weapons (i.e. crushers and slashers, such as maces and swords), and frequently used battle standards and war suits. These armies also shared similar forms of military organization, although their order of battle varied widely.

The military similarities between most Mexican city-states and the Aztecs were superficial, however. Even though there was general access to Aztec tactics and weapons, how and whether these were incorporated depended on the size and composition of the various armies, which is particularly illustrated by the use of the *atlatl*. In major conventional armies, such as the Aztecs', the *atlatl* was used to disrupt opposing army formations. But armies too small to train large numbers of specialists discontinued use of the *atlatl*, replacing it with the bow which, in these forces, was essentially a lower-class tool turned to military use. As a result, *atlatls* remained important in large conventional armies but they were discarded elsewhere.

Groups among whom this was true include the petty Mixtec and Zapotec kingdoms of Oaxaca, the Totonacs of the Veracruz coast, the Huaxtecs of the northern Gulf coast, the Mazahuas in the Valley of Toluca, many Nahuatl-speaking city-states scattered throughout central Mexico, and the Maya city-states of Yucatan. Although the Aztecs had not yet conquered all of these groups, neither did they pose a significant military obstacle. Even though these small kingdoms and city-states posed little obstacle in and of themselves, united they could become formidable opponents. In most of Mesoamerica, there is little evidence of the emergence of such larger political groupings at this time, but even regional powers could become powerful magnets for the disaffected and grow to threaten Aztec dominance.

Two such regional powers existed and confronted the Aztecs when the Spaniards arrived. One, the Tarascan empire centred in the modern state of Michoacan, was probably the most powerful group facing the Aztecs. Theirs was a multi-ethnic empire incorporating Tarascan, Otomi and Nahuatl speakers, many of whom had fled Aztec expansion. Much of the mechanics and underlying strategy of Tarascan warfare was similar to, though less sophisticated than, that of the Aztecs and the Tarascan empire was also organized as a hegemonic system. The Tarascans had the same weapons inventory as the Aztecs, but used these in different proportions, relying extremely heavily on bows and arrows.

The Tarascans had defeated the Aztecs in a minor battle when King Axayacatl (ruled 1468–81) invaded their territory, but they were nevertheless not a major military power: they had a relatively small population and made little provision for the specialized military training of commoners. Most Tarascan soldiers were unarmoured and fought with bows and arrows; only the elite used armour and shock weapons, yet their heavy reliance on archery gave the army great defensive strength. They were considerably less formidable offensively because they lacked large numbers of hand-to-hand combatants and consequently did not use the *atlatl*. Although the Tarascans successfully expanded within the area around their capital, their early attempts to expand toward the east against Nahuatl-speaking cities failed and any further efforts were thwarted by the Aztecs' pre-emptive conquest of the area. Nevertheless, their heavy reliance on archery gave the Tarascans a decisive defensive advantage in their own territory, where they had ample ammunition and a favourable logistical situation. These tactical advantages and the advantage of operating within a large hinterland that denied aggressors logistical support, combined to thwart Aztec thrusts deep into Tarascan territory. Nevertheless, the Aztecs remained a significant threat so the Tarascans built a series of fortifications on the major routes from Aztec-allied areas. Responding in kind, the Aztecs built counter-fortifications, but their main expansionary thrust was around Tarascan territory. Bypassing the fortifications, the Aztecs conquered and incorporated the surrounding groups as part of a long-term strategy to strangle the Tarascans, a process cut short by the Spanish conquest.

The second major power to confront the Aztecs was the Tlaxcallan confederacy made up of Nahuatl-speaking city-states in central Mexico. Individually, these city-states were too weak to resist the Aztecs, but joined into shifting alliances. At various times, this alliance included Tlaxcallan, Cholollan, Huexotzinco, Atlixco and Tliliuhqui-Tepec; thus united, it was a significant threat. Unlike some of their other adversaries, these fought wars the same way as the Aztecs and used the full complement of Mesoamerican weapons, although their commoners received less formal training than did most of the Aztecs.

Even though the Aztecs could muster a larger and better trained army, Tlaxcallan controlled a powerful confederacy and, even in victory, the Aztecs would have been badly mauled. Thus, they dealt with the Tlaxcallan confederacy through a series of flower wars, pinning them down while they were completely encircled, cut off, and finally crushed. This was a decades-long process, but by the time the Spaniards arrived, the Aztecs had already completed their encirclement, they had escalated the ferocity of their battles, and Tlaxcallan's final defeat was perhaps no more than a decade away. The Aztecs were dealing effectively with the Tarascans and the Tlaxcaltecs, but both remained threats, in part owing to their military potential, but primarily because of their political potential to lure and unite other disaffected Mesoamerican groups.

In brief, Tenochtitlan was the capital of the mightiest empire in

Mesoamerica. However, it did not rule unchallenged over a unified region. Even within the empire, individual tributaries could, and did, revolt almost at will if the Aztecs proved too weak to compel continued allegiance. This was because the various parts of the empire were not politically, economically, ideologically or socially integrated into the whole. The Aztecs thus ruled over an empire with a remarkably varied social and political mosaic. Moreover, there was little incentive for independent groups to become part of the empire, but whether the Aztecs were resisted depended largely on the balance of power. Thus, the only large powers anywhere near Tenochtitlan – the Tlaxcallan confederacy and the Tarascan empire – remained free. Nevertheless, both of these powers were being slowly encircled and their days were numbered. The Aztecs were undoubtedly the greatest power in Mesoamerica and, without external intervention, there was no major threat to the internal security of Tenochtitlan.

3 THE DISCOVERY OF YUCATAN

As we have seen, Spanish expectations about what they would find in Mexico were conditioned by the peoples they had already encountered in the New World. Compared to Mesoamerica, the Spanish conquests of the Indies, Central America and Florida were relatively easy. Although they were often fierce warriors, the Indians in these places lacked the arms and organization to mount a sustained military challenge that would seriously threaten Spanish exploration or settlement. Guns, crossbows, steel swords and armour had proved decisive against native forces, so when Governor Velásquez of Cuba dispatched Francisco Hernández de Córdoba on yet another journey of exploration, this time to the as-yet unknown Yucatan Peninsula, there was every reason to think that his force of three ships and 110 soldiers would be adequate.[1]

Córdoba left Cuba on 8 February 1517 and reached Cape Catoche, Yucatan, three weeks later, having been delayed by a storm. There, for the first time in the New World, the Spaniards encountered cities, states and organized resistance. Nevertheless, they felt that they had a right to enter Indian communities, freely trade with the inhabitants, and ultimately conquer them under Spanish laws, as they had in the Indies. The Maya of Yucatan lived in organized cities and provinces under their own kings and their laws also governed foreign contacts and trade, all of which precluded the Spaniards' plans. Since the two sides held conflicting attitudes about what actions were permissible, this first Spanish/Mesoamerican contact was almost guaranteed to provoke a clash. Moreover, each side was confident of its superiority – the Maya by virtue of their numbers and the Spaniards by virtue of their military technology and their culture. [2]

1 Díaz del Castillo 1908–16, 1:8, 11–12; 1977, 1:41, 43; Martyr d'Anghera 1970, 2:6.

2 Alfonso el Sabio 1972, 2:228; Díaz del Castillo 1908–16, 1:14; 1977, 1:45. Where the data conflict, I am following the dating of Wagner (1942a:26; 1942b:47–8; 1944) for the expeditions of Córdoba, Grijalva and Cortés, respectively.

The Spanish accounts claim that the natives' friendly overtures induced them to come ashore where they were then treacherously ambushed. The Indian version went unrecorded, but they may have had both advance knowledge of these bearded white men and reason to fear them. Christopher Columbus's ships had encountered sea-going Maya traders at the end of the fifteenth century, and in the following decades native societies must have been unsettled by ship sightings, shipwrecked foreigners washing up on their shores, and stories of the devastation overtaking the native societies of the Caribbean. Moreover, Córdoba and his men belied their peaceful intentions by disembarking heavily armed with crossbows and harquebuses.[3]

The Spaniards could not have known Maya political etiquette and most likely misconstrued events at their initial encounter. The Spaniards were probably received in peace until they seized, or appeared to be seizing, Maya property without permission, initiating the eventual clash. The Spaniards were familiar with such native weapons as bows, lances, slings and shields which they had seen in the Indies. But this was certainly their first encounter with natives who fought in well-ordered and armoured military units following an organized combat sequence as in European warfare. The battle that met Córdoba's men began with an initial barrage of arrows and slingstones that wounded fifteen Spaniards (two subsequently died) and this was quickly followed by the Maya closing for hand-to-hand combat. The Spaniards were immediately placed on the defensive but their weaponry prevailed. Neither side was prepared for the other – not the Spaniards for Indian organization nor the Maya for Spanish weaponry. Spanish swords were no sharper than native ones but kept their edges longer and could be used for forward thrusts as well as for vertical and lateral slashes; the impact of the fifteen crossbows and ten harquebuses must have been devastating psychologically as well as physically. [4]

Clubs and swords had effect, but Spanish steel armour was proof against most Indian projectiles except perhaps darts cast from very close range. Indeed, Spaniards' wounds were typically limited to the limbs, face, neck and other vulnerable areas not protected by armour, which meant that the Spanish soldiers faced considerably less risk than did their Indian adversaries whose entire bodies were vulnerable. Moreover, Spanish infantry arms were also superior.

3 Colón 1984:274; Cook and Borah 1971:376–410; Díaz del Castillo 1908–16, 1:14–16; 1977, 1:45–6; Wilson 1990:94–6.
4 Díaz del Castillo 1908–16, 1:20; 1977, 1:49.

Their pikes and metre-long swords had Indian equivalents, but the Spanish steel versions were stronger and retained their edges far longer. The Spaniards' main advantage, however, lay with their crossbows and harquebuses. Military crossbows of that period weighed 5.5–6 kilograms (15–16 pounds) and fired 1.5–3 ounce wooden bolts with metal heads for distances of over 320 metres (350 yards) in an arc, or 64 metres (70 yards) point blank, compared to a probable maximum range of 180 metres (600 feet) for Indian bows. However, reloading was slow, limiting crossbow fire to only one bolt per minute compared to between six and ten arrows by bow for the same time. Nevertheless, crossbows had the advantage of greater range and power while demanding far less skill than bows.[5]

Spanish harquebuses measured 1–1.5 metres (3 feet 3 inches to 5 feet) long, weighed 8–9 kilograms (17 pounds 8 ounces to 20 pounds), and fired a 47–140 gram (2–6 ounce) lead ball up to 137 metres (150 yards), although it was effective for only about half that distance. In addition, reloading was very slow, limiting the harquebus's rate of fire to no more than one round every one and a half minutes.[6]

Despite these low rates of fire, the greater range and impact of crossbows and harquebuses gave the Spaniards unprecedented hitting power in Mesoamerica, allowing them to fire into armoured opponents with deadly effect. Because of their weight, however, crossbows and harquebuses could not be used for long as the soldiers' arms became unsteady after half an hour's rapid fire. Also, since crossbows and harquebuses were most effective at point-blank range, they could be used only in two ranks so their fire was not as concentrated as arrow barrages: archers in the back rows could lob volleys over the front ranks, they could coordinate fire for up to six ranks, and they could do so at a much higher rate of fire.[7]

Fifteen Indians were killed in this initial clash between Spanish and Maya forces before the rest broke off contact. The attacking force probably numbered only in the hundreds – too few to force a decisive result against 110 well-armed Europeans. In the face of this

5 Brereton 1976:37; Burne 1955:28; Foley, Palmer and Soedel 1985:104; Payne-Gallwey 1986:14–20, 37; Pope 1965:91; Pope 1923:334–40; Rodgers 1939:108; Salas 1950:183.

6 Brereton 1976:37; Contamine 1984:143, 147; Pope 1965:91; Salas 1950:207, 209, 213. See also the illustrations of the step-by-step reloading procedure in Gheyn (1986:9–181).

7 Pope 1965:91.

defeat, the Maya abandoned their town to the Spaniards, who looted the houses and temples of whatever gold they could find. They also took two Maya prisoners, who were later baptized Julianillo and Melchorejo and eventually taught Spanish so that they could serve as translators.[8]

The Spaniards returned to their ships and sailed west along the coast until 29 March 1517 when they reached the town of Campeche, which they renamed San Lázaro. They travelled slowly because they sailed only during the day, so news of the earlier battle probably preceded them and the Maya knew the Spaniards were vulnerable to greatly superior numbers. The Spaniards were not likely to take any more Maya by surprise and they were cautious in initiating further contacts: Córdoba was neither authorized nor equipped to make forays inland and much of his exploration was carried out from the safety of his ships. The Spaniards already knew what the area offered and that gold was scarce, yet they repeatedly landed – perhaps for trade and exploration, but certainly for food and water.[9]

Because of the duration of the expedition and the small size of the ships, the Spaniards could not carry all the supplies they needed. Some additional food was hunted by the soldiers in the relative safety of rural and forested areas, but the main reason the Spaniards stopped at Maya cities was their insistent need for water. Each man required at least 1.9 litres (2 quarts) of drinking water per day – 208 litres (55 gallons) per day for the original complement of soldiers, in addition to the needs of the sailors. However, the Yucatan Peninsula is essentially a large limestone slab almost completely devoid of surface water. Although rainfall is plentiful, the runoff does not flow into rivers and streams but instead drains into the rock and collects in natural cisterns, called *cenotes*. It was the presence of these natural reservoirs that permitted the growth of cities in Yucatan and dictated their locations. Such water sources were virtually impossible to see from shipboard so the Spaniards could be assured they had found one only when they sighted a city. This meant that whatever other motivations they may have had, and despite the obvious dangers of doing so, the Spaniards were forced to stop at Maya cities.

Though fearful of an attack, the Spaniards landed all their forces near Campeche to refill their water casks. They were led into

8 Díaz del Castillo 1908–16, 1:17; 1977, 1:47.
9 Díaz del Castillo 1908–16, 1:18; 1977, 1:47; Martyr d'Anghera 1970, 2:9.

the city by a party of Indians but left when ordered and sailed another ten days before reaching the political centre of Chanpoton, where they once again landed for water. The well-armed Spaniards camped ashore where they anxiously remained on the defensive. They were surrounded by a force of Indians during the night and were attacked at dawn. The Maya wounded more than eighty Spaniards with a barrage of arrows, darts and stones, and then advanced for hand-to-hand combat. The Spaniards repulsed them, despite being greatly outnumbered – allegedly by two hundred to one – because their arms and armour were superior to those of the Indians and because once the Maya had closed, only their first few ranks could actively engage the Spaniards and the significance of their numerical advantage diminished. Once they pulled back to relative safety, the Indians again used their superior numbers to fire into the Spanish camp; when Maya reinforcements arrived, the Spaniards could no longer hold out and, in close formation, broke through and fled toward their boats under constant assault. The battle had lasted only an hour but the Spaniards were decisively defeated: of the 110 Spanish soldiers, fifty were killed, two were carried off alive, and all but one survivor were wounded, some dying soon thereafter.[10]

Now shorthanded, the Spaniards were forced to abandon one of their ships, which they burned. They set sail and eventually reached Cuba on 20 April 1517, where Córdoba soon succumbed to his wounds. Word of these events spread throughout Cuba: in just two and a half months, a new land of great cities and gold had been discovered, but it was also a dangerous land of large armies that had defeated the Spaniards.

We can only speculate about the reaction among the Maya, but there must have been considerable ill-ease. True, half of Córdoba's men had been killed at Chanpoton, but the Spaniards were formidable fighters and the Maya had won with great difficulty and loss of life. Moreover, the Spaniards possessed wonders never before seen, including large sailing ships, harquebuses, crossbows and other steel arms and armour, and they were of very different aspect with their pale faces, pronounced facial hair, and blue as well as brown eyes. Still, their stay was brief and without significant impact: they initiated no sustained trade, no political upheaval, no religious revolution. Córdoba's arrival left few traces and, had the Spaniards

10 Díaz del Castillo 1908–16, 1:18, 20–1; 1977, 1:48–9; Martyr d'Anghera 1970, 2:10.

not come again, his presence would probably have faded into legend.

Córdoba's visit had even less impact on the Aztecs. His landings were all in the Maya area well beyond Aztec control. Nevertheless, merchants linked the two areas and the Aztecs had outposts at Xicallanco and Cimatlan, so some word of these unusual events must have reached their capital of Tenochtitlan. There are no direct records of Córdoba's visit in native accounts, but there are stories of wondrous and troubling events: comets, temples burning, the lake boiling, a wailing woman at night, two-headed men, and a miraculous bird with a mirror on its head. These were later said to be omens foretelling the destruction of the Aztec world but they may have reflected distorted accounts of strange invaders that must have gone through many tellings before they reached Tenochtitlan.[11]

Inspired by the discovery of gold and other wealth in Mesoamerica, Governor Velásquez dispatched a second expedition, led by Juan de Grijalva. Very conscious of the danger, Grijalva left Cuba with a larger and better-armed second expedition. With four ships (three caravels and one brigantine, which soon turned back), two hundred men and a Maya interpreter, Grijalva reached Cozumel on 3 May 1518. Expecting to be attacked, he disembarked with a hundred armed men on 6 May and, finding the town abandoned, claimed it for the king. The Spaniards then reconnoitred the Yucatan coast but did not land before sailing on in search of Campeche. Grijalva's failure to land at any large settlement suggests a very cautious approach. Nevertheless, like Córdoba, he also needed water but rather than stopping at cities where his reception was uncertain, he sailed on, straining his supplies, until he reached Campeche, the one city where Córdoba had resupplied without being attacked.[12]

Sorely in need of water, on arrival, Grijalva and a hundred fully armed men went ashore, taking several cannons – weapons that Córdoba had not possessed. Unopposed, he placed the cannons near a temple in the centre of town and landed another hundred men. When a Maya force approached, Grijalva said through his interpreter that the Spaniards wanted only food and water and would then leave. Disregarding Maya warnings, the Spaniards

11 Acosta 1954:236–7; 1970–73, 2:508–10; Durán 1964:247–60; 1967, 2:467–503; Muñoz Camargo 1966:169–72; Sahagún 1975:1–8; 1989:31–3.

12 Díaz 1942:69–70, 72; 1950:5, 7, 10; Martyr d'Anghera 1970, 2:12; Oviedo y Valdés 1942:88–94, 96–9; 1959, 2:118–25. I am not relying on the account of Grijalva's expedition written by Díaz del Castillo (1908–16; 1977) because its reliability is disputed. Wagner (1942b:18–21) questions whether he was even there.

marched through the town in defensive formation until they reached a well where they took water. The Maya brought food and gifts and asked Grijalva to leave, which he declined to do as he still needed more water. The next morning the Maya attacked, but they were driven back when the Spaniards fired their cannons, killing three Indians and putting the rest to flight.[13]

The type of cannon that Grijalva used is uncertain but all were ships' guns, as would be expected for a coastal reconnaissance. Gun ports cut through the sides of men of war were a very recent innovation in Europe and were not yet employed in ships in the Indies. Instead, guns were mounted on the rail topside, which favoured light cannons called falconets.[14]

Falconets of the day were 1–1.6 metres (3 feet 3 inches to 5 feet 3 inches) long, 6–7 centimetres (2.3–2.7 inches) in calibre, typically weighed 225 kilograms (500 pounds), but could get as large as 500 kilograms (1,100 pounds). They fired a 1.7–5.5 kilogram (12 ounce to 2 pound 8 ounce) ball for 140 metres (460 feet) point blank, but could reach a maximum distance of 2,000 metres (6,600 feet). Falconets could be fired twice as rapidly as other cannons and harquebuses because they were breechloading: each gun was equipped with two or three chambers that were loaded and then sequentially placed in the breech, braced, and fired, which was much quicker than loading and firing muzzleloaders, which had to be swabbed out and reloaded down the same barrel. However, this higher rate of fire was achieved at a cost of significantly lower muzzle velocity. Chambers fit the barrel poorly, leaking gas and producing far greater windage than muzzleloading cannons. Still, this was a minor disadvantage against opponents who lacked comparable weapons, and the falconets played havoc with Indian formations. Their one significant drawback was their lack of mobility. The falconets were not mounted on wheeled carriages and had to be carried into position, so a rapidly shifting tactical situation often meant that they could not be moved with the battle, limiting their use.[15]

The cannons inflicted psychological as well as physical damage on the Indians, but the Spaniards' main advantage lay in their defensive formation that, against steel arms and armour, the Maya

13 Díaz 1942:73–4; 1950:11–13; Oviedo y Valdés 1942:99–102, 105–6; 1959, 2:125–9. Díaz (1942:73; 1950:11) says five cannons but Oviedo y Valdés (1942:99, 104) reports only three – two medium-sized bronze cannons and one of iron.
14 Pope 1965:58; Rodgers 1939:337.
15 Arnold 1978:243; Contamine 1984:147; Rodgers 1939:339–40; Salas 1950:216; Stone 1961:160, 162; Tarassuk and Blair 1982:54; Vigon 1947:37, 46.

were unable to penetrate. The Spaniards continued to kill Maya and burn their houses, but when they pursued the fleeing Indians, they became separated and their formation broke down. Some Spaniards followed Grijalva while others followed their standard. Once they were divided, the Maya turned on the Spaniards in individual combat and forced them back, killing one and wounding forty. Only the covering fire of cannons, harquebuses and crossbows staved off total defeat and the Spaniards retreated to their camp. There, they tended their wounded and were unmolested until, after securing the needed water, they left.[16]

Grijalva then sailed to Chanpoton. Aware that Córdoba had lost half his men there, Grijalva scared off the canoes that approached his ship by firing two cannon shots and then left without attempting to land. On 31 May 1518 the Spaniards reached Laguna de Términos, a large bay fed by rivers southwest of Yucatan's limestone shelf. At last, here was an area of abundant fresh water where the Spaniards could replenish their supplies without having to enter a city. Everyone went ashore, made camp, gathered food and water, and repaired their ships, remaining until 8 June before they sailed on past the Grijalva River. There they were followed by more than two thousand Indians in canoes who shot arrows at them, which the Spaniards answered with a cannon shot, killing an Indian.[17]

The next day, the Spaniards were approached by many canoes of Indians with whom they were able to trade for gold. The following day with considerable ceremony, an Indian lord dressed Grijalva in an elaborate gold ornamented costume and Grijalva reciprocated, dressing the noble in Spanish attire. The exchange had little more significance for the Spaniards, but it was to give the Indians of central Mexico, and especially the Aztecs, their first tangible evidence of the arrival of these strangers. The Spaniards arrived at Coatzacualco on 11 June 1518 and then sailed to Isla de Sacrificios. There, they also traded for gold but, despite the desire of his men to establish a settlement, Grijalva sailed on. They passed the town of Nauhtlan (renamed Almería by the Spaniards) before reaching a much larger one, where twelve canoes of Indians attacked the ships and were repulsed by artillery fire.[18]

16 Díaz 1942:74; 1950:13; Oviedo y Valdés 1942:106; 1959, 2:129.

17 Díaz 1942:75; 1950:13–15; Oviedo y Valdés 1942:112; 1959, 2:134.

18 Díaz 1942:75–6, 79–80; 1950:15–16, 19–21; López de Gómara 1964:15–18; 1965–66, 2:16–19; Martyr d'Anghera 1970, 2:16. Oviedo y Valdés 1942:114; 1959, 2:135–6. See Oviedo y Valdés (1942:111; 1959, 2:133–4) for a detailed list of the dress and gifts presented to Grijalva.

The Spaniards then retraced their route, finally reaching Chanpoton, where Grijalva disembarked with a hundred men to secure badly needed food and water. They were again attacked by Indian canoes, which were driven off by artillery fire after which the Spaniards decided to take and burn the town. However, since it was well defended and fortified with wooden palisades, the Spaniards left and sailed on to Campeche, where Grijalva landed with his men and four cannons. There he fended off an Indian attack and took food and water for the return trip to Cuba.[19]

As with Córdoba's expedition, Grijalva's landings had local impact on the groups contacted but caused little long-term or fundamental change. Whether or not stories of these contacts reached Tenochtitlan through merchants trading in the Maya area, Grijalva's expedition had sailed along the Gulf coast into areas dominated by the Aztecs. The noble who had so ceremoniously dressed Grijalva in fine attire was an Aztec who wanted to find out about these strangers so he could send this information and the goods he had received to Moteuczoma (i.e. Montezuma). Thus, the Aztecs learned of the Spaniards' arrival in concrete terms, but who they were and the significance of their presence remained unclear. [20]

The Aztec king and his advisers discussed the situation but kept it secret from the people. They decided that the coast should be watched in case the strangers returned and Moteuczoma accordingly dispatched men to do so. This did not, however, resolve the matter of who or what the strangers were.[21]

It is a widely accepted interpretation that the Aztecs thought that the Spanish leader was the returning god, Quetzalcoatl. This interpretation may well be more or less accurate. To understand who and what these Spaniards were, the Aztecs drew on their own background in order to interpret them in a meaningful way. The Spaniards were unlike any people seen before and they had technological capabilities that seemed godlike, so a supernatural origin had to be considered, especially in the Aztec worldview where gods could play direct roles in human affairs. After considerable thought and discussion, the notion that the strangers might be gods

19 Díaz 1942:80–2; 1950:21–4; Oviedo y Valdés 1942:125, 130, 132–3; 1959, 2:141–2, 145–6.

20 Acosta 1954:238; 1970–73, 2:513; Ixtlilxochitl 1969:3; 1975–77, 1:450; Sahagún 1975:5–6; 1989:34–6.

21 Acosta 1954:238; 1970–73, 2:513; Durán 1964:268; 1967, 2:513; Sahagún 1989:37.

was accepted – not, apparently, as a fact, but as a disturbing possibility.[22]

Even if the Aztecs had determined that these strangers were only mortal men, there was little they could have done to prevent their return. The Aztecs had faced sustained threats elsewhere in Mesoamerica, but these were predictable, as we have seen. Any attack would have been limited to specific times of the year, the armies would have travelled through a limited number of mountain passes, and their advance would have been fairly open because of the slowness of the march. The Spaniards, by contrast, presented an unprecedented situation. The sailing ships offered little warning of their approach and they could land anywhere along hundreds of miles of coastline, easily thwarting any defensive forces posted to intercept them. Until the Spaniards fully landed, the Aztecs had no feasible defensive strategy.

Governor Velásquez began preparing for a third expedition to Mexico even before Grijalva returned to Cuba, and appointed a young man, Hernán Cortés, as its leader. Cortés had learned much about Mesoamerica from the earlier expeditions and some of his men had also been on those voyages and had first-hand experience with the groups they set out to contact and subdue. Nevertheless, support among his Spanish backers in Cuba was decidedly mixed. Political calculation and intrigue affected the staffing and equipping of the expedition and greatly affected the course of action subsequently adopted in Mexico.

Governor Diego Velásquez provided the political authorization for this third expedition, as well as its primary financial backing, as he had with the two previous ones. However, Cortés was a controversial choice for commander: there were more experienced men available. However, Velásquez distrusted them. Cortés's selection was also encouraged by the judicious lobbying of his allies – notably Andrés de Duero, the governor's secretary, and Amador de Lares, the king's accountant – who had formed a secret partnership with Cortés. In addition to the ships, men and provisions supplied by Velásquez, Cortés used his own money as well as borrowed funds to fit out the expedition so he also had a significant financial stake in its outcome.

More than 350 men were recruited for the expedition, but except for Cortés and a few of his more prominent followers, little is

22 Acosta 1954:238; 1970–73, 2:514; Durán 1964:264; 1967, 2:507; Sahagún 1989:37–8, 41; 1975:5, 9.

known about these men. Most of those who settled the Indies during the early decades were from Andalusia and Castile, supplemented by a scattered sample of other Spanish provinces, Portugal, Italy, and a smattering of other countries. Many pretended to *hidalgo* (lesser noble or gentleman) status but the accuracy of this claim is questionable, especially in light of the better-known social background of the conquistadors who went to Peru. About one-quarter of these were *hidalgos*, but the rest were plebeians, and less than one-third of the total could read and write. Successful men in the Indies generally remained where they were or returned to Spain. Those who went on exploratory expeditions were relatively new arrivals, had not fared well financially, lacked high social positions, and most were single or had left their families in Spain. Thus the conquistadors were not triumphal noblemen of Spain, but the relatively unsuccessful residue of the Caribbean experience.[23]

Although Cortés had already assembled most of the men and fleet for the expedition, Velásquez began turning against him amidst many disquieting rumours about his trustworthiness and ambitions, as well as Cortés's own political manoeuvrings. Forewarned of Velásquez's doubts about him and alert to the possibility that he might remove him as leader, Cortés left Santiago de Cuba early and sailed to Port of Trinidad a few days later where he secured more arms, supplies and horses, as well as additional men who were among his staunchest supporters.[24]

On learning of Cortés's precipitous departure, Velásquez sent orders to the local authorities to have him imprisoned and the fleet detained, but Cortés had the support of his men who were too formidable a force for local officials to challenge. Thus, after ten days, the fleet sailed for Havana, where still more men summoned by Cortés had gathered. Velásquez sent orders for Cortés to be arrested there, too, but again without effect, and the fleet sailed for Yucatan on 10 February 1519.[25]

Spanish ships of the day did not sail well against the wind so the timing of each expedition's departure depended primarily on the prevailing winds. The Gulf of Mexico and the Caribbean enjoyed winds from the east for only about three months of the year, so

23 Boyd-Bowman 1973:3–5; Gibson 1975:292; Lockhart 1972:19–20, 31–6; Mörner 1976:747–8; Sauer 1966:198; Wagner 1944:3–5.

24 Díaz del Castillo 1908–16, 1:70; 1977, 1:81; López de Gómara 1964:19; 1965–66, 2:19–20.

25 Díaz del Castillo 1908–16, 1:90; 1977, 1:94; López de Gómara 1964:20–1; 1965–66, 2:21; Martyr d'Anghera 1970, 2:26; Tapia 1950:31–3, 45–7; 1963:19–20, 26–7.

further Spanish voyages of exploration were generally timed to take advantage of these and to avoid the hurricane season and the prevailing northers. However, the political situation forced Cortés to sail earlier in the year than the previous two expeditions, while weather conditions were still less than ideal.[26]

Cortés reached Yucatan with eleven ships and as many as 450 soldiers, including thirteen harquebusiers and thirty-two crossbowmen, four falconets and ten brass cannons. The exact nature of these cannons is not known but they were probably muzzleloading field guns of the day. Their size is also unknown, but they were doubtless larger than the falconets and would have had greater range and accuracy, although they would also have been less mobile. In addition, Cortés brought sixteen horses, a number limited by their scarcity and expense in the Indies as well as the difficulty in carrying them on the open decks of the ships, where they had to be supported by large belly slings lest they fall and injure themselves on the rolling deck.[27]

This expedition was significantly larger and stronger than earlier ones, but what is most apparent is not the simple increase in soldiers, but the disproportionately large number of ships. Cortés had more than twice as many men as Grijalva but almost four times as many ships. Cortés did bring more equipment, but the primary reason for the greater number of ships was logistical.

Both of the previous expeditions had relied on local supplies, as was common on all Spanish expeditions throughout the circum-Caribbean area. But the unique conditions of the Yucatan Peninsula fostered unnecessary clashes as the Spaniards had to enter cities in search of water and food. Moreover, they typically did so by force, but the timing was dictated by need rather than a favourable military situation, which led to casualties that could have been avoided had Spanish supplies been adequate. Cortés's response to this problem was to embark on his expedition with a much larger store of supplies; although he still depended on local resupply, his needs were significantly less pressing, giving him greater freedom to consider social and military factors in deciding whether to make or avoid contact.[28]

26 Chaunu 1979:96–7; Chaunu and Chaunu 1955–59, 7:28–9; Haring 1918:208.
27 Cortés 1963:11; 1971:11; Díaz del Castillo 1908–16, 1:85, 92; 1977, 1:91, 96; López de Gómara 1964:23; 1965–66, 2:23; Tapia 1950:36; 1963:22; Vigon 1947:473. Wagner (1944:157) suggests that the field guns were *culebrinas*, capable of firing a 7–11 kilogram (18–30 pound) shot, but this is far from certain.
28 López de Gómara 1964:23; 1965–66, 2:23.

Cortés's expedition followed the same route as the first two and landed at Cozumel, where Grijalva's expedition had gone ashore. This was a friendly town and Cortés enforced a policy of no looting, a practice designed to ensure friendlier relations, and one that was made feasible by Cortés's greater supplies.[29]

Both previous expeditions had seen native temples, idols and direct evidence of human sacrifice, but had made little attempt to convert the Indians to Christianity because the Spaniards were militarily vulnerable and could ill afford to alienate the Indians further. Moreover, whereas the earlier expeditions had lacked priests, at least one accompanied Cortés. Cortés, however, did break the statues of native gods and replaced them with a cross and an image of the Virgin, perhaps because conversion justified his conquest, although he did not do this everywhere. While on Cozumel, Cortés dispatched one of his ships to find Spaniards rumoured to be held captive among the Maya. One, Gerónimo de Aguilar, was found and returned to become a trustworthy translator of Maya but the second, Gonzalo Guerrero, had assimilated into Maya society, refused to return, and in fact had led the attack against Córdoba's forces at Cape Catoche two years before.[30]

Cortés then sailed along the coast of Yucatan until he reached Potonchan, bypassing Chanpoton because of adverse tides. The Spaniards landed near the city and camped on the beach that night, despite Maya protests and the arrival of a reported twelve thousand warriors. The next day, Cortés decided to enter the town, even though it was strongly fortified with log barricades. He put the crossbowmen, harquebusiers and cannons in the smaller boats and sent them up the Grijalva River toward the town, while a force of two hundred men under Alonzo de Avila approached it by land. Their boats were met by canoes full of warriors and Cortés ordered Aguilar to read the *requerimiento* (summons) in the Maya language. The *requerimiento* was a Spanish legal statement written just before 1514 during Spain's early years of overseas expansion. It demanded that the Indians recognize the authority of the Church, pope and king; refusal meant coercive subjugation, loss of property, and

29 Aguilar 1963:137; 1977:66; Cortés 1963:11; 1971:11; Díaz del Castillo 1908–16, 1:90–2; 1977, 1:94–6; López de Gómara 1964:26–8; 1965–66, 2:25–7; Tapia 1950:32–3; 1963:20.
30 Aguilar 1963:137; 1977:66; Alfonso el Sabio 1972, 2:228; Cortés 1963:15; 1971:17–18; Díaz del Castillo 1908–16, 1:97–8, 100–3; 1977, 1:99–100, 102–4; López de Gómara 1964:28, 30–2; 1965–66, 2:28–32; Martyr d'Anghera 1970, 2:28–31; Tapia 1950:33–4; 1963:20–1.

punishment befitting traitors, and its reading before each battle legally absolved the conquistadors of responsibility for their wars. Even if Aguilar's translation was adequate and if he was close enough to be heard clearly, which is unlikely, the *requerimiento* would have been meaningless to the Maya. In any case, the reading had no effect and the Maya allegedly fired first. The Spaniards responded with crossbow, harquebus and cannon fire, pushing the Indians back to the town and destroying their barricades. At that point, Avila's force arrived from the rear and the combined Spanish forces routed the Indians and Cortés took possession of the town in the name of the king.[31]

Dividing forces in the face of superior numbers had led to disastrous consequences for the earlier expeditions, but there was a logic to Cortés's actions. His land force was large enough to fend off an attack and was not plunging into the unknown, but was marching along a known path to a fixed destination – the town. His sea force, although smaller, had the advantage of cannons, and they were more mobile so, even if they were repulsed, they could retreat to the ultimate refuge of the ships. Thus, neither Spanish contingent was dangerously vulnerable to the Maya; dividing his forces allowed Cortés to confront the Indians from the sea while his land forces surprised them from the rear, leading to a rout.

The next day, two Indians brought Cortés a gift of gold ornaments and again asked him to leave. In response, Cortés demanded food and the Indians promised to bring it. But the Spaniards' situation deteriorated when Melchorejo fled during the night. Melchorejo was one of the Maya who had been captured during Córdoba's expedition and who was to serve as a translator on this one; his flight caused the Spaniards to worry that he might divulge crucial intelligence to the Indians. Their anxiety increased when the Indians did not return with the promised food so, after two days, Cortés sent out two foraging parties. Each of these numbered more than a hundred men but both were attacked and forced back to their camp. Stretched out along trails, even forces as large as two hundred men were vulnerable to Maya attack when they were not supported by artillery or additional soldiers. Therefore, the next day Cortés landed the rest of his men and at least ten of his horses – the first to reach Mesoamerica.[32]

31 Cortés 1963:15–16; 1971:18–20; Díaz del Castillo 1908–16, 1:106–10; 1977, 1:106–8; Gibson 1966:38–9; López de Gómara 1964:37–40; 1965–66, 2:36–9.
32 Cortés 1963:17; 1971:20; Díaz del Castillo 1908–16, 1:113–16; 1977, 1:110–12; Tapia 1950:38; 1963:23.

With horsemen and cannons, a force of three hundred Spaniards marched on the Maya, reaching a savanna near the town of Centla. From there, the foot soldiers advanced without the horsemen, who had difficulty crossing a swamp. Again, the *requerimiento* was read and a battle ensued. The Spaniards had little idea of the size of the opposing force when they set out, but neither did the Maya since only slightly more than two hundred Spaniards had engaged in the earlier clashes. Now they faced three hundred Spaniards and, just as the battle began, their rearguard arrived with another hundred men. Seventy Spaniards were wounded in the opening barrage and one was killed after the Maya closed for hand-to-hand combat. But the Spaniards fought in close formation and successfully defended themselves, even though the Maya now completely surrounded them.[33]

Spanish arms and armour were superior to native arms but the Maya adapted to the situation by pulling back beyond sword range, while sustaining their barrage of arrows, darts and slingstones. This reduced their vulnerability to Spanish swords and pikes, but cannons played havoc with the tightly packed Indian formations. This tactic nevertheless favoured the Maya so the Spaniards advanced to re-establish contact, regain the advantage of superior swords and armour, and avoid the murderous barrage.

After two hours of fighting, Cortés's horsemen arrived, and charged from the rear. Dividing forces was a common tactic in Mesoamerica and would not have been totally unexpected, but the Maya were surprised by the appearance and speed of the horses. Nevertheless, the horses did not afford the Spaniards a significant strategic advantage because the terrain was broken, heavily wooded, boggy in places, and generally unknown. In fact, the infantry were able to reach their objective faster than horsemen because they could more easily traverse such barriers. But once the cavalry arrived, they could gallop across the open, flat battlefield so quickly that the Maya had little time to react. Armed with four-metre lances, the stirruped riders held the weapons rigidly under their arms, hitting the enemy with the combined power and momentum of both rider and horse, penetrating native armour and riding through their formations. Mounted lancers thus not only gave the Spaniards the same ability to disrupt enemy formations as crossbows, harquebuses and cannons, but also allowed them to pursue and even outpace the enemy, striking repeatedly with their lances.[34]

33 Cortés 1963:17–18; 1971:21.
34 Finer 1975:102; Salas 1950:187.

The battle lasted another hour before the Indians fled into the woods but it was the horses that proved decisive. Aside from the psychological impact of these unknown, but powerful creatures, mounted lancers provided the perfect counter to established Indian tactics. To this point, the Maya had been able to maintain a cohesive front, even when the foremost fighters fell, but the great force that could be channelled into the lances enabled the Spaniards to punch through their lines, disrupting their formations and allowing foot soldiers to pour through, now striking the Maya from flanks and rear. Many Maya soldiers were killed with very low immediate Spanish losses, although more than thirty-five Spaniards died later in Vera Cruz of wounds they received in this battle. Among the Maya taken prisoner were two captains whom Cortés sent back to their rulers with gifts and a peace entreaty. In response, thirty Maya nobles returned the next day, pledged fealty, and gave the Spaniards gifts of food, gold, cloth and twenty women, including Malinche, whose ability to speak both Maya and Nahuatl would later enable Cortés to speak to the Indians of central Mexico. Having subdued the Maya, Cortés felt safe enough to begin their forced conversion to Christianity: he had the statues of Maya gods removed from their temples and replaced with a cross. The Spaniards remained near Potonchan for five days, tending their wounded and then, having been told that the Maya got their gold and jewels from Mexico, sailed away from the Maya area.[35]

The three Spanish expeditions to the Yucatan Peninsula had met with a variety of responses from the groups they contacted, ranging from an apparent eagerness to trade, to hostility, to armed resistance, and to flight. Much of this may be understood strictly in terms of military strength – smaller towns offered less resistance. But this masks a more important reality: Maya towns were part of larger political units so the arrival of invading strangers put the dependent towns in a dilemma. Without direction from their political lords who resided elsewhere, any attack was risky, not only militarily from the Spaniards but also politically from their own leaders. As a result, smaller towns typically did not resist the Spaniards, but larger cities that housed political leaders capable of making decisions of war and peace frequently did.

In their successive expeditions, the Spaniards learned which

35 Aguilar 1963:138; 1977:67; Cortés 1963:18–19; 1971:21–3; Díaz del Castillo 1908–16, 1:118–20, 126–9, 153; 1977, 1:113–15, 119–21, 136; López de Gómara 1964:46–8, 51; 1965–66, 2:44–7, 49; Martyr d'Anghera 1970, 2:35; Oviedo y Valdés 1959, 4:9; Tapia 1950:39; 1963:23–4.

towns were likely to resist and acted accordingly. Moreover, the Spaniards could be more daring in their military actions because they could always fall back to the security of their ships if they miscalculated whereas the Maya, tied to their fields and towns, risked all. But whether successful or not, these clashes taught the Spaniards much about Indian warfare. Spanish tactics changed and adapted throughout the course of these three expeditions. They learned that minimal combat units of around two hundred men were necessary to resist massive Indian attacks, that harquebuses and crossbows were effective against Indian armour, that artillery was extremely disruptive and, finally, that mounted lancers could disrupt formations and force the Indians to flee. This learning process was not one-sided, however, as the Indians also adapted to Spanish warfare. Nevertheless, what the Maya learned and how they adjusted to Spanish weapons and tactics had little impact on the course of Spanish expansion because they were soon left behind. But the Spanish took their understanding of, and adaptation to, native warfare with them to central Mexico, which gave them a significant advantage over those Indians they were yet to encounter.

4 THE CONQUEST OF CENTRAL MEXICO

On 21 April 1519 Cortés's fleet reached the natural harbour on the central Veracruz coast where Grijalva had stopped and traded previously and which was renamed San Juan de Ulua. The ships were met by canoes full of Indians whom Tentlil, the Aztec governor of the region, had sent to collect information about the identity and motivations of these bearded strangers. The Indians were fed and given trade goods before they left; the next day, Cortés landed his men, artillery and horses, then built and fortified his camp.[1]

Although central Veracruz was the homeland of the Totonac people, it was under Aztec control and the next day, the Aztec governor and four thousand unarmed men arrived from Cuetlachtlan with loads of food for Cortés. They then gave Cortés more gifts, including many gold objects, and Cortés gave the Indians Spanish goods in return. Indeed, the Spaniards saw much more gold in Veracruz than in the Maya area, confirming what they had been told. It was the Spanish greed for gold that sealed the Aztecs' fate.[2]

The Aztecs' primary purpose in meeting the Spaniards was to gather information for Moteuczoma. Reports of strange people had reached Tenochtitlan for years, coming not only from the Maya area, but also from this very coast where Grijalva had also put ashore; Aztec accounts of strange events allegedly foretold the Spanish arrival. The very nature of the intruders was in question and one conquistador, Bernal Díaz del Castillo, reported that the Aztec leaders asked for a Spanish metal helmet to see if it was like that worn by one of their gods. Accordingly, a helmet was sent to Moteuczoma.[3]

1 Acosta 1954:238; 1970–73, 2:513; Aguilar 1963:138; 1977:67; Anales de Cuauhtitlan 1975:68; Chimalpahin 1965:121, 234; Cortés 1963:19; 1971:23; Díaz del Castillo 1908–16, 1:130–1, 136–7; 1977, 1:122, 125–6; López de Gómara 1964:54; 1965–66, 2:52–3; Tapia 1950:40; 1963:24.

2 Aguilar 1963:67–8; 1977:138; Cortés 1963:19; 1971:24; Díaz del Castillo 1908–16, 1:137–40; 1977, 1:126–7; López de Gómara 1964:56; 1965–66, 2:54; Martyr d'Anghera 1970, 2:38; Sahagún 1975:5–6; Tapia 1950:41; 1963:25.

3 Díaz del Castillo 1908–16, 1:141; 1977, 1:128; Muñoz Camargo 1966:174–5; Sahagún 1975:1–3, 5, 9.

The Aztec nobles were accompanied by artists who faithfully drew and painted images of everything they saw, including the Spaniards, their ships, horses, dogs and all of their arms and armour. Noting this great interest, the Spaniards demonstrated their weapons for the Aztecs, charging their horses and firing their cannons. Tentlil ordered a camp built nearby for two thousand Indians who were to provide food for the Spaniards, and messengers were sent with the pictures to tell Moteuczoma all they had seen.[4]

A week later, Tentlil returned with more than a hundred porters and at this time gave Cortés still more lavish gifts. Among these, Moteuczoma sent Cortés gifts normally offered to the gods Quetzalcoatl, Tezcatlipoca and Tlalocateuctli, which suggests that the Aztecs did indeed think that the Spaniards might be gods; Cortés dutifully forwarded these gold and turquoise inlaid objects to Spain. The Aztecs relayed Moteuczoma's message that the Spaniards remain where they were and not come to Tenochtitlan. Moteuczoma's presentation of gifts may be interpreted in two ways. He may have been acknowledging that the Spaniards were gods, or he may have been tacitly acknowledging Aztec subservience – both religious and political. The presentation of lavish gifts was not simply an honour but, in the Mesoamerican political world, an admission of hegemonic vassalage. However, this subordination, whether religious or political, was conditional rather than complete. Moteuczoma was offering Cortés recognition of his superior rights if he would stay away and not come to Tenochtitlan. The Aztecs were accustomed to enforcing conditions on vassal cities and it was a type of relationship they understood: whatever apprehension they may have felt, they were trying to incorporate the Spaniards into their world – politically, religiously and conceptually.[5]

In response, Cortés said that he must see Moteuczoma or his own king would be displeased. He also refused to move his camp to another village six or seven leagues away as the Aztecs had also requested. This request may have been an attempt to keep Cortés away from the Totonacs, but it was also a test of his relationship with Moteuczoma. Had Cortés moved, his compliance with the request would have helped clarify the relationship as negotiable

4 Acosta 1954:239; 1970–73, 2:515; Díaz del Castillo 1908–16, 1:140–2, 145; 1977, 1:127–9, 131; López de Gómara 1964:57–9; 1965–66, 2:55–7; Sahagún 1975:6.

5 Acosta 1954:238; 1970–73, 2:514; Cortés 1963:28–32; 1971:40–5; Díaz del Castillo 1908–16, 1:147; 1977, 1:132; Martyr d'Anghera 1970, 2:45–7; Sahagún 1975:11.

rather than dominant. But without more information, Moteuczoma dared not directly challenge the Spaniards' apparent claim to dominance and the parameters of the relationship remained unclear.[6]

After Cortés refused to move his camp, most of the Indians stopped trading and stopped bringing food. In addition, the Aztecs decamped on 12 May 1519, leaving the Spaniards fearful of an attack that never came. Perhaps Moteuczoma thought that withdrawing support would force these strangers to leave, but the Spaniards already knew of the great wealth of Tenochtitlan and, with the Aztecs gone, other groups began to play a supportive role. Three days after the Aztecs withdrew, the Spaniards were visited by five Totonac Indians, who had not dared come while the Aztecs were there. Having heard of the Spanish successes among the Maya, they came to offer their services. This was the Spaniards' first inkling that the Aztecs had enemies, and was one of two major events that set Cortés's course irrevocably toward conquest, the second being Cortés's manipulation of his legal status, which freed him from Velásquez's restraints.[7]

Cortés's relations with the local Indians were important, but even more so was consolidating his support among the Spaniards. Many wanted to return to Cuba, especially Velásquez's supporters. Since the expedition had been authorized by Governor Velásquez, Cortés remained legally bound by the governor's restrictions, which forbade any campaign of conquest. But in a clever bit of legal manipulation, Cortés founded the town of Villa Rica de la Vera Cruz and established its own legal structure so that it now functioned as a political entity directly under the authority of Emperor Charles V (King Charles I of Spain). The town council appointed by Cortés then decided that the expedition had fulfilled Velásquez's mandate and therefore the authority granted by the governor had now lapsed. They then proceeded to elect Cortés as captain directly under the king's authority. This dubious legal

6 Díaz del Castillo 1908–16, 1:142–5; 1977, 1:130–1; López de Gómara 1964:61; 1965–66, 2:58. The length of a league in early colonial Mexico is uncertain. Roland Chardon (1980a:295; 1980b:150; 1980c:465) notes that there were two types in use at that time, the statute league and the common league. Statute leagues, used for juridical matters, were approximately 4.19 kilometres in length whereas common leagues were about 5.5 kilometres. In practice, leagues varied by terrain, being shorter uphill than downhill. What a league actually measures is travel time: five leagues is essentially shorthand for a full day's trip, regardless of the actual linear distance traversed.

7 Díaz del Castillo 1908–16, 1:150–3; 1977, 1:134–5; López de Gómara 1964:61; 1965–66, 2:58–9; Martyr d'Anghera 1970, 2:59; Tapia 1950:42; 1963:25.

manoeuvre neatly freed Cortés of the restraints placed on him by Velásquez and permitted him to act as he saw fit. However, the likelihood of this legal sleight of hand being upheld by the king depended on Cortés's success: it was essentially a political rather than a legal matter. If Cortés failed in his efforts, he laid himself open to charges of treason and other criminal acts against one of the king's loyal governors but if he succeeded in bringing new lands and wealth into Spanish hands, the king's support would be assured and Velásquez's objections would be pushed aside.[8]

The Spaniards in the New World were accustomed to making decisions without the immediate political approval they would have needed in Spain because of the vast distances separating them from their king. It took two to three months for a ship to reach Mexico from Spain and four and a half months to go back. Moreover, to achieve this, ships had to sail at times of the year when the winds favoured them. Usually, this was between April and August for departures from Spain and May to June for the return. Otherwise, the ships had adverse winds and the journeys were substantially longer. As a result, an inquiry to the king from the New World would leave in summer, regardless of when it arose during the year, and the earliest response would not be received until the following summer. Each further clarification of instructions would require an equal amount of time, with an additional year's lag if the instructions failed to arrive until after the New World fleets had sailed for the year. Consequently, New World functionaries were accustomed to making decisions that would have to be approved formally long after the fact. This relative autonomy played a major part in Governor Velásquez's concern in trying – and failing – to select a reliable commander for his third expedition. The great time lag between the New World and the Old is also what allowed Cortés to take the seemingly desperate political chances he did – because there was little that could be done to stop him in his own attempt to conquer Mexico and he would either have succeeded or not by the time the king could act; by then, his political situation would probably be significantly different.[9]

This legal manoeuvre was carried out without the knowledge of Velásquez's supporters, who protested when they found out. To quieten them, Cortés said that anyone who so wished could return

8 Cortés 1963:20–1; 1971:25–7; Díaz del Castillo 1908–16, 1:153, 155–7; 1977, 1:136–9; Ixtlilxochitl 1975–77, 2:202; López de Gómara 1964:67–8; 1965–66, 2:64–5.
9 Chaunu and Chaunu 1955–59, 7:28–31; Haring 1918:208, 227; Rees 1971:128.

to Cuba, but through judicious inducements, he eventually won them over, primarily by promising an increase in their share of the proceeds from the expedition. Moveover, by cutting out Velásquez, there would now be more booty to distribute among the men.[10]

With his legal status resolved and the dissension among the members of his expedition quelled, Cortés then marched to nearby Cempohuallan, the home of the Totonacs who had visited the Spanish camp. He reached the town on 3 June 1519 and was greeted with gifts of food and lodging. Several Maya groups had pledged nominal fealty to Cortés and had given him supplies, but none had turned against their own lords. The Totonacs were the first Mesoamerican group to indicate a willingness, even an eagerness, to end support not for their own political lords who governed legitimately, but for the Aztecs, a different ethnic group, who were the Totonacs' political masters through right of conquest. This was a real watershed for Cortés. The Totonacs had been conquered by, and paid tribute to, the Aztecs, and the Totonac ruler complained of this to Cortés, indicating that he paid allegiance not out of loyalty but fear. This was the first indication to Cortés that there were significant grievances and potential political cleavages among the Aztec tributaries, and he moved quickly to exploit these to his own advantage.

Cortés could not hope to conquer the empire with so few men, regardless of the military superiority they had demonstrated in the past. They could still be overwhelmed and destroyed through sheer numbers of Indians. If a conquest of Mexico was envisioned, the Spaniards had only two alternatives. One was to enlist the help of more Spanish troops from the Indies, but this was not feasible given Cortés's political difficulties with the governor of Cuba; in any case, there were probably not enough soldiers in all the Indies to have accomplished the task unaided. The other alternative was to divide his enemies, which was the course of action chosen. Throughout the entire Conquest period, Cortés consistently sought to split and factionalize the Aztecs and their tributaries so that he would face less opposition. Accordingly, Cortés promised to see that the Totonacs' burdens were relieved and Cempohuallan's ruler agreed to become a Spanish subject which, at a minimum, ensured material support in the form of food, lodging and porters.[11]

10 Cortés 1963:25–7; 1971:37–8; Díaz del Castillo 1908–16, 1:158–62; 1977, 1:140–1.
11 Cortés 1963:34; 1971:50; Díaz del Castillo 1908–16, 1:162–6; 1977, 1:142–5; López de Gómara 1964:62–3; 1965–66, 2:60.

Toward mid-June 1519, the Spaniards marched further up the coast toward another town, Quiahuiztlan, with fifteen horsemen, three hundred Spanish foot soldiers and over four hundred Indian porters. The Spaniards anticipated difficulty in conquering the fortified town but, to their surprise, they were welcomed. Quiahuiztlan's rulers also complained of the treatment they received from the Aztecs and Cortés again promised to do all he could, a pledge he would soon fulfil. When five Aztec tribute collectors arrived, summoned the Totonac rulers, and chastised them for feeding and housing the Spaniards without Moteuczoma's permission, Cortés ordered the Totonacs not to pay any more tribute or obey Moteuczoma, and to take the Aztecs prisoner. The Totonacs obeyed and seized the tribute collectors, but Cortés later had the prisoners secretly brought before him, pleaded ignorance as to why the Totonacs had imprisoned them, and released two of them so they could assure Moteuczoma that the Spaniards were friends. When the Totonacs discovered that two captives were missing, Cortés feigned outrage and ordered the other three to be put on board his ship and guarded, but he secretly freed them as well. Nevertheless, Cortés gained Totonac pledges of fealty by promising to defend them from Moteuczoma's wrath. Still unsure as to who might best serve his interests, Cortés was playing the two sides against each other.[12]

The ruler of Cempohuallan knew far better than Cortés what his pledge of fealty to the Spaniards was worth. Such pledges were not unusual in Mexico and were only as good as the new allies' ability to keep their subjects safe from Aztec retribution. If Cortés proved unable to do so, the Totonacs would quickly resubmit to the Aztecs, so the king's pledge was little more than a promise of support, provided the Spaniards proved capable of defending this new political claim. The Aztecs had dealt with such uprisings before, typically reconquering rebellious cities and demanding increased tribute. But changing allegiance was an act that guaranteed devastating reprisals and was not done lightly or without a strong partner. The Totonacs doubtless saw the Spaniards as powerful, but their shift in allegiance was also forced by Spanish actions. Whether or not the Cempohualtecs played an active role in seizing the tribute collectors, they would have been held responsible for their imprisonment by the Aztecs, in effect forcing the Totonacs to ally

12 Díaz del Castillo 1908–16, 1:166–74; 1977, 1:146–51; Ixtlilxochitl 1975–77, 2:203–4; López de Gómara 1964:69, 72–3, 76–80; 1965–66, 2:66, 69–70, 72–6; Tapia 1950:42–3; 1963:25.

with the Spaniards; Cortés's duplicitous actions cemented this realignment in the minds of the Aztecs.

Such local alliances were crucial to the Spaniards' success because Cortés was not equipped to march overland without Indian support. His expedition had been planned for coastal exploration and although his men and horses could march inland, they were ill-equipped to transport the many supplies that such a trek demanded. The Totonacs had, indeed, offered the Spaniards an opportunity to gain allies while dividing their opponents, but Cortés overestimated what he had gained and underestimated what he still faced. So far, the Spaniards had defeated all the Indians they had met, but these were armies from provincial areas, not an imperial army that had expanded over and subdued most of central Mexico during the preceding ninety years. However, Cortés did not know that this was what was in store for him, because the Aztecs he had encountered thus far had refused to fight. The Totonacs appeared to be valuable allies since they numbered in the tens of thousands, but the advantage of this alliance was more apparent than real.

For one thing, the Totonacs could not mount very formidable armies. The lowlands produced cotton and some Totonac towns manufactured quilted cotton armour, but this was exported commercially and did not reflect local military use. While the Totonacs could muster many soldiers, theirs was not a professional army like the Aztecs'. They had a core of elite warriors, but most of their soldiers were commoners performing tributary service. Moreover, the Totonacs, like most smaller Mesoamerican states of the time, had abandoned the deadly *atlatls*. The Totonacs may have appeared militarily advantageous to Cortés, but their organizational weakness belied their numbers and gave the Spaniards a distorted view of what imperial Mesoamerican armies were like; this misperception was the basis for Cortés's subsequent decisions on how to proceed against the Aztecs.[13]

Secure in their Totonac alliance, the Spaniards began building the city of Villa Rica de la Vera Cruz, including a fort with wooden walls, loopholes, watchtowers and barbicans. In his chronicle, Díaz del Castillo claimed that Moteuczoma learned of the Totonac rebellion and had raised an army to march against them and the Spaniards, but such a course of action is inconsistent with Moteuczoma's other known behaviour and is highly unlikely. Moteuczoma did send a party of high nobles to Cortés with a

13 Acuña 1982–87, 5:190.

message of thanks for having freed the two Aztecs, but they also relayed complaints that the Spaniards had instigated the rebellion. In response, Cortés complained of the withdrawal of the earlier Aztec party, although he assured Moteuczoma that he knew that this discourtesy was not the result of his orders. He explained that the Totonacs were now vassals of the king of Spain, and that he and his followers were coming to Tenochtitlan to place themselves at Moteuczoma's service and thereafter the Totonacs would follow Aztec commands. The respect that these noble Aztecs showed Cortés impressed the Totonacs, further buttressing the Spaniards' reputation and cementing their Totonac allegiance.[14]

The Cempohualtecs then asked Cortés's help against Tizapantzinco, whose Aztec garrison was destroying their crops. This put Cortés in an awkward position: he did not want to alienate the Aztecs, but Totonac support was his more immediate concern. Without it, an inland expedition was impossible because Cortés needed Totonac manpower as well as logistical and intelligence support en route, and their continued friendship was vital for the security of the settlement at Vera Cruz. Thus, Cortés decided to assist them and set out with four hundred soldiers, fourteen horsemen, crossbowmen, harquebusiers, a hundred porters to carry the cannons, and four thousand Indian warriors. But the Aztecs had already left when Cortés reached Tizapantzinco, so he disarmed the remaining Indians and forced an alliance between the two groups before returning to Cempohuallan. This overt action against the Aztecs cemented Cortés's alliance with the Cempohualtecs, who then gave the Spaniards eight women, all daughters of kings and nobles.[15]

As we have seen, intermarriage between ruling families of allied towns was a common way of strengthening political ties in Mesoamerica; although the presentation of women had little actual effect on the Spaniards, it had great political significance for the Cempohualtecs in cementing this new political alliance. They could now expect Aztec reprisals and, without Spanish aid, the Cempohualtec position was hopeless. They were dependent on the Spaniards and Cortés took advantage of this to increase the division between the Aztecs and Totonacs and simultaneously tie Cempohuallan's rulers to him, which he did through religious conversion. Conversion was a prominent feature of the Conquest, or

14 Aguilar 1963:139; 1977:69; Cortés 1963:34; 1971:50; Díaz del Castillo 1908–16, 1:174–7; 1977, 1:151–3; López de Gómara 1964:81–2; 1965–66, 2:77–8.
15 Díaz del Castillo 1908–16, 1:178–80, 182–5; 1977, 1:154–5, 157–9; Ixtlilxochitl 1975–77, 2:205; López de Gómara 1964:82–3; 1965–66, 2:78–9.

at least in how the Spaniards later wrote of these events. But whatever the sincerity of the Spaniards' religious beliefs and obligation to convert non-believers – after all, one of the Spaniards held captive among the Mayas had abandoned his faith – this was as much a legal requirement justifying war as it was a religious imperative. There was a priest among the Spaniards, but his presence was apparently incidental and Cortés's expedition did not include members of any regular orders to whom the conversion of the natives was entrusted. In any case, Cortés's use of conversion was thoroughly political. The prominence of temples and the ongoing human sacrifices reflected a powerful role for religion in native society, and Cortés challenged native beliefs only when it was politically feasible.

When Cortés first reached Cempohuallan, he asked that slaves being held for sacrifice be released. When this was rebuffed, he did not insist as that would have threatened the fledgling alliance that he sought. But after the Totonacs' open break with the Aztecs, they were dependent on the Spaniards and Cortés's position was greatly strengthened. He then took advantage of his increased power to destroy the Totonac idols and erect a cross and an image of the Virgin, despite protests by the native rulers. Nevertheless, only seizing and threatening to kill their leaders kept the Totonacs from attacking the Spaniards over this affront. The Totonacs' knowledge of Christianity was superficial at best, but this was common in many missionization efforts. The Church was content with the acceptance of the outward manifestations of Christianity, leaving fuller understanding for the future. So superficiality alone does not throw suspicion on Cortés's sincerity in his missionizing role, but his timing does. Cortés's aim in forcing even superficial religious conversions was primarily political, both in justifying his actions to the Spanish throne and in cementing his alliances in Mexico. Though protesting, Cempohuallan's leaders were no longer in a position to resist Spanish demands: they had to accept the destruction of their old gods and the introduction of new ones or risk loss of Spanish support, which would mean their sure destruction at the hands of the Aztecs. But the Totonac leaders also lost the religious support of their own priests and probably needed the Spaniards to retain their political positions: the destruction of the Totonac gods marked more of a change in political support than in religious belief of the indigenous leadership.[16]

16 Díaz del Castillo 1908–16, 1:186–90; 1977, 1:160–3.

Thereafter, the Spaniards returned to Vera Cruz where a ship from Cuba had landed, bringing eleven men and two horses. The ship also brought news that King Charles had granted Velásquez authority to trade and establish settlements, which was a direct threat to the new legal position that Cortés was working to create. Cortés decided that he had to act and, in an effort to present his claim, he sent the king not only the royal fifth of the goods collected, to which he was legally entitled, but also all the gold collected thus far. This he dispatched to Spain by ship on 26 July 1519, some two months after he landed on the Veracruz coast. Against Cortés's explicit orders, the ship stopped in Cuba; word of its purpose reached Velásquez, who tried to capture it. He failed and the ship sailed for Spain, but the obvious perfidy prompted Velásquez to make ready a large fleet under Pánfilo de Narváez to take Cortés captive.[17]

Even as he forged an alliance with the Totonacs, Cortés's support among the Spaniards wavered. When some of Velásquez's supporters conspired to seize a ship to sail to Cuba, Cortés arrested the conspirators and ordered the two principal conspirators hanged, the pilot's feet cut off, and the sailors given two hundred lashes each. Not all of these sentences were actually carried out, however, because Cortés was concerned about the loss of men. Each death or defection reduced his forces and the likelihood of a successful incursion into the interior. Yet with the Spaniards' divided loyalties, Cortés had little hope of united support for his plans as long as escape to Cuba was possible. Accordingly, he stripped the ten remaining ships of their equipment, including anchors, cables and sails, and sank them. The sinkings were carried out in secret and caused outrage among many of the Spaniards, especially those loyal to Velásquez, but left them with little option except to follow Cortés. The now shipless sailors were added to his army, as were six men captured later from a ship sighted near Vera Cruz.[18]

With no hope of returning home, Cortés and his army forged ahead with their plans to overthrow the Aztecs. The Totonac alliance was critical to these plans because the Spaniards lacked the needed supplies or the means to transport them overland: without

17 Cortés 1963:21–2, 27–8; 1971:28, 37–46; Díaz del Castillo 1908–16, 1:192–4; 196–9; 1977, 1:164–9.
18 Aguilar 1963:138–9; 1977:68–9; Cortés 1963:34–6; 1971:51–3; Díaz del Castillo 1908–16, 1:206, 208–9, 211–15; 1977, 1:174–80; López de Gómara 1964:89–90; 1965–66, 2:85–6; Martyr d'Anghera 1970, 2:62; Tapia 1950:43–4; 1963:25–6.

wagons or draught animals, these would only add to their already considerable load of arms and armour. But the Totonac alliance profoundly altered the Spaniards' capabilities. They would now be accompanied by Indian allies to carry supplies, serve as guides, aid in the fighting and ease their passage through towns en route. With an inland trek now possible, Cortés put Juan de Escalante in command of Vera Cruz with 60 to 150 soldiers and prepared for the march.[19]

Cortés asked the king of Cempohuallan for forty or fifty warriors and two hundred porters, which he received; in mid-June 1519 Cortés left Cempohuallan with three hundred Spanish soldiers accompanied by Indians carrying the artillery. Cortés had four falconets and ten larger cannons, referred to as lombards. Large numbers of native porters meant that the falconets could accompany the army, but the heavier lombards were not very mobile. Their weight was a minor hindrance as long as they were on ships or used in encampments near the shore, but there were not enough Spaniards to carry them inland for any appreciable distance. Therefore, some of the cannons were left in Vera Cruz. These were probably the lombards because they placed greater demands on porters and presumably would not be essential against the Indians, who lacked firearms, but they would be useful in Vera Cruz as they would be more effective against any forces sent by Velásquez.[20]

Moteuczoma could not have remained ignorant of events on the coast, no matter how imperfect his intelligence may have been. A major tributary had rebelled, another had been conquered, and the Spaniards were marching toward Tenochtitlan against his expressed wishes. Yet the Aztecs still took no offensive action. Why was Moteuczoma so passive? Between the landings of Grijalva and Cortés, Moteuczoma had consulted with his priests and advisers: how the Spaniards should be treated was not his decision alone, but

19 Díaz del Castillo 1908–16, 1:208–9, 268; 1977, 1:176–7, 216; López de Gómara 1964:91; 1965–66, 2:87; Martyr d'Anghera 1970, 2:61. Throughout the rest of the volume, I frequently refer to the side opposing the Aztecs as the Spaniards, or the Spaniards and their allies. In fact, non-Spaniards vastly outnumbered Spaniards for most of this time, but I nevertheless use Spaniards to refer to that side since they form a continuing presence and the composition of their Indian allies varies.

20 Díaz del Castillo 1908–16, 1:140–1, 211, 217–18; 1977, 1:128, 177, 181; Ixtlilxochitl 1975–77, 2:208; López de Gómara 1964:93; 1965–66, 2:89; Martyr d'Anghera 1970, 2:61. The Lienzo de Tlaxcala (Chavero 1964:14, 15, 17, 47) and Muñoz Camargo (1981:258v, 260, 275) depict cannons on gun carriages, but these pictures were executed decades after the Conquest and probably reflect cannons of that time rather than the earlier pieces actually used in the Conquest.

was also the considered opinion of his counsellors. Moteuczoma probably played a major, if not pivotal, role in deciding to take no action, but this decision was one in which all the advisers had a stake, and not even the king could disregard or change it without risking his political support. Thus, unmolested by the Aztecs, Cortés's force marched toward Tenochtitlan, passing through Xicochimalco and Ixhuacan and then descending into a cold, uninhabited desert. Their food was exhausted and several Indians whom Cortés had brought from Cuba died of privation and exposure. The Spaniards and their allies marched for three days before reaching Tzauhtlan, where they were again given shelter and food.[21]

As elsewhere, Cortés had the town's ruler instructed about Christianity and asked him to stop human sacrifice and idol worship, but he did not insist. The people of Tzauhtlan were Aztec tributaries and destroying their temples and idols would have provoked a violent response, precisely the result that the Spaniards could least afford. The issue could be forced only if the people were dependent on the Spaniards, as they would be if they rebelled against the Aztecs. Thus, leaving intact the religious practices of Aztec loyalists, the Spaniards enjoyed a relatively unmolested inland trek. As long as the Aztecs took no offensive action, neither would their tributaries.[22]

Despite the recommendation of Tzauhtlan's ruler that he march to Tenochtitlan by way of Cholollan, Cortés followed the advice of the Cempohualtecs, who warned that the Chololtecs were treacherous and allied with the Aztecs, and chose instead to go through Tlaxcallan, which was hostile to the Aztecs. Cortés demanded and received twenty noble warriors from Tzauhtlan to accompany him and marched onward to Iztac-Maxtitlan. There, Cortés learned that the Tlaxcaltecs were armed against them, so he dispatched Cempohualtec messengers with an appeal for friendship. But the Tlaxcaltecs did not respond.[23]

What the Tlaxcaltecs understood is uncertain. They must have been aware of the Spaniards' arrival on the coast and of their progress inland. But since many of the accompanying Indians were

21 Díaz del Castillo 1908–16, 1:218–20; 1977, 1:181–3; López de Gómera 1964:94–5; 1965–66, 2:89–91; Martyr d'Anghera 1970, 2:64–5; Oviedo y Valdés 1959, 4:13. See Wagner's (1944:141–4) reconstruction of the route.
22 Díaz del Castillo 1908–16, 1:221; 1977, 1:183–4.
23 Díaz del Castillo 1908–16, 1:223, 225–7; 1977, 1:185–7; López de Gómara 1964:97; 1965–66, 2:93; Martyr d'Anghera 1970, 2:66; Muñoz Camargo 1984:233–4; Oviedo y Valdés 1959, 4:15.

Aztec tributaries and Cortés had just spent a number of peaceful days in towns allied with the Aztecs, the Spaniards were naturally presumed hostile. The Spaniards continued toward Tlaxcallan until they saw a small party of armed Indians. Their horsemen advanced to capture them, but the Indians fought back, wounding three horses and killing two, and wounding two riders. This was part of a standard Mesoamerican stratagem in which a small force attacked and then fell back, enticing the enemy forward into a compromising position. When the Spaniards pursued them, a concealed force of perhaps three thousand ambushed the Spaniards in what should have been a decisive blow, but the Spaniards were saved by their crossbows and harquebuses, weapons hitherto unknown in central Mexico.[24]

The battle took place on level ground where the Spaniards could use their rapid-firing artillery, harquebuses and crossbows, and the Indians were gradually forced back. The cannons and harquebuses were effective but probably functioned at less than optimum: the Spaniards had been on the march and had time to do little more than assemble into formations. This haste had no effect on the use of lances, crossbows and swords, but it did on firearms, as there was no time to properly prepare their gunpowder. Although often impure, gunpowder of the day was usually one-half saltpetre, one-third charcoal and one-sixth sulphur. However, the jostling of transport caused these ingredients to stratify and they required remixing for effective use: when the Spaniards were attacked, they either had to delay combat to remix the powder, or had to fire poorly mixed powder that was less effective.[25]

Tlaxcaltec weapons proved effective, especially missiles directed against unarmoured soldiers. Arrows depended on penetration which was largely thwarted by Spanish armour, but slingstones drew their effect from the force of impact, against which steel armour offered only partial protection, and provoked many Spanish complaints. Four Spaniards were wounded in this battle and one later died, as did seventeen Tlaxcaltecs.[26]

The Indians were beaten back, but the Spaniards had suffered a

24 Aguilar 1963:139–40; 1977:70–1; Díaz del Castillo 1908–16, 1:228–9; 1977, 1:188; Ixtlilxochitl 1975–77, 2:208; López de Gómara 1964:99–101; 1965–66, 2:94–6; Martyr d'Anghera 1970, 2:68–9; Oviedo y Valdés 1959, 4:16; Tapia 1950:48; 1963:28–9.

25 Davis 1943:39; Díaz del Castillo 1908–16, 1:229–30; 1977, 1:188–9; Martyr d'Anghera 1970, 2:68–9; Rodgers 1939:340; Tarassuk and Blair 1982:49.

26 Díaz del Castillo 1908–16, 1:230; 1977, 1:188.

serious shock and were in for more in the days to come. The Tlaxcaltecs were professional soldiers, skilled beyond any whom the Spaniards had yet encountered in Mesoamerica. They attacked in unison, used complementary shock and projectile weapons, and displayed a high degree of expertise. Cortés's assessment of his risk could only have been based on the groups he had seen thus far, but these warriors were a much greater threat than he could reasonably have anticipated. Had the Spaniards made a more informed and realistic assessment of the risks they faced, dissension would doubtless have been greater and the expedition would have been endangered, if it was attempted at all.[27]

The Tlaxcaltec attack was even more threatening politically than militarily. Cortés had promised aid to his Indian allies so that if he retreated now he would be perceived as weak and his promises meaningless. At best, his allies would cease all aid; at worst they would turn on him. Cortés had gambled that he could overcome all potential adversaries, which was not altogether unreasonable based on his experiences to that point. The situation he encountered, however, was vastly different from what he had anticipated, but having staked all on succeeding, the threat to his alliances prevented him from following the most prudent military course – withdrawal.[28]

The battle ended at dusk, but the next day, 2 September 1519, six thousand Tlaxcaltec warriors marched toward the Spanish camp. Cortés then released three Tlaxcaltec prisoners with the message that he did not want war. Releasing captives with peace entreaties was a standard Spanish tactic throughout the Conquest, the goal being to acquire allies at minimal cost. This was consistent with Cortés's overall strategy of dividing the enemy; unlike his earlier battles, now it was also vital to Spanish survival. If negotiations failed, the battle would be lost eventually, despite the Spaniards' technological advantages. The Tlaxcaltecs attacked anyway but were driven back by cannon, harquebus and crossbow fire; once again the Spaniards followed their retreating enemies, right into another ambush. Surrounded and assailed on all sides, the Spaniards were afraid to charge with their horses lest they fail to maintain their defensive formation and be routed. They were too hard pressed to take offensive action, but Spanish firepower proved especially effective against the tightly massed Tlaxcaltecs, who finally withdrew. This

27 Díaz del Castillo 1908–16, 1:238; 1977, 1:194–5; Martyr d'Anghera 1970, 2:69.
28 Díaz del Castillo 1908–16, 1:253–6; 1977, 1:205–7.

allowed the Spaniards to fall back to some more easily defended nearby temples, though at a cost of one Spaniard dead, fifteen wounded and four or five horses killed.[29]

The Spaniards' position was precarious: they did not dominate the battlefield, they were seriously threatened, and they could adopt only a defensive stance. However, if they stayed on the defensive, the battle would degenerate into a war of attrition that the Spaniards would inevitably lose, given the Tlaxcaltecs' great numerical superiority. But attacking the Tlaxcaltec main forces was not feasible since any advance would inevitably open gaps in the Spanish formations, with disastrous consequences. Therefore, the Spaniards directed their offensive at nearby towns where their speed and power could be demonstrated without revealing the weaknesses that would be evident in a conventional encounter. They also hoped to restock their rations, but had no success. The Spaniards thus sent out a party of two hundred soldiers, seven horsemen, a few harquebusiers and crossbowmen and their Indian allies, attacked some towns and captured twenty Indians, but failed to find any food.

Cortés had experienced little difficulty in securing local supplies to this point, but the Tlaxcaltecs followed a scorched earth policy that left virtually nothing behind; once within Tlaxcallan's territory, the Spaniards could no longer count on local towns to provide food. They could rely only on the food carried with them, yet the few accompanying porters could supply a force of that size for only a few days, which left the Spaniards dangerously underprovisioned. So once again the Spaniards released prisoners to plead for peace, but these entreaties were also rejected.[30]

The Tlaxcaltecs attacked again the next day, beginning the battle in conventional Mesoamerican fashion with a barrage of arrows, slingstones and darts before advancing for hand-to-hand combat; the Spaniards avoided being overwhelmed by the sheer mass of the attackers only by keeping them back with superior firepower. To concentrate and increase their effectiveness, Cortés divided his men, ordering some to reload crossbows and harquebuses while others fired. He directed the mounted lancers to make short forays, their primary effect being to disrupt the Tlaxcaltecs' formations, rendering them vulnerable to counter-attack and frustrating their own attack. The Spaniards, by contrast, faced no weapons equally

29 Díaz del Castillo 1908–16, 1:231–4; 1977, 1:189–92.
30 Díaz del Castillo 1908–16, 1:229–30, 235; 1977, 1:188–9, 192–3.

disruptive of their own formations; the Tlaxcaltecs eventually withdrew, but the clash left all of the horses wounded, one Spaniard dead, and sixty more wounded.[31]

Having fared poorly in a frontal daylight assault, the Tlaxcaltecs next tried a night attack which, in Mesoamerica, was generally restricted to small-scale raids. The main difficulty in a night attack is maintaining communications in the dark to deploy forces properly: launching a night attack suggests that Spanish firepower was taking a heavy toll and the Tlaxcaltecs doubtless hoped that this change in tactics would be more successful. Cannons, harquebuses and crossbows all had greater effective ranges than Indian weapons and this larger killing zone meant that if the Tlaxcaltecs tried to close for hand-to-hand combat, they had to do so through this lethal field of Spanish fire. The Tlaxcaltecs were vulnerable longer because they had to charge right into the guns, whereas the outnumbered Spaniards generally did not advance. Furthermore, since the Tlaxcaltec archers and slingers remained back behind the frontline troops, their fire was even less effective than that of the Spaniards. A night attack, however, reduced this Spanish advantage by concealing the targets in darkness.

A standard Spanish tactic was to watch enemy arrows in flight and dodge or deflect them, so the farther away the archers were, the easier this was to accomplish. But a night attack also neutralized this advantage, leaving the Spaniards vulnerable to now-unseen arrows. The Spaniards could still shoot back, but at only one-sixth the rate of fire of the Tlaxcaltecs. The Spaniards depended on accuracy that the night now denied them, while the higher rate of bow, sling and *atlatl* fire allowed the Indians to pour multiple volleys into the massed and immobile Spaniards.[32]

Ten thousand warriors, led by their commanding general Xicotencatl, attacked the Spaniards' camp. But in an effort to limit their exposure to the devastating Spanish fire, the archers, slingers and atlatlists held back in units so that they did not have to manoeuvre. From the protective darkness, they assailed the hemmed-in Spaniards on three sides while the Tlaxcaltec swordsmen quickly rushed across the killing zone and engaged them hand to hand, forcing the Spaniards to defend themselves with swords and

31 Díaz del Castillo 1908–16, 1:237–9; 1977, 1:194–6.
32 This common practice was mentioned by Díaz del Castillo (1908–16, 1:43–4; 1977, 1:64) only when they were confused by clouds of locusts and the Spaniards were unable to distinguish these from arrows and could not defend themselves in the usual fashion.

pikes, offering a fairer match for the native weapons. These tactics minimized the Spanish advantage in firepower, but the mounted lancers managed to disrupt the Tlaxcaltec formations and expose their vulnerable flanks to Spanish steel. Unable to reassemble in the dark, the Tlaxcaltec attack ultimately failed. [33]

Despite this success, the Spaniards' position was eroding badly: over forty-five had been killed since leaving Vera Cruz, another dozen were ill, several horses had been slain, and their food supplies were dwindling. How serious this last problem was is uncertain, but all their food and arms had to be carried with them, and both were being consumed at prodigious rates. Most of the food was carried by two hundred Indian porters from Cempohuallan, occasionally augmented along the way. On average, each porter carried 23 kilograms (50 pounds: roughly 23–24 man/days of food), although this was replenished en route through Spanish demands on local towns. But since there were two Spanish or Indian soldiers for every porter, Cortés's forces could carry only eight days' supply and once in hostile territory, this was rapidly exhausted.[34]

Equally serious, Spanish arms were dwindling, too. Unlike swords, lances and pikes, projectiles are exhausted in use and the Spaniards had a limited supply. Most crossbow bolts were probably not recovered after battle and at one shot per minute, each hour of combat cost sixty bolts – 2.2–4.1 kilograms (6–11 pounds) or 72–131 kilograms (200–350 pounds) for all thirty-two crossbows. Each harquebus could fire as fast as once every one and a half minutes, expending forty 47 gram (2 ounce) balls per hour plus an equal weight of powder, for a combined total of 3.7 kilograms (10 pounds) – 49 kilograms (130 pounds) for all thirteen harquebusiers per hour. In addition, the four falconets each fired shot weighing 0.28–0.93 kilograms (12 ounces to 2 pounds 8 ounces) with a similar weight of powder at least as rapidly as the harquebuses, for a total hourly cost of 22–75 kilograms (60–200 pounds). Thus, an hour of vigorous combat with all crossbows, harquebuses and falconets consumed 150–260 kilograms (400–700 pounds) of largely unretrievable armaments – a total of eight to fourteen porter loads.

Each porter diverted to the task of carrying powder, shot and bolts reduced Cortés's ability to march by twenty-three man/days, or one day's supply for the entire company for every twenty-nine porters so diverted. And each hour of vigorous combat cost the

33 Díaz del Castillo 1908–16, 1:227–8, 230–1; 1977, 1:187, 189.
34 Díaz del Castillo 1908–16, 1:242–3; 1977, 1:198.

army from one-third to one-half a day's food supply. At these rates, even if half the porters carried powder and shot, the Spaniards could fight actively for only seven to twelve and a half hours and they could subsist on their own food supplies for just four days. How many porters were engaged in transporting arms versus food is unknown, but since all the armaments had to be transported from Vera Cruz, Cortés had to have made this decision from the outset and he underestimated the magnitude of the opposition he would meet. Considering the food required to support his men on some of the long stretches between sizeable towns, Cortés must have used at least a hundred porters for this purpose so, after having repulsed the Tlaxcaltecs, his supply situation must have been precarious.

The Spaniards would have been lost if the Tlaxcaltecs had encircled and contained them. Besieged, they would have been completely cut off from further supplies and been unable to threaten nearby towns. As it was, the Spaniards successfully attacked undefended towns and, while they were too few to be a significant military threat, their perceived menace was doubtless much greater in Tlaxcaltec eyes. The Tlaxcaltecs did not try sustained encirclement, probably because this ran counter to Mesoamerican military practices, which were strongly shaped by logistical constraints. Offensive armies typically lacked the logistical support to remain in the field for long: if defeated, they usually withdrew. A major defeat or even a draw generally sent the invaders away, so encirclement and a war of annihilation was unusual and unnecessary. That the Spaniards did not withdraw, as the Tlaxcaltecs could justifiably expect, was less a tribute to their skills than to their lack of alternatives.

Once again, Cortés sent messages of peace, coupled with threats to kill all the Tlaxcaltecs and destroy their country if a peace was not reached within two days. It was beyond Cortés's ability to carry out this threat, but the Tlaxcaltecs could not have known this with certainty. The Spaniards' limited success in battle and their precarious position further eroded support in Cortés's own camp. His men were near mutiny, demanding that they return to the coast, but doing so would have unravelled the fragile alliance Cortés had fashioned and signalled the end of his aspirations in Mexico. Once more, through cajoling and promises, he persuaded the men to stay.

Returning to the offensive, perhaps as much to forage for food and encourage his men as to bolster his threat to the Tlaxcaltecs, Cortés attacked the Otomi town of Tecoac, routed the defenders, and sacked it. The Spaniards next marched on the town of

Tzompantzinco, one league away, but its inhabitants fled. When the Spaniards did not harm the town, the lords of Tzompantzinco approached with food and apologized for not bringing it to their camp when first asked.[35]

Although mounted lancers played an important role in these offensive thrusts, they were not decisive alone. Horsemen had speed and mobility and could disrupt the enemy, but they could not hold what they had taken. Foot soldiers were needed to hold an objective so, except for scouting and short forays, the horsemen accompanied the foot soldiers, which reduced the horses' speed and mobility to that of the party as a whole. By this time, Cortés's forces were reduced to approximately 250 Spaniards (and not all were fit), about ten horses (all wounded), about 200 non-combatant porters, and fewer than 100 Indian warriors who, judging by their low losses, played a minimal role in combat. Facing thousands of enemy soldiers, Cortés's ultimate defeat was inevitable. The Spanish forces were battered and badly divided but the Tlaxcaltecs did not know this; while Cortés continued to make forays against nearby villages and small towns, he was able to maintain a facade of success.[36]

The Tlaxcaltecs were now reconsidering their own position. They had received a series of messengers – Cempohualtecs as well as released Tlaxcaltecs – asking for peace and bringing information about Spanish actions elsewhere. Moreover, the Spaniards appeared to be successful: even though some Spaniards and horses had been killed, Tlaxcaltec losses were higher. Moreover, the disparity between their respective casualties probably seemed much greater as the Tlaxcaltecs had an accurate view of their own losses but not of Spanish casualties, which Cortés tried to conceal. But just as the Spaniards were divided over what to do, so too were the Tlaxcaltecs, perhaps even more so. Tlaxcallan did not have a paramount ruler who could make authoritative decisions about war but was ruled by the kings of four confederated kingdoms, each with its own ruler. Provincial decisions depended on a consensus among these rulers and support for the war against the Spaniards had eroded. Some Tlaxcaltec units had refused to join in the last major daytime battle, as had Tlaxcallan's most important ally, Huexotzinco.[37]

Tlaxcallan's failure to achieve a decisive victory and their

35 Aguilar 1963:141; 1977:73; Díaz del Castillo 1908–16, 1:244, 249; 1977, 1:199, 202–3; Tapia 1950:51; 1963:30.
36 Díaz del Castillo 1908–16, 1:242–3; 1977, 1:198.
37 Díaz del Castillo 1908–16, 1:238–9; 1977, 1:195.

significant losses shifted this consensus and the rulers decided to seek peace with the Spaniards. In retrospect, the Tlaxcaltec decision to ally with the Spaniards may appear radical, but forming this type of alliance was a common Mesoamerican political tradition. Moreover, it was a conservative act. Because opinion was divided, independent towns – especially Huexotzinco – could well decide to negotiate a separate peace with the Spaniards, which would undermine Tlaxcallan's authority and weaken its position. Dissenters would be found no matter what course was followed, but an alliance with the Spaniards would preserve Tlaxcallan's rulers' authority and strengthen it by the addition of Spanish arms. Thus, this decision reinforced, rather than undermined, the traditional power structure.[38]

Had they been defeated quickly, the Spaniards would have been little more than a ripple in Mesoamerican political history. But once the Spaniards were recognized as a powerful force, the Tlaxcaltecs had only three major choices. They could continue the battle until they decisively defeated the Spaniards, they could cease fighting in hope that the Spaniards would simply go away, or they could seek an alliance with them.

The decision to ally with Cortés was made in view of Tlaxcallan's geopolitical situation. The Tlaxcaltecs had been engaged in a series of wars with the Aztecs for decades, but now found themselves and their allies in a situation that continued to erode, completely encircled by Aztec tributaries and largely cut off from external trade. Without a profound alteration of the political situation, Tlaxcallan's defeat by the Aztecs was only a matter of time. Recognizing the superiority of Spanish arms, the Tlaxcaltecs now saw an alliance with the Spaniards as a means to shift the balance of power in a way more favourable to themselves.

Spanish cannons, harquebuses, crossbows and horsemen could all disrupt enemy lines at a distance and in a way that Indian arms could not match; once a breach was opened, their formations were extremely vulnerable. Even when combat was hand to hand, the Spaniards greatly benefited from their armour. Although many of the Spaniards did not have steel armour, they did have some and all had cotton armour, so the most vulnerable parts of their bodies were protected, in contrast to most of their attackers. Thus, while the Spaniards enjoyed greater firepower that prevented their enemies

38 Chimalpahin 1965:234; Díaz del Castillo 1908–16, 1:246–7; 1977, 1:201; Ixtlilxochitl 1975–77, 2:211–13; López de Gómara 1964:114–16; 1965–66, 2:102–3; Tapia 1950:54–5; 1963:32.

from engaging them in organized formations and could disrupt the enemy front much more easily than could Mesoamerican armies, they were too few to exploit these breaches fully. If they joined forces with large Indian armies, however, these allies could exploit the breaches created by the Spaniards while maintaining the integrity of their own units, since other Indian armies lacked the Spanish edge in arms and armour, and they could wreak havoc on the enemy.

Both sides recognized the Spaniards' advantages and both may even have realized that an alliance between them could produce an exceptional fighting force in which the Spaniards would serve as shock troops for the vastly larger Indian support forces. But the decision to seek an alliance did not lie with the Spaniards, as they were being battered and in danger of annihilation. It lay with the Tlaxcaltecs, since only they could halt the attack and initiate an alliance, Spanish claims to the contrary notwithstanding.

A Tlaxcaltec victory over the Spaniards would have been pyrrhic at best. It would have cost so many dead and wounded that continued resistance to the Aztecs would have been greatly undermined and the Tlaxcaltecs' own conquest hastened. If, however, the Tlaxcaltecs allied with the Spaniards, the regional balance of power might shift to their advantage. They would suffer no more casualties against the Spaniards, they would gain a numerically small but powerful ally and even more importantly, they would deprive the Aztecs of one. The Tlaxcaltecs could have defeated the Spaniards or simply withdrawn: their decision to seek an alliance was a deliberate choice and theirs alone. This decision was not without opposition: the rulers ordered their general, Xicotencatl, to return home and not to attack again, but he refused. They then sent messages to his subordinates not to obey him; after three more such demands, Xicotencatl finally desisted. Even then, he sent spies into the Spaniards' camp on the pretext of delivering food, but Cortés seized and interrogated them, cut the thumbs off some and the hands off others, and sent them back.[39]

Such harsh dealings stood in stark contrast to his treatment of earlier captives. Previously, Cortés desperately needed a cease-fire and gradually released his prisoners unharmed with requests for peace. But once the situation shifted to his advantage, Cortés traded

39 Cortés 1963:42; 1971:61; Díaz del Castillo 1908–16, 1:247, 258–9; 1977, 1:201, 209–10; Ixtlilxochitl 1975–77, 2:209; López de Gómara 1964: 106–7; 1965–66, 2:101–2; Martyr d'Anghera 1970, 2:72–3; Oviedo y Valdés 1959, 4:18; Tapia 1950:52; 1963:31.

the olive branch for the sword and mutilated the Tlaxcaltecs as an exercise in political terrorism.

The Tlaxcaltecs had not been defeated: their decision to make peace was a political rather than a military one. Four nobles approached the Spanish camp and said that they had fought because they believed the Spaniards were Aztec allies and that the first battles were carried out by the Otomi without orders from the Tlaxcaltecs. Both of these claims were probably true, at least in part. Since Aztecs accompanied the Spaniards and they had just come from an Aztec tributary town, Cortés did indeed appear to be their ally. The claim that the initial attacks were carried out by the Otomi was probably also true. The Tlaxcaltecs allowed the Otomi fleeing from the Aztecs to settle in villages on their borders to serve as buffers and to guard against encroachment. Thus, it is probable that the earliest attacks were, in fact, initiated by the Otomi although this was doubtless known to Tlaxcallan's rulers. In any case, these disclaimers enabled the Tlaxcaltecs to offer, and Cortés to accept, a peace at the status quo without requiring either retaliation or retribution. Accordingly, Cortés promised the Tlaxcaltecs assistance against the Aztecs, gave them gifts, and asked that a delegation be sent with fuller powers to make peace. Soon, Xicotencatl and a delegation of Tlaxcaltec nobles reached Cortés's camp and pledged fealty. Cortés accepted them as vassals and promised to travel to the city of Tlaxcallan soon.[40]

Aztec emissaries accompanied Cortés throughout his trek so Moteuczoma learned of these events shortly after they occurred. Cortés's negotiations with their enemies was very disturbing to the Aztecs: they asked him to defer any decision for six days while they sent this news to Moteuczoma and awaited a reply, and Cortés agreed. Nobles soon arrived from Tenochtitlan with gifts and a message from Moteuczoma, asking Cortés not to go to Tlaxcallan because the people were treacherous. Spanish accounts claim that Moteuczoma also offered to become Cortés's vassal and pay him tribute, but this is at odds with both his subsequent actions and his refusal to invite the Spaniards to Tenochtitlan. Nevertheless, the Aztecs' offer put the Tlaxcaltecs in an awkward position. They had offered peace and an alliance, but Tenochtitlan was Cortés's primary goal and he was still negotiating with the Aztecs. If an agreement was reached, Tlaxcallan's position would be very precarious, so the

---

40 Aguilar 1963:142; 1977:74; Díaz del Castillo 1908–16, 1:261–2, 265–6; 1977, 1:211–14; Muñoz Camargo 1966:185, 187–8; 1984:235–6.

Tlaxcaltec rulers travelled to Cortés's camp to meet him and beg forgiveness for the battles.[41]

The Aztecs were clearly the more powerful group, but faced with Moteuczoma's courteous intransigence, the Tlaxcaltec offer of material assistance could not be refused. Cortés tacitly accepted the Tlaxcaltecs' offer, requested porters to carry his cannons, which were quickly supplied; the next day, the Spaniards marched to the city of Tlaxcallan, entering on 23 September 1519, just five months after landing in Veracruz.[42]

Even though he entered into an alliance with the Tlaxcaltecs, Cortés was intent on preserving his relationship with Moteuczoma and asked that the accompanying Aztec nobles be admitted to Tlaxcallan and lodged with him, and this was permitted. Once in Tlaxcallan, the rulers presented Cortés with gifts and with their daughters, a common means of cementing alliances in Mesoamerica.[43]

Cortés erected an altar, a mass was said, and the next day, he instructed the Tlaxcaltecs about Christianity and asked them to adopt it, but did not insist when the rulers said that their priests and people would rebel if they were forced to adopt the new religion. However, they did permit one of the temples to be cleaned so that a cross and an image of the Virgin could be erected, and the daughters of the rulers were baptized. But as with both previous and subsequent groups, the religious conversion of the Tlaxcaltecs was not immediate. They allowed Christian images to be erected since, as polytheists, the addition of foreign gods was acceptable. But rejecting their own gods as the messianic monotheistic Christianity demanded was not acceptable; forcing the issue could undermine the kings' support among both priests and commoners. However, the Spaniards sought conversions to secure their political alliance and native rulers declared public conversion only after their political fates were inextricably tied to the Spaniards. This guaranteed continued Spanish support without which the rulers were vulnerable, not only to the Aztecs, but also to the internal unrest that such conversions would engender.[44]

41 Aguilar 1963:142; 1977:75; Díaz del Castillo 1908–16, 1:264–71; 1977, 1:213–18.

42 Aguilar 1963:142; 1977:74–5; Díaz del Castillo 1908–16, 1:274; 1977, 1:218–19; López de Gómara 1964:117–18; 1965–66, 2:111; Oviedo y Valdés 1959, 4:20; Tapia 1950:53; 1963:32.

43 Díaz del Castillo 1908–16, 1:272–3, 277–9; 1977, 1:218, 221–2; López de Gómara 1964: 118; 1965–66, 2:112; Muñoz Camargo 1966:191; 1984:237–8.

44 Díaz del Castillo 1908–16, 1:277–82; 1977, 1:221–5; López de Gómara 1964:121; 1965–66, 2:115.

Once in Tlaxcallan, Cortés sought information about the Aztecs and was told about their large army and given a description of Tenochtitlan and its defences, but he still underestimated the Aztec threat. He knew Moteuczoma had not been able to conquer Tlaxcallan despite many attempts, which led him to believe that this new-found ally was at least roughly comparable in power to the Aztecs. True, the Tlaxcaltecs had prevailed defensively where the advantage should have been theirs, but this nevertheless indicated a significant military capability, much of which Cortés had already witnessed. What Cortés could not have appreciated was that the Tlaxcaltecs had not enjoyed this success in a conventional war but were locked in a flower war with the Aztecs.[45]

As mentioned, the goal of a flower war was to pin down strong opponents, encircle and slowly strangle them, and this had been underway in Tlaxcallan for decades. Once it was isolated and without allies, it would be finally defeated, as had been the fate of the Chalca city-states. Thus, Cortés's assessment of the relative strength of his allies was based on a misunderstanding. The Tlaxcaltecs had not enjoyed this success against the Aztecs in a series of conventional clashes: victory in these would have supported his assessment. But Cortés's estimate of his allies' strength was seemingly supported by two other facts: Moteuczoma's continued gift-giving and his failure to attack.[46]

Whenever an Indian group offered vassalage to the Spaniards, whether freely or following conquest, they gave them gifts in acknowledgement of this new status. But the Aztecs had brought the Spaniards gifts from the outset, leading them to believe that Moteuczoma too was offering vassalage. Offering gifts, however, did not necessarily mean political subordination, but the Spaniards either did not recognize that or chose not to. The Aztecs' gifts were offered in homage to possible gods, not in vassalage to men, so the two sides viewed the significance of gift-giving very differently. But even had the Aztecs offered gifts in political homage, it was within the Mesoamerican tradition of hegemonic rule in which the goal was to acknowledge tacit vassalage and pay tribute to be left in peace. But Cortés functioned with a European notion of political domination: not satisfied with moderate exaction and indirect control through the existing political regime, he sought the ouster of that regime, direct rule, and the undivided wealth that this would offer.

45 Díaz del Castillo 1908–16, 1:283–5; 1977, 1:225–7; López de Gómara 1964:122–3; 1965–66, 2:115–16; Tapia 1950:55–6; 1963:33.
46 Hassig 1988:128–30, 171, 225–6, 232, 235, 256.

That the Aztecs were acknowledging vassalage was further supported in the eyes of the Spaniards by Moteuczoma's failure to attack thus far, which was indeed strange. However, this can be attributed to three factors. First, Moteuczoma was still uncertain about the identity and intentions of these strangers and was reluctant to attack them until he was. Second, to reduce his vulnerability to overthrow by domestic challengers, Moteuczoma had reorganized Aztec imperial society to broaden his political support by drawing on nobles in tributary towns. This was an admirable strategy as long as Tenochtitlan remained the dominant power, but the arrival of the Spaniards and their alliance with city-states to the east significantly changed this, undermining Moteuczoma's external political support, in effect weakening him at home. This made changing his original position on the Spaniards dangerous if it now supported the position of any potential challenger, such as Cuitlahua. Third, even if he had wanted war, Moteuczoma could not marshal a large army at that time. Only during the dry period following the harvest were large numbers of men available for such service, when there were adequate food supplies to sustain them en route, and roads were passable and streams fordable by large armies. This is why Aztec wars took place primarily between December and April. During the summer rainy season, most of the commoners were engaged in agricultural and related pursuits and could not be diverted without damage to the economy. Moteuczoma did have a corps of elite soldiers – perhaps a few thousand – but these were too few for an assault against the Spaniards and their allies in distant Tlaxcallan. Thus, Moteuczoma's failure to attack was soundly based, but this was probably misinterpreted as weakness by the Spaniards. Thus, Cortés entered into an alliance seriously miscalculating the Aztecs' actions as well as their strengths and those of the Tlaxcaltecs.[47]

47 Hassig 1988:220–3.

5 THE MARCH TO TENOCHTITLAN

Cortés stayed in the city of Tlaxcallan for seventeen days before resuming his march to Tenochtitlan on 10 October 1519, but when he did, he went by way of Cholollan where, according to conventional accounts, one of the least explicable events of the trek occurred. Cholollan was an Aztec ally and, according to Spanish accounts, the Tlaxcaltecs tried to dissuade Cortés from going there. Cortés's own stated purpose in going to Cholollan was to gather supplies since it was a large city, but this claim does not ring true. Cholollan was no closer to Tenochtitlan than was Tlaxcallan, where supplies were already available, so a logistical purpose for the trip is unlikely. If supplies actually were a concern, Cortés would have been significantly better off obtaining them from allied Huexotzinco, which was a full day's march closer to Tenochtitlan.[1]

Cortés demanded entry and the Chololtecs reluctantly invited the Spaniards to their city, where they went, accompanied by five to six thousand Tlaxcaltec warriors. Cortés's actual reasons for going to Cholollan were not logistical but strictly political and military. Cholollan had traditionally been allied with Tlaxcallan and Huexotzinco and had only recently become an Aztec ally. Thus, whatever the Tlaxcaltecs told Cortés about Cholollan was doubtless tinged with hostility and their perceived betrayal. Cortés was not primarily interested in fighting the Indians' battles, but there were sound military reasons to want to conquer Cholollan, which he accomplished through treachery.[2]

Cortés covered most of the five leagues to Cholollan before making camp for the night, where he was welcomed by nobles bringing food. At the request of the Chololtecs, the Tlaxcaltecs

1 Aguilar 1963:143; 1977:76; Díaz del Castillo 1908–16, 1:290–2; 1977, 1:230–1; Ixtlilxochitl 1975–77, 2:214; López de Gómara 1964–123–4; 1965–66, 2:116–17; Martyr d'Anghera 1970, 2:78–9; Oviedo y Valdés 1959, 4:22.

2 Chimalpahin 1965:234; Cortés 1963:48–9; 1971:70–2; Díaz del Castillo 1908–16, 1:297–8; 1977, 1:235; Muñoz Camargo 1984:247–8; Sahagún 1975:29; 1989:57; Tapia 1950:56–7; 1963:33.

remained there and the Spaniards entered Cholollan the next morning, accompanied only by the Cempohualtecs and the Tlaxcaltecs who carried the cannons. There they were well housed and fed for two days before the food inexplicably stopped arriving. According to Spanish accounts, the Cempohualtecs reported that the Chololtecs planned to attack the Spaniards, aided by a hidden Aztec army. Cortés had the Chololtecs assemble in the main courtyard, placed armed Spaniards at every entrance, and then massacred the enclosed and unarmed Indians.[3]

Despite nearly unanimous Spanish support for this account of the Cholollan massacre, it does not ring true. There probably never was an Aztec army waiting to attack the Spaniards. The Aztecs had not attacked the Spaniards before this and it is unlikely that Moteuczoma even had twenty thousand soldiers available to send to Cholollan as reported, since it was still during the agricultural season. And even if he had, only three days had lapsed between Cortés's arrival in Cholollan and the alleged reports of that army, barely enough time for a message to be sent to Tenochtitlan, much less raise, arm, supply and dispatch an army. Thus, an armed Aztec threat does not seem credible, although Cortés may well have accused Moteuczoma of sending one to keep him on the defensive.[4]

There was, however, a massacre that was probably a deliberate act by Cortés to destroy Cholollan which he intended as a warning to other hostile cities. Cholollan straddled the main route between the Tenochtitlan and Vera Cruz, posed a major danger to any communications between the two, and would have threatened Cortés's rear once he marched on to Tenochtitlan. His need for reliable links to Vera Cruz had been brought home to him by the rapid exhaustion of his shot and gunpowder in the war with Tlaxcallan. Vera Cruz was the only available source for these essential armaments and his access could not be impeded. Moreover, having established an alliance with Tlaxcallan, Cortés felt less constrained in his dealings with Aztec tributaries.

In short, there was no sound logistical reason to go to Cholollan

3 Aguilar 1963:144; 1977:77; Chimalpahin 1965:234; Cortés 1963:49–50; 1971:73–4; Díaz del Castillo 1908–16, 2:1–5, 7, 13, 15; 1977, 1:236–9, 242–3, 245; Ixtlilxochitl 1975–77, 2:216; López de Gómara 1964:124, 126–9; 1965–66, 2:117, 119–22; Martyr d'Anghera 1970, 2:81–2; Muñoz Camargo 1966:213; 1984:250–1; Oviedo y Valdés 1959, 4:22–3; Sahagún 1975:29; 1989:58; Tapia 1950:57–8, 60–1; 1963:33–6.
4 Díaz del Castillo 1908–16, 2:10–11; 1977, 1:242. As Wagner (1944:175) points out, this alleged army seems to have evaporated as there is no further mention of it despite having been invoked previously to justify the massacre.

but there was animus between that city and his new ally, Tlaxcallan, which threatened Cortés's plans. Thus, his decision to go to Cholollan can best be understood as political, to secure his rear and his lines of resupply, and chastise his friends' enemies. Cortés's actions cannot be seen exclusively in terms of his own interests. He had no first-hand knowledge of the Chololtecs and no compelling need to attack them for his own purposes. However, the attack may well have been orchestrated by the Tlaxcaltecs as a litmus test of Spanish loyalty. If they attacked the Chololtecs, they would prove themselves by undermining a now-despised enemy. But this would also be an assault on an Aztec ally, so it would put the Spaniards in opposition to Moteuczoma, a position from which they could not easily withdraw. This forced the Spaniards to demonstrate their loyalty at a point when the Tlaxcaltecs had risked nothing. The attack thus cemented Cortés's relationship with the Tlaxcaltecs and was probably instigated in retribution for Cholollan's recent shift in allegiances. In a single stroke, Cortés killed the king, much of the political leadership, and the cream of the Chololtec army. After the massacre, Cortés appointed a new king and forced an alliance between the Tlaxcaltecs and the Chololtecs. At the same time, he laid the blame for the massacre on Moteuczoma. But even though the Spaniards described themselves as the motivating force behind the events of the Conquest, it is highly improbable that Cortés understood the situation well enough to have known the weak points in the system and exploited them. The most significant of these was royal succession.[5]

As we have seen, kingship in Mesoamerica was not typically locked into a strict hereditary succession system, such as male primogenitor. Kings came from among the upper nobility – often the king's son or brothers – but which one was chosen depended on political support from both that city and its allies. Even after a king was selected, there were still other contenders for the throne; these divisions were probably strongly felt in Cholollan since it had shifted its fundamental alliance away from the Tlaxcaltecs to the Aztecs. The Chololtec king must have been the primary supporter and beneficiary of this switch, but there were doubtless other nobles with political and kin ties to Tlaxcallan, and many were legitimate contenders for the throne.

Cortés also could not have known how the institution of

5 Díaz del Castillo 1908–16, 2:17; 1977, 1:246; López de Gómara 1964:130; 1965–66, 2:122.

kingship operated in Mesoamerica or who among the Chololtecs fell into what camps. But the Tlaxcaltecs did, and when Cortés claimed to have chosen a new ruler, he may have thought himself a kingmaker, but it is likelier that he was a pawn of Tlaxcaltec and Chololtec factional politics. Killing the king and many of his noble supporters left the field clear for a successor with pro-Tlaxcallan sympathies and political support – one who may have actually played a role in the preceding events. Cholollan's shift in allegiance was not the agonizing movement of a monolith from one position to the opposite, but a subtle shift that allowed an existing faction to take power. In this coup, a Spanish hand was on the sword but Indian minds guided it, as only they understood the distribution of power in Cholollan and who would support the insurgent position.

Moteuczoma must have been thoroughly dismayed at this attack on, and wanton destruction of, his allies, who had peacefully received the Spaniards. This can only have reinforced his reluctance to have Cortés come to Tenochtitlan. Moteuczoma dispatched a delegation of nobles to greet Cortés and learn his true intentions, but he also sent soothsayers and magicians to stop him supernaturally. These, however, had no effect and, having exhausted both diplomacy and magic, Moteuczoma ordered the main road from Cholollan to Tenochtitlan to be planted with magueys (century plants). This traditional means of sealing off roads and signalling a breach in relations was a last-ditch effort to deter the Spaniards.[6]

After two weeks in Cholollan, Cortés marched to Calpan, a dependency of Huexotzinco. There, according to Spanish accounts, he was told that there were two roads to Tenochtitlan but that one was blocked and the Aztecs had set up ambushes along it. There is no evidence to support the latter contention but, in any case, Cortés took the other path and reached Amaquemecan after two days. There, people from the neighbouring towns and cities, including Chalco, Amaquemecan, Chimalhuacan and Ayotzinco, brought presents to the Spaniards and complained about the Aztecs. Cortés promised them that they would soon be free.[7]

Cortés may have been influenced by advice from his allies, but there are sound reasons for doubting the accuracy of the Spanish

6 Sahagún 1975:31, 33, 37; 1989:59–62, 64.
7 Aguilar 1963:145; 1977:78; Chimalpahin 1965:234; Cortés 1963:51–4; 1971:76–9; Díaz del Castillo 1908–16, 2:28–31; 1977, 1:254–7; Ixtlilxochitl 1975–77, 2:217; López de Gómara 1964:134–6; 1965–66, 2:126–8; Martyr d'Anghera 1970, 2:88–9; Oviedo y Valdés 1959, 4:28–9; Sahagún 1975:37; 1989:64–5.

version of events. Calpan was on the east side of the mountains ringing the Valley of Mexico and there were indeed two major routes to Tenochtitlan, skirting the 5,230 metre (17,159 feet) high mountain, Iztac-Cihuatl. The main route went through a 3,000 metre (9,843 feet) high pass to the north whereas the other road was smaller and a more difficult trek through a 3,500 metre (11,483 feet) high pass to the south.

Part of Cortés's claimed rationale for choosing the southern route was to avoid an Aztec ambush, but this was an unlikely threat as there had been no ambushes before. Moreover, the Aztecs were following Cortés's progress and could have ambushed him by dispatching a force to the south pass as easily as to the north, and intercepting him well before he ended the two-day march since they did send emissaries to meet him there. In fact, since the south pass was more rugged and narrow, an ambush there would have been far easier.[8]

Cortés most likely selected the southern route because of what lay at the other end. The north pass emptied out into the Tetzcoco area, which strongly supported Moteuczoma, whereas the south pass led to the Chalca city states. These cities were conquered by the Aztecs in 1464 after fighting a bitter flower war for eighty years. Their kings were removed, the cities were ruled by Aztec governors until 1486, and the area became a major breadbasket for the Aztecs. The Chalca cities thus deeply resented their subordination to Tenochtitlan, they had had earlier ties to Huexotzinco and, of all the cities in the Valley of Mexico, they were the most promising for Cortés's purposes.

The Spaniards then marched from Amaquemecan to Ayotzinco where Moteuczoma's nephew, King Cacama of Tetzcoco, met to accompany them into Tenochtitlan. The next day, they crossed the Cuitlahuac causeway and reached Ixtlapalapan, where they were greeted by the rulers of the surrounding cities. And the following day, 8 November 1519, escorted by these rulers, the Spaniards travelled along the causeway into Tenochtitlan where they were greeted by Moteuczoma.[9]

8 Sahagún 1975:31.

9 Acosta 1954:240; 1970–73, 2:518; Aguilar 1963:145–6; 1977:79–80; Alvarado Tezozómoc 1975:148–9; Chimalpahin 1965:121, 235; Cortés 1963:55–8; 1971:81, 84; Díaz del Castillo 1908–16, 2:35–41; 1977, 1:259–63; Durán 1964:287, 290; 1967, 2:536, 541; Ixtlilxochitl 1969:4–5; 1975–77, 1:451, 2:217–18; López de Gómara 1964:136–9; 1965–66, 2:128–30; Martyr d'Anghera 1970, 2:89–90, 93–4; Muñoz Camargo 1966:215; 1984:251; Oviedo y Valdés 1959, 4:30–1; Sahagún 1975:37, 43–4; 1989:65–9; Tapia 1950:59; 1963:38.

Perhaps the best Conquest-era description of Tenochtitlan was penned by the Anonymous Conquistador, who wrote that Tenochtitlan, built in the lake, was two and a half to three leagues in circumference and tied to the shore by three high causeways. The city had wide, beautiful streets and canals, many large plazas, numerous temples, and houses and gardens as beautiful as any in Spain. Here, deep within enemy territory, Cortés and fewer than three hundred Spaniards and a few thousand Indian allies walked into the capital of the most powerful empire in Mesoamerica. Why did he take this seemingly foolhardy step? Was it a sense of cultural or military superiority? Perhaps. Certainly, these factors cannot be discounted. But it may be better explained by examining how Moteuczoma and Cortés each understood their respective positions.[10]

Moteuczoma may have had several reasons for allowing the Spaniards into Tenochtitlan without overt opposition. He may still have been uncertain about the Spaniards' status as men or gods, and his army was still limited by the pre-harvest lack of manpower. But a major reason why Moteuczoma did not oppose Cortés's entry was political. He knew about the massacre at Cholollan and that the new king had assumed power with Spanish help and that his own politically divided city and region also harboured dissident factions. Any opposition to Cortés could embolden these groups and threaten his position, so Moteuczoma was conciliatory. This ostensibly offered Cortés a strong ally and effectively blocked this option for any emergent dissident faction. In light of the reception the Spaniards received in the Chalca cities, Moteuczoma did not move against them lest this splinter the political coherence of the Valley of Mexico, but it left him to face Cortés in a weakened position. Thus, Moteuczoma's acquiescence to Cortés's arrival, which appears inept from a Spanish-centred perspective, was considered and logical in terms of the political dynamics of Mesoamerican society. But even if he wanted to oppose Cortés's entry, Moteuczoma lacked the forces at that time to take decisive offensive action, although they would be adequate to seize and kill Cortés once he entered Tenochtitlan.

This may explain why Moteuczoma permitted the Spaniards to enter Tenochtitlan, but not why Cortés would voluntarily do so and place his vastly smaller force in such a dangerous position. Part of his assurance doubtless arose from his having successfully subdued

10 Conquistador Anónimo 1941:42–8; 1963:178–81; López de Gómara 1964:156–60; 1965–66, 2:147–51; Martyr d'Anghera 1970, 2:91–2, 108–9.

or allied with all of his opponents so far. However, most of the towns he had encountered were small, holding only thousands of inhabitants, with the largest cities holding a few tens of thousands, and he had successfully allied with Tlaxcallan, multiplying his strength many fold. Thus, Cortés was doubtless buoyed by his initial successes and his greatly bolstered position following his alliance with Tlaxcallan and the defeat of Cholollan.

At the same time, Cortés's experience in Spain would have led him to believe that he could subdue any potential force in Mexico. The largest city that Cortés is likely to have seen was Seville, which held between 60,000 and 100,000 inhabitants. Moreover, the largest city in Europe was Paris, with between 100,000 and 150,000 people, at a time when London held fewer than 60,000. Thus, Cortés probably based his assessment of the Aztec threat on the military forces he had met so far, the size of cities in Europe, and the Mesoamerican towns seen to that point.[11]

When Cortés entered the Valley of Mexico, he passed through numerous towns and cities, but none larger than about 30,000 inhabitants until he reached Tenochtitlan, which held at least 200,000 people – far more than any city he had ever encountered before – and the entire Valley of Mexico that formed the capital's metropolitan area held from 1 million to 2.65 million people. He had doubtless been told of the size and splendour of Tenochtitlan, but given the general inaccuracy of descriptions and the tendency to exaggerate by Indians and Spaniards alike, he had probably discounted these stories and assessed the potential threat in terms of the size of cities he knew. When Cortés reached Tenochtitlan and it proved to be vastly larger than anticipated, he was no longer in a position to retreat.[12]

Cortés's strength did not lie primarily in his own men. He was almost entirely dependent on Indian supplies, labour and now auxiliary troops. These were ensured as long as his alliance with them lasted, but that depended on their perception of him as powerful and able to defend them against Aztec retaliation. A retreat in the face of the obvious power of the Aztec empire would have undermined Cortés's position. The Aztecs would have been emboldened and, even more disastrous for the Spaniards, his allies would have abandoned him, with the Tlaxcaltecs retreating to their

11 Mols 1974:41.
12 Calnek 1976:288; 1978:316; Denevan 1976b:81–2; Sanders 1970:449; Sanders, Parsons and Santley 1979:154. But see also Hardoy (1973:154–5), who puts the population of Tenochtitlan at 300,000.

home province, allied Indians seeking Aztec forgiveness for their transgressions, and wavering towns reaffirming their allegiance to the Aztecs. In short, having made the decision to go to Tenochtitlan, Cortés was now confronted with the enormity of his opponents but by that time he had no way out. He had to continue fearlessly into the city or risk the abandonment of all his allies. Since Cortés could not retreat to Cuba without facing charges of treason, any mis-step at this point would leave him at the mercy of the Aztecs.

6 MOTEUCZOMA'S TENOCHTITLAN

By whatever plan or miscalculation, the Spaniards found themselves in Tenochtitlan, the largest city in the New World and capital of Mexico's greatest empire. Moteuczoma presented the Spaniards with gifts, fed them, and housed them in the palace of Axayacatl, the sixth Aztec king. Whatever his private thoughts, Moteuczoma publicly befriended Cortés.[1]

If Moteuczoma still felt that the Spaniards may have been gods, this idea surely faded quickly with first-hand contact. Perhaps Moteuczoma did want Cortés inside Tenochtitlan where he could be seized and killed, or perhaps he was biding his time until the war season, when he could again raise a large army and deal with the Spaniards as well as the Tlaxcaltecs and all the rebellious provinces to the east. But whatever the king's motivations, Cortés did enter Tenochtitlan where Moteuczoma embraced him, which would have stilled any public rift among the Aztec rulers and nobles.[2]

The Valley of Mexico that the Aztecs presided over was cut by political and ethnic divisions. There were nine major ethnic groups within the valley, including the dispersed Otomi. The others, centred in city-states or larger polities, were the Mizquicas and Cuitlahuacas in their respective towns, the Aztecs (or Mexica) in Tenochtitlan, the Colhua on the Ixtapalapa Peninsula, the Chalca in the southeastern corner of the valley, the Xochimilca to the south, the Tepanecs on the west side, and the Acolhua on the east. By the time Cortés arrived, these had all been incorporated into the Aztec empire, through acquiescence, conquest or cooption, but dissident factions existed everywhere.[3]

Tenochtitlan was a formidable city: its population was enormous and it commanded great resources. Moreover, the

1 Acosta 1954:240; 1970–73, 2:519; Aguilar 1963:146; 1977:80; Cortés 1963:59–60; 1971:87; Díaz del Castillo 1908–16, 2:43, 54–5; 1977, 1:264–5, 267; Ixtlilxochitl 1975–77, 2:218; López de Gómara 1964: 140; 1965–66, 2:131.
2 Díaz del Castillo 1908–16, 2:58; 1977, 1:269.
3 Gibson 1964:9–20.

Spaniards knew that it was located on an island connected to the mainland by only three major causeways that could easily be severed, trapping them inside the city. The causeway over which they had entered Tenochtitlan was wide, able to accommodate eight horsemen abreast, but it could be cut by removing its wooden bridges and it was defended by merloned fortifications. The city also held large, well-stocked armouries.[4]

The danger of their position quickly became apparent and the Spaniards began to believe that Moteuczoma had enticed them into Tenochtitlan in order to kill them. Whether or not this was true, once inside the capital, they were certainly in a precarious position. Most of the Tlaxcaltecs remained outside the city and, separated by causeways, could not be of much assistance; even with their technological advantages, the few hundred Spaniards could easily be overwhelmed and destroyed. Despite the shift of Aztec opinion against the Spaniards, Cortés could not withdraw without undermining the support of his allies. His only hope lay in Aztec restraint.[5]

Word soon reached Cortés that the Aztecs had attacked the Totonacs at Nauhtlan for refusing to pay tribute. The Totonacs asked the Spanish garrison at Vera Cruz for help and Juan de Escalante led a force of forty to fifty Spanish soldiers, with two horsemen, two cannons, three crossbows, two harquebuses and eight to ten thousand Totonacs against the Aztecs. But once the attack began, the Totonacs fled and seven Spaniards were killed before the survivors also fled, leaving the Aztecs victorious and the region in turmoil. The Spaniards were obviously neither immortal nor invincible: if they could not defeat the Aztecs, other towns loyal to the Spaniards would defect, endangering the garrison at Vera Cruz, cutting Cortés's lines of communications to the gulf, and precipitating even more defections.[6]

Cortés could not risk leaving Tenochtitlan but neither could he ignore this reversal, so he exercised the only available option, went before Moteuczoma, and seized him. With Moteuczoma in Spanish

4 Aguilar 1963:145; 1977:79; Cortés 1963:58; 1971:83–4; Díaz del Castillo 1908–16, 2:64–5, 85–6; 1977, 1:273–4, 287–8; López de Gómara 1964:152, 159; 1965–66, 2:143–4, 150; Tapia 1950:58–9; 1963:37.

5 Díaz del Castillo 1908–16, 2:85–7; 1977, 1:287–8; López de Gómara 1964:168; 1965–66, 2:159.

6 Cortés 1963:60–1; 1971:87; Díaz del Castillo 1908–16, 2:87, 89–90; 1977, 1:288–91; Ixtlilxochitl 1975–77, 2:218–19; Martyr d'Anghera 1970, 2:97–8; Oviedo y Valdés 1959, 4:33.

hands, the rest of the Aztecs could be easily controlled and Cortés would not have to fear an armed attack or face the cut off of his food and water. The king went without resisting and Cortés held him captive for the entire eight months that he stayed in Tenochtitlan, indirectly ruling the city. Why Moteuczoma cooperated with Cortés so freely is not known. Perhaps he was weak or simply too concerned for his own safety to take decisive action against the Spaniards. Or perhaps it was a calculated political decision: if he continued to rule, even under the influence of Cortés, he retained power. Refusal would have paralysed the Aztec government, strengthened the position of other power contenders who had opposed allowing the Spaniards into Tenochtitlan in the first place, and ultimately led to Moteuczoma's ouster as others struggled for the throne. He may also have been passive initially in order to find out more about the Spaniards or to wait until the war season when his armies would reassemble but, if the latter, he did not act after he had been taken prisoner. Why Moteuczoma would cooperate is puzzling, but he did; fear for his personal safety is a less likely explanation than fear for his political future.[7]

From captivity, Moteuczoma ordered the leader of the Aztec army that had attacked Nauhtlan to be seized and brought to Tenochtitlan. There, truthfully or not, he denied that Moteuczoma had ordered the attack and, at Cortés's insistence, the king had him burned to death – a European rather than a Mesoamerican form of capital punishment and one that horrified the Aztecs. This act generated considerable resentment in Tenochtitlan but reaffirmed Cortés's authority among his allies and, on learning what had happened, the Totonacs resumed supplying Vera Cruz.[8]

Although Cortés ruled through Moteuczoma, the imprisoned king did not provide the secure control that he had expected. Selection for, and retention of, the Aztec throne depended on ability and performance but, held hostage by the Spaniards, Moteuczoma now appeared weak. Aztec tributaries were not organizationally

7 Acosta 1954:241; 1970–73, 2:519–20; Aguilar 1963:148; 1977:82; Chimalpahin 1965:235; Cortés 1963:61–3; 1971:88–91; Díaz del Castillo 1908–16, 2:87, 93–6; 1977, 1:288, 292–6; Ixtlilxochitl 1975–77, 2:218–19; López de Gómara 1964:169–71; 1965–66, 2:159–62; Martyr d'Anghera 1970, 2:98–100; Tapia 1950:59–61; 1963:38–9.

8 Aguilar 1963:149; 1977:83; Cortés 1963:62–3; 1971:91; Díaz del Castillo 1908–16, 2:97–8; 1977, 1:295–6; Ixtlilxochitl 1975–77, 2:221–3; López de Gómara 1964:170, 176–7; 1965–66, 2:160–1, 166–7; Martyr d'Anghera 1970, 2:98–9; Oviedo y Valdés 1959, 4:34–5.

integrated into the Aztec state and their control depended on cooperation reinforced by their perception of the Aztec king's ability to act decisively. The single previous weak king to rule the Aztec empire, Tizoc, had been assassinated after a prolonged period of inaction. Weakness also struck at the interests of the nobles as both they and the empire depended on tributary revenues whose flow would quickly dry up if not enforced. Moreover, there was never a shortage of able and eligible nobles qualified to become king, and Moteuczoma warned Cortés of this.[9]

Reaction to Moteuczoma's weakness did not emerge first among the nobles of Tenochtitlan where his power was most obvious, but in allied Tetzcoco, where, with the help of the kings of Coyohuacan, Tlacopan, Ixtlapalapan and Matlatzinco, King Cacama conspired to attack the Spaniards. Even though Moteuczoma's authority was eroding, directly challenging his commands remained dangerous. With too many conspirators and divided loyalties, word leaked out and Moteuczoma learned of Cacama's plot and told Cortés.[10]

Although he lacked unanimous support for his planned overthrow at this point, Cacama was determined to continue. However, his own domestic support was weak because Tetzcoco's nobles had been divided over his own succession to the throne. When Tetzcoco's King Nezahualpilli died in 1515, Cacama was placed on the throne largely through Moteuczoma's insistence, but it was this very support that he had now defied. At Cortés's insistence, Moteuczoma dispatched six loyal nobles to Tetzcoco, captured Cacama with the help of Tetzcoca dissidents, and sent him to Tenochtitlan. He also seized and imprisoned the rulers of Coyohuacan, Ixtlapalapan and Tlacopan; on the king's advice, Cortés made one of the Moteuczoma's sons, Cocozca, king of Tetzcoco.[11]

Moteuczoma assembled his nobles and ordered them to pledge fealty to Cortés, which they did, but resentment was growing against both Moteuczoma and the Spaniards. Then, at Cortés's insistence, Moteuczoma ordered tribute to be gathered and delivered to the

9 Díaz del Castillo 1908–16, 2:98; 1977, 1:296; López de Gómara 1964:178–9; 1965–66, 2:168.
10 Cortés 1963:68; 1971:97; Díaz del Castillo 1908–16, 2:115–16; 1977, 1:308–9; López de Gómara 1964:182; 1965–66, 2:171–2; Martyr d'Anghera 1970, 2:103; Oviedo y Valdés 1959, 4:40; Tapia 1950:68; 1963:40.
11 Chimalpahin 1965:235; Cortés 1963:68; 1971:97–8; Díaz del Castillo 1908–16, 2:116–22; 1977, 1:309–10, 312–13; López de Gómara 1964:183–4; 1965–66, 2:172–3; Martyr d'Anghera 1970, 2:104–5; Oviedo y Valdés 1959, 4:40–1.

Spaniards. Cortés controlled Moteuczoma but he lacked a full understanding of the nature and limits of the king's power. Moteuczoma's tenure in office depended on proper actions, yet most of what he ordered at Cortés's insistence was contrary to Aztec interests and his support among both the people and the nobility eroded.[12]

While the Spaniards were seizing control of Tenochtitlan, in Cuba, Governor Velásquez had assembled a powerful fleet – 19 ships (one small ship sank en route), at least 800 soldiers, over 20 cannons, 80 horsemen, 120 crossbowmen and 80 harquebusiers – to capture Cortés under the command of Pánfilo de Narváez. Spanish accounts claim Moteuczoma learned that Narváez had landed before Cortés did, which was probably true, and that he sent emissaries to greet him. First word of Narváez's arrival did come by Aztec messengers, but a conspiracy between Moteuczoma and Narváez to attack Cortés and force his withdrawal was improbable in the light of Moteuczoma's weak response to his own seizure and continued imprisonment.[13]

Although Governor Velásquez had known of Cortés's disobedience since the previous summer, an expedition sent in reprisal could not sail until the favourable winds of spring. Thus, it was not until around 20 April 1520 that Pánfilo de Narváez and his men landed at San Juan de Ulua with orders from the governor to seize Cortés and return him to Cuba. When Cortés learned of this, he marched to the coast, reached Narváez's camp at Cempohuallan about 27 May, and prepared to attack. With only 266 men against Narváez's 800 plus, Cortés launched a surprise attack after midnight, resulting in the capture of Narváez and the surrender of his men. Narváez's swift defeat by vastly inferior forces was less a testament to Cortés's military skills than to his duplicity. There is significant evidence that Cortés had negotiated, or was in the midst of negotiating, an arrangement to settle their dispute peacefully, so Narváez was not expecting an attack. Cortés had also sown seeds of dissension within Narváez's camp and when the attack came, many of the defenders did not fight, nor were the cannons used. Narváez

12 Díaz del Castillo 1908–16, 2:125, 135; 1977, 1:315, 321; López de Gómara 1964:184–5; 1965–66, 2:173–4; Oviedo y Valdés 1959, 4:42–4.
13 Aguilar 1963:149; 1977:83; Cortés 1963:81–2; 1971:113–15; Díaz del Castillo 1908–16, 2:153–4, 157–8; 1977, 1:333, 336; López de Gómara 1964:191; 1965–66, 2:180; Martyr d'Anghera 1970, 2:127; Muñoz Camargo 1966:215; Oviedo y Valdés 1959, 4:52–3; Tapia 1950:75; 1963:44.

was thereafter imprisoned in Vera Cruz and his men joined Cortés, although with widely varying degrees of enthusiasm.[14]

Events in Tenochtitlan had not gone as smoothly for the Spaniards as they had on the coast, however. When Cortés left for Vera Cruz, he placed Pedro de Alvarado in charge in Tenochtitlan. Alvarado was left in command of a force of eighty soldiers, including fourteen harquebusiers and eight crossbowmen, as well as five horses, some cannons and all the remaining powder; their quarters were fortified and stocked with a large quantity of maize brought from Tlaxcallan. Yet during Cortés's absence, Alvarado massacred thousands of Aztec nobles during the festival of Toxcatl. He maintained that the Aztecs planned to attack the Spaniards, but this was almost certainly untrue, despite dissension among the Indians and general hostility toward the Spaniards for holding Moteuczoma prisoner. The most important of the eighteen monthly festivals, the feast of Toxcatl, involved human sacrifice and a dance and procession by warriors carrying a figure of the god Huitzilopochtli. The festival was a major celebration of Aztec war gods and the participating warriors were dressed in their finery rather than in functional combat gear. Alvarado probably did perceive a threat – apparently extracting this information from some Indians by torture – but it was not real. Alvarado's limited forces would have had a minimal chance of succeeding in a conventional battle against the Aztecs, so he wanted the advantage of striking first.[15]

The festival of Toxcatl was held in the courtyard before the Great Temple, which was accessible through only four entrances. Alvarado blocked these, then entered with his fully armed Spaniards and began the slaughter of the unarmed Aztecs. Most were trapped inside and killed by Spanish swords, but some escaped over the walls. How many died will never be known with certainty but the sixteenth-century priest, Diego Durán, estimated that the courtyard held eight to ten thousand nobles, most of whom were killed. When word of the massacre spread, the people gathered their arms and attacked the Spaniards, killing seven, wounding many, and driving the rest back to their fortified quarters. Once behind their defences,

14 Aguilar 1963:150; 1977:84–5; Cortés 1963:113–27; 1971:81–9; Demanda 1971, 1:437–44; Díaz del Castillo 1908–16, 2:153–220; 1977, 1:333–79; López de Gómara 1964:192–205; 1965–66, 2:181–92; Martyr d'Anghera 1970, 2:129–31; Muñoz Camargo 1966:216; 1984:251; Oviedo y Valdés 1959, 4:52–60; Tapia 1950:76–82; 1963:45–8.
15 Aguilar 1963:151; 1977:85; Díaz del Castillo 1908–16, 2:171; 1977, 1:346; Ixtlilxochitl 1975–77, 2:227; Sahagún 1981:9–10, 66–77; Tapia 1950:75–6; 1963:45.

the Spaniards managed to drive the Aztecs back with artillery fire. The Aztecs could certainly have destroyed Alvarado's forces although the cost would have been high, so they besieged the Spaniards but did not attempt an all-out effort to destroy them. This may have occurred as a result of the Aztecs' disarray following the loss of so many leaders, a mourning period following their funerals, the continued imprisonment of Moteuczoma, and their uncertainty over unseating a reigning king. Once besieged, Alvarado sent two Tlaxcaltecs to tell Cortés what had happened. Whatever Alvarado's true reasons for massacring the Aztecs, it did have profound consequences for the positions of both the Aztecs and the Spaniards. The attack decimated the Aztec forces, not only killing thousands, but also killing the very best soldiers – the seasoned veterans and noble warriors who participated in the festival. The slaughter greatly reduced both the number of elite troops now facing the Spaniards and destroyed much of the army's command structure which, at a loss of only seven men, was a major coup for the Spaniards. Politically, however, it turned the tide against both the Spaniards and Moteuczoma.[16]

Even with superior firepower and a much higher kill ratio, the Spaniards could not hope to prevail against the great crush of Aztecs inside Tenochtitlan. To this point, they had been shielded by Moteuczoma, whom they held prisoner. But each act on behalf of the Spaniards and against Aztec interests further undermined Moteuczoma's position as he lost more and more noble support. Moteuczoma's eventual loss of authority was probably inevitable but the Toxcatl massacre was the ultimate outrage and his support vanished virtually overnight. Thus, whatever military gains Alvarado enjoyed from this massacre were purchased at a tremendous political cost.

When Cortés learned of the rebellion in Tenochtitlan, he sent word to Alvarado that he was returning and then began the march with an army swollen by men from Narváez's forces, that now numbered over 1,300 soldiers, 96 horses, 80 crossbowmen and 80 harquebusiers. At Tlaxcallan, Cortés was joined by 2,000 Tlaxcaltec warriors; the entire party marched by way of Tetzcoco, reaching Tenochtitlan on 24 June 1520 and entering the city unopposed.

16 Acosta 1954:241; 1970–73, 2:520; Chimalpahin 1965:121; Códice Aubin 1980:85; Cortés 1963:89–90; 1971:128; Díaz del Castillo 1908–16, 2:219–20; 1977, 1:379; Durán 1964:297–8; 1967, 1:21–2, 2:548; 1971:77; Ixtlilxochitl 1969:7–9; 1975–77, 1:453–4, 2:228; López de Gómara 1964:207–8; 1965–66, 2:194–5; Muñoz Camargo 1966:216; Sahagún 1975:51–57; 1989:74–8.

Tenochtitlan's streets were completely deserted, perhaps to show Aztec opposition and displeasure, as they claimed, but allowing Cortés back into the city had military implications too. Outside, he could move freely, use his horses effectively, receive military and logistical support from his allies, and retreat to safer areas if need be. Once inside Tenochtitlan, however, all these advantages were forfeited. Cortés must have recognized the potential danger but probably felt that he could rectify the situation with Moteuczoma's help, suggesting either a fundamental misunderstanding of Aztec kingship or a failure to grasp how badly the situation had deteriorated.[17]

Augmented by Narváez's men, the force that returned to Tenochtitlan was much larger and better armed than the one that had left and Cortés felt he was now in a much stronger position. But only Moteuczoma had held the Aztecs at bay previously and he no longer could: for the first time since he reached Tenochtitlan in November, Cortés faced a strictly military challenge. He rejoined the forces left inside Tenochtitlan, but now the city was a trap. Cortés could repulse virtually any Aztec assault on his stronghold with his artillery, but he was also cut off. Some messengers made their way in and out of the city, but large groups could not: Cortés was cut off from allied support, food, and additional supplies of shot and powder.

The Spaniards were besieged in their quarters for twenty-three days. The causeway bridges were raised to cut off a Spanish retreat and Aztec soldiers controlled the city. Resistance was so fierce that Spanish sallies with forces as large as four hundred men were attacked and forced back with serious losses. The Aztecs continued to assault the Spaniards' quarters and all of Cortés's attempted forays were forced back. The Aztecs had seized the offensive: any Spanish notion that they ever had the upper hand vanished as they realized that they had not dominated the Aztecs but had been merely tolerated by them.[18]

Spanish arms and tactics were proving insufficient under this withering assault: in desperation, Cortés decided to build three war machines, large movable towers that could each protect twenty to twenty-five men who could fire out through loopholes. However,

17 Cortés 1963:90–1; 1971:128–30; Díaz del Castillo 1908–16, 2:220–2; 1977, 1:379–81; Ixtlilxochitl 1975–77, 2:229; López de Gómara 1964:206; 1965–66, 2:193; Oviedo y Valdés 1959, 4:60.
18 Aguilar 1963:152; 1977:88; Chimalpahin 1965:121; Cortés 1963:91; 1971:130; Díaz del Castillo 1908–16, 2:228–9; 1977, 1:384–5; López de Gómara 1964:211; 1965–66, 2:197; Martyr d'Anghera 1970, 2:132; Sahagún 1975:59.

these machines did not prove decisive and were destroyed in battle; moreover, Spanish attempts to burn the city were thwarted by the crisscrossing canals. Having failed in all of his military efforts, Cortés tried to negotiate a withdrawal, but to no avail. He then brought Moteuczoma onto the roof to order his people to stop the attack, but the king was struck down. Spanish and Indian accounts of Moteuczoma's death conflict. The Spaniards claim that he was struck by Aztec stones while attempting to stop his people's attacks on Cortés's men. Since the Aztecs deeply disapproved of his actions and had repudiated his leadership, this version is plausible, especially since at least one ineffectual Aztec king, Tizoc, had been killed previously by his own people. The Aztecs, however, claim that Moteuczoma was killed by the Spaniards. Whether or not this was done to gain the four-day respite while the people mourned their king, holding Moteuczoma prisoner had now become a liability rather than an asset. His captivity could still inspire Aztec attacks but if he were released, he would be ignored at best and could unite his people against the Spaniards at worst. There was little to be gained by keeping Moteuczoma alive and much to be gained if he died, so the Aztec account is also plausible and, in the light of both earlier and later Spanish actions, probable.[19]

Following Moteuczoma's death and cremation, Cuitlahua, king of Ixtlapalapan, son of King Axayacatl, and younger brother of Moteuczoma, was elected king, but the formal investiture did not take place until 16 September 1520, almost three months later. Cuitlahua had consistently opposed the Spaniards so Cortés released an Aztec prisoner with a message that Moteuczoma's nephew, who was with the Spaniards, should rightfully be the king, not Cuitlahua, arguing from the principle of hereditary succession that dominated in Europe. Even in his current predicament, Cortés was trying to manipulate the political situation by dividing Aztec loyalties or, more likely, he still failed to grasp the dynamics of Aztec kingship. This effort failed and the assault continued.[20]

19 Acosta 1954:241; 1970–73, 2:521; Aguilar 1963:153; 1977:88; Alvarado Tezozómoc 1975:149; Chimalpahin 1965:236; Códice Aubin 1980:82, 86; Cortés 1963:93; 1971:132; Díaz del Castillo 1908–16, 2:232–8; 1977, 1:387–91; Durán 1964:302–5; 1967, 2:551; Ixtlilxochitl 1969:9; 1975–77, 1:454, 2:229; López de Gómara 1964:212; 1965–66, 2:198–9; Martyr d'Anghera 1970, 2:135–6; Muñoz Camargo 1966:217; 1984:252; Oviedo y Valdés 1959, 4:62–3; Sahagún 1975:65–6; 1989:84–5.
20 Alvarado Tezozómoc 1975:159; Chimalpahin 1965:236; Díaz del Castillo 1908–16, 2:239; 1977, 1:391; Ixtlilxochitl 1975–77, 2:230; Myers 1982:211–12, 236, 244, 284–6.

Food, water and gunpowder were all running out: the Spaniards had to escape or die. This show of weakness would certainly affect Cortés's political alliances, but the choice was now flight or death, so Cortés decided to sneak out of Tenochtitlan late at night when the Aztecs would be least alert. The Spaniards were in the centre of the city and would have to fight their way out no matter which direction they went. Tlaxcallan was the Spaniards' objective, so a retreat directly east would be shortest. However, this required crossing Lake Texcoco for almost 25 kilometres (15.5 miles) and making their way through the dyke that enclosed the western portion of the lake. This would all have to be done while under attack if they were discovered, which was virtually certain since a water escape would require hundreds of canoes, many more than could be secured secretly. And even if this route were feasible, taking it would require the abandonment of all the horses and probably the cannons as well. [21]

Because a canoe escape was not feasible, the Spaniards had to choose between the three major land routes along the causeways. The north causeway went to Tepeyacac, the smallest of the three termini and thus probably the least dangerous, but this route also required the longest march through Tenochtitlan. The south causeway went to Coyohuacan and Ixtlapalapan, but the water was deepest along this route and the exit towns were hostile. The western route, which Cortés used, went to Tlacopan, also a large and hostile city, but it required the shortest march inside Tenochtitlan and thus offered the least chance of detection. But since the Spaniards would be very vulnerable strung out along a road, carrying all their supplies, and accompanied by their allies, prisoners and dependants, marching undetected was also crucial. The Spaniards would be leaving their fortifications, which was all that had stood between them and the Aztecs.

The Aztecs had removed the causeway bridges and widened and deepened the openings to keep the Spaniards from fleeing, so Cortés ordered a portable wooden bridge to be built that could span these breaches. The Spaniards began their escape just before midnight on 30 June 1520: a heavy rainstorm hid their movements and they crossed one breach but were seen at the second and an alarm was raised, forcing them to abandon their bridge. Attacked on the

21 Acosta 1954:242; 1970–73, 2:521; Chimalpahin 1965:236; Díaz del Castillo 1908–16, 2:241–2; 1977, 1:393; López de Gómara 1964:217; 1965–66, 2:203; Martyr d'Anghera 1970, 2:141; Muñoz Camargo 1966:218; Oviedo y Valdés 1959, 4:64–5.

causeway and from canoes on either side, the Spaniards fled since they could not form defensive formations or even see the arrows shot at them in the dark. Cortés finally reached Tlacopan, but many Spaniards had been killed, as were their noble prisoners, most of the Tlaxcaltecs and Huexotzincas, and some horses; all of the cannons were lost.[22]

Some Spaniards were cut off and could not get out of Tenochtitlan, so they turned back, returning to their quarters where they were again besieged for some days before they were all killed. The Spaniards who escaped had actually passed out of the city proper before they were seen by an Aztec woman getting water and the alarm was raised. At dawn, they reached Popotlan, near Tlacopan, but were surrounded by attacking Aztecs. The Spaniards were then driven toward Tlacopan and finally rested at Otoncalpolco, where they were met by the people of Teocalhueyacan. The alarm was raised in all the surrounding towns but the people of Teocalhueyacan nevertheless aided the Spaniards.[23]

Although the Spaniards usually speak only of the Tlaxcaltecs, Tlaxcallan was only the most prominent of several allied cities and provinces that also included Huexotzinco, Atlixco and Tliliuhqui-Tepec, all of which were represented in the forces supporting Cortés. The people of Teocalhueyacan were Otomi but, under Aztec pressure, many had migrated east and settled in Tliliuhqui-Tepec, so they helped Cortés because of their close ties to his Tliliuhqui-Tepec allies. Indeed, this source of assistance may have been known to Cortés before he left Tenochtitlan and was perhaps a key factor in determining his route.[24]

The Spaniards had to march around the lakes to reach Tlaxcallan; although Cortés would perhaps have received some aid from the Chalca cities, he was also more vulnerable to attack by causeways and from canoes in the densely populated southern end of the valley than in the less populous north. Moreover, the land rose much more sharply from the lakes in the southern end of the valley and the Spaniards would have been funnelled along a

22 Acosta 1954:242; 1970–73, 2:521–2; Aguilar 1963:151, 153–6; 1977:87, 89–97; Chimalpahin 1965:122; Conway 1953:8, 17, 22, 25, 28, 30; Cortés 1963:97–8; 1971:137–8; Díaz del Castillo 1908–16, 2:242, 244–7, 249; 1977, 1:393–8; Ixtlilxochitl 1975–77, 2:230; López de Gómara 1964:219–22; 1965–66, 2:205–7; Muñoz Camargo 1966:218–20; 1984:253; Oviedo y Valdés 1959, 4:65, 68.

23 Durán 1964:304–5; 1967, 2:556; Ixtlilxochitl 1975–77, 2:232; López de Gómara 1964:222–3; 1965–66, 2:208; Sahagún 1975:67–9; 1989:87–9, 91.

24 Carrasco Pizana 1950:280; Ixtlilxochitl 1969:10; 1975–77, 1:454; Sahagún 1975:76–7; 1989:90, 93.

narrower strip of land where their movements would be easily anticipated and Aztec attacks would be more effective. Thus, the Spaniards marched north from Teocalhueyacan under constant assault. They had lost all of their cannons and most of their crossbows, but were able to keep the attackers at bay with short cavalry charges. The Spaniards reached Tepotzotlan that night, which was abandoned, and left the next morning, spending the following night in Citlaltepec. They reached Xoloc the next might and fought a major battle near Zacamolco the following day. But faring poorly, the Spaniards finally withdrew.[25]

Although the Spaniards were under assault to varying degrees throughout their flight, the fighting was relatively light during most of the transit around the northern lakes. Part of this may be attributed to the four days of mourning in Tenochtitlan for the nobles killed during Cortés's flight, including Cacama and the sons and daughters of Moteuczoma, but four other factors probably played larger roles. First, the northern end of the valley simply held fewer people, so there were no significant local forces available to fight the Spaniards. Second, there was little surplus food available this early in the agricultural season in the north to support either Spaniards or Aztecs. Indeed, the Spaniards were so hungry that they ate horses killed in battle. Third, troops and supplies could be brought by canoes from Tenochtitlan but the lakes were still very low and travel would have been difficult, if not impossible. And fourth, the Aztecs could not have marshalled large offensive armies: as it was the rainy season, most of the men were still engaged in agricultural pursuits. So while larger forces could be mobilized against the Spaniards in and around major towns, at this time the Aztecs were not equipped to dispatch and support large forces for any appreciable period or at any significant distance. Thus, throughout much of their flight from Tenochtitlan, most of the soldiers whom the Spaniards fought were drawn from the cities they passed near: in the north, these were small and few.[26]

Once they completed their transit of the north, the Spaniards re-entered more populous areas and were once again attacked in force. The Spaniards could not simply transfer Old World tactics to fight the Indians because they were typically outnumbered and surrounded. Instead, they fought most of these clashes from

25 Cortés 1963:98–100; 1971:138, 140–1; Díaz del Castillo 1908–16, 2:249–51; 1977, 1:398–9; Muñoz Camargo 1966:225; 1984:256; Sahagún 1975:76-8; 1989:93-4.

26 Cortés 1963:100; 1971:141; Díaz del Castillo 1908–16, 2:249; 1977, 1:398.

defensive formations, which minimized the problems of coordinating movements and maximized the effectiveness of their weapons. Harquebuses and crossbows both had greater range than Indian weapons, allowing the Spaniards to engage the enemy while still beyond the reach of return fire, and had greater effect so the Spaniards could more easily disrupt opposing troop formations and throw the attackers into disarray. But more important were the horses. Groups of armoured horse lancers mounted rapid charges into advancing formations. And while gaps created by crossbow and harquebus fire could often be closed before the opposing sides met, cavalry charges created gaps that could be exploited by follow-on troops. Thus, Spanish successes were less a matter of individual than technological and organizational superiority: they were better able to maintain their protective formations while disrupting those of their enemies and attacking their exposed flanks.

The Aztecs nevertheless persisted in their practice of surrounding the Spaniards, in part because of their training but also because it was an effective, though costly, tactic. They could not prevent a breakout, but the Aztecs typically attacked in several different commands so even though the Spaniards could disrupt one, the rest remained intact. Moreover, even when the Spaniards broke through, their rear elements were less able to withdraw as a cohesive unit, leaving the weakest Spanish units to face the most cohesive Aztec ones. Thus, even though encirclement could not contain the Spaniards, it was effective against the withdrawing Spanish forces.

After retreating from the battle near Zacamolco, the Spaniards reached Otompan the next day where Aztec troops had gathered and they fought another fierce battle before marching on. The next day, they reached the territory of Tlaxcallan, having lost over 860 Spanish soldiers, five Spanish women who had arrived with Narváez, and over 1,000 Tlaxcaltecs in the five days of flight from Tenochtitlan. They desperately needed a safe haven so they marched toward the city of Tlaxcallan, uncertain and anxious about what kind of reception they would receive.[27]

27 Aguilar 1963:156; 1977:92; Cortés 1963:100–1; 1971:142; Díaz del Castillo 1908–16, 2:252–4; 1977, 1:400–2; Durán 1964:305–6; Martyr d'Anghera 1970, 2:144; Sahagún 1975:79; 1989:96–7.

7 FLIGHT AND RECOVERY

During their flight from Tenochtitlan, the Spaniards were at their most vulnerable: they had left their fortifications, they had lost their cannons, many crossbows and a number of horses, their supplies were running out, and they were strung out on a march through enemy territory. However, the Aztecs did not mount a sustained assault. Certainly, logistical and manpower limitations hindered Aztec movements, but their political disarray was probably the main factor that allowed the remnants of Cortés's forces to slip away.

The war season was still five months away and Aztec forces had not been assembled and retrained for war, so large armies were not available to assault Tlaxcallan. Moreover, Tenochtitlan's political leadership was in disarray; as the Spaniards were in flight and seemed to be no further threat, the Aztecs turned their attention to the more immediate problems of shoring up support among their tributaries.

Escape, however, was only part of Cortés's problem. Having fled in the face of certain defeat, his political alliances were now unsure. He had been able to create political ties through his military superiority – often perceived rather than demonstrated – but this had now been shown to be false. Thus, as he marched toward Tlaxcallan, Cortés was anxious over his reception so he ordered the Spaniards not to seize anything from the people there, despite their desperate need. When they reached the town of Huei-Otlipan, the Spaniards were received and fed, but this was done for pay rather than from tributary obligation. Clearly, Cortés's political standing had changed and Tlaxcallan's rulers debated their continued alliance. Opinion was divided in Tlaxcallan, as it was in Tenochtitlan. General Xicotencatl had always opposed the Spaniards and was even more opposed after they fled Tenochtitlan. Had Tlaxcallan been a defecting Aztec ally, they would probably have shifted their allegiance back. But Tlaxcallan was an independent enemy state and had few options. Their own political position had been eroding long before Cortés arrived: they were now more tightly encircled by Aztec tributaries, Cholollan had recently defected to the Aztecs, and Huexotzinco's loyalty was suspect. Short of becoming an Aztec ally – and probably a subservient one – their best choice was to continue their support for the Spaniards.[1]

After several days, the rulers of Tlaxcallan and Huexotzinco came to Huei-Otlipan to greet Cortés and to re-cement the alliance. Then they marched to the province's capital on 11 July 1520. Once there, the Spaniards were relatively safe. Cortés's remaining 440 Spaniards, twenty horses, twelve crossbowmen and seven harquebusiers were all wounded, and they rested there and tended their wounds for approximately three weeks. Even in Tlaxcallan, Cortés's security was not absolute. The Aztecs could penetrate the province, as they had previously, but this did not occur because Tenochtitlan remained in turmoil. However, Tlaxcaltec support was not a foregone conclusion and they exacted major concessions from Cortés for their continued help should he defeat the Aztecs. These included the right to tribute from Cholollan, Huexotzinco and Tepeyacac, command of a fortress to be built in Tenochtitlan, an equal division of the spoils that the Spaniards would receive from all the towns and provinces conquered, and perpetual freedom from tribute themselves.[2]

Moteuczoma and many other rulers were dead; although Cuitlahua had been chosen king, he had not yet consolidated his position. When the Aztecs conquered other cities, they usually left the local kings to rule as before, as long as they fulfilled their new tributary obligations. But without instituting major structural changes in the tributary towns, their allegiance to Tenochtitlan was essentially voluntary, based on their perception of the Aztecs' ability and willingness to back up their demands by force should a vassal default in his obligations. This efficient system required little military or administrative expense by the Aztecs to maintain the flow of tribute into their capital. But the perception of Aztec power that undergirded this compliance depended primarily on the king.

An Aztec king's ability to enforce his will was rarely challenged in the case of an established sovereign, but new rulers had to prove

1 Cortés 1963:101; 1971:142–3; Díaz del Castillo 1908–16, 2:256–7, 260–2; 1977, 1:403, 406–7; Durán 1964:306; 1967, 2:558; Ixtlilxochitl 1975–77, 2:233–4; Martyr d'Anghera 1970, 2:144; Muñoz Camargo 1966:229; 1984:258.
2 Chimalpahin 1965:236; Cortés 1963:101, 103; 1971:143–4; Díaz del Castillo 1908–16, 2:256–63; 1977, 1:403–7; Información 1870–75, 20:17, 21, 140, 145; Martyr d'Anghera 1970, 2:145; Muñoz Camargo 1966:236; 1984:261; Oviedo y Valdés 1959, 4:71; Sahagún 1975:80.

themselves. Thus, between his selection and coronation, each king-elect normally led his army on a campaign: in part to secure sacrificial victims for his investiture ceremony but, more practically, to demonstrate his military prowess and resolve. A successful demonstration would re-cement Aztec vassal ties without the need for actual reconquest throughout the entire empire. Cuitlahua could not immediately demonstrate this prowess. As a result, many Aztec tributaries were divided over whether to continue their obedience or to rebel, especially since Tlaxcallan and the Spaniards offered a powerful alternative alliance partner. And this uncertainty reached the highest ranks, with nobles falling into conflicting factions. Cuitlahua could not demonstrate his prowess until the war season began some months hence, and he died of smallpox before it arrived.

Cortés's situation was very different from the Aztecs'. He had lost men and arms, but his forces were still powerful enough to undertake offensive actions. Their primary effectiveness was in being the spearhead for Indian troops and their losses only marginally reduced this role. Moreover, as long as Tlaxcallan remained loyal, Cortés had no empire requiring attention in the wake of his defeat, but there was nevertheless an urgency to his actions. He had to renew his efforts immediately to avoid defections of both Indians and Spaniards and he had to succeed before Velásquez could send another force against him.

One factor working in Cortés's favour was disease. Among the members of Narváez's party who reached Mexico was one infected with smallpox. This disease swept into the Valley of Mexico, touching off an epidemic such as the Aztecs had never seen before, killing some 40 per cent of the population of central Mexico in a year. The smallpox plague reached the Valley of Mexico after mid-October, lasted sixty days in Tenochtitlan and ended by early December. Among its victims was Cuitlahua, who died on 4 December 1520, having ruled for only eighty days. Smallpox was unknown in indigenous Mesoamerica and the native populations were devastated by the disease because they lacked previous exposure and therefore had no immunity. Initial infection is followed by an incubation period of about twelve days during which there are no obvious symptoms. Then begins a three-to-five day period of fever, head- and back-aches, prostration and vomiting, followed by the onset of the smallpox rash during which the illness appears to subside, although this also signals the beginning of the infectious phase. The rash lasts for about eight days, after which scabs form and then fall off six days later; five days into the rash, the fever returns. The disease runs its entire course from infection to recovery in about twenty-six days, giving the survivor permanent immunity. But death, if it occurs, usually happens toward the end of the disease cycle, in the last four or five days.[3]

If Cuitlahua did, indeed, die on 4 December, he must have been infected as early as 10 November and been unable to perform his royal functions after about 22 November. Thus, the empire would have been effectively leaderless during the crucial period when the Aztecs would normally be preparing for war. But beyond the impact on Cuitlahua, the pathology of smallpox would have given rise to successive outbreaks in Tenochtitlan every two to three weeks throughout the epidemic, incapacitating even the survivors for over two weeks each, further disrupting the Aztecs' ability to plan.[4]

Smallpox unquestionably affected the course of the Conquest, but this was not a simple result of massive Aztec deaths. The smallpox epidemic spread and devastated the Indian populations friendly to the Spaniards, so the net effect was to reduce the numbers on both sides. The epidemic did make a difference, however, on the leadership of the two sides. Aztec leaders were devastated; although new ones emerged, they lacked both the experience of their predecessors and the time needed to consolidate their rule and reaffirm allegiances with tributaries. Leaders on the pro-Spanish side were also lost, but these were then replaced by more loyal supporters, and the Spaniards themselves had greater immunity and did not die from the epidemic. Thus, the Spanish leadership remained intact and the devastation allowed Cortés to consolidate his support among the newly installed leadership while that of the Aztecs was divided and in tatters.

Cortés's men were nevertheless dispirited. Many, especially those who had come with Narváez, wanted to retreat to Vera Cruz before the Indians rose against them, and Cortés cajoled and placated them, but refused to withdraw. Leaving central Mexico would mean an eventual return to Cuba or Spain, where his life was still in danger,

3 Aguilar 1963:159; 1977:96–7; Alvarado Tezozómoc 1975:160; Baxby 1981:16–17; Behbehani 1988:83, 89–90; Códice Aubin 1980:86; Cook and Borah 1971:80–2; Crosby 1973:35–63; Díaz del Castillo 1908–16, 2:218–19, 273; 1977, 1:378, 414; Fenner, Henderson, Arita, Jezek and Ladnyi 1988:5, 183, 189, 195, 236–7; Hopkins 1983:204, 207; Ixtlilxochitl 1969:11; 1975–77, 1:454, 2:236; Joralemon 1982; López de Gómara 1964:204; 1965–66, 2:191–2; McNeill 1977:183–8; Ricketts and Byles 1966, 1:26–8, 34–6, 39; Sahagún 1975:83; 1989:102.
4 Behbehani 1988:89.

and he was determined to reassert his power and dominate the Indians of the region.[5]

While recuperating in Tlaxcallan, Cortés must have given his defeat great thought and at least one thing was very clear: despite his initial confidence and the bolstering that this received with the addition of Narváez's men and equipment, his strategy of controlling Tenochtitlan from within was hopelessly flawed. To conquer Mexico, Cortés would have to secure his lines of communication with Vera Cruz, which was his only source of resupply for Spanish arms, he had to neutralize any threat to his rear before attempting another advance on Tenochtitlan, he had to re-cement his Indian alliances through demonstrations of force, and he had to secure a reliable source of food. Previously, all this had been guaranteed by Moteuczoma, but the Aztec political apparatus had irrevocably slipped from Cortés's grasp and he lacked the forces to confront the Aztecs directly. To remedy this situation, Cortés decided to chip away at any Aztec tributaries that threatened him or his future plans. Badly depleted of both men and equipment, Cortés sent to Vera Cruz for any soldiers and all the gunpowder and crossbows. These were delivered, but only seven men were available, four of whom were sailors who were less skilled as soldiers.[6]

The Aztec empire was particularly vulnerable to factionalization. Not only were tributaries often divided internally, but also their allegiance to the Aztecs extended only as far as their own interests converged; anything more was based on fear of Aztec reprisals. This factionalization had been brought home to Cortés at Teocalhueyacan where he had been helped even while under assault from the Aztecs. If the Spaniards could conquer an Aztec tributary and promise protection from reprisals, a shift in allegiance was simple and consistent with traditional patterns of alliance formation in Mesoamerica. A campaign to the east of the Valley of Mexico would meet relatively small forces and, if successful, could achieve many of the Spaniards' military objectives, demonstrate their political power, ease the process of convincing others to become allies, and simultaneously deprive the Aztecs of support from these towns.

While Cortés was besieged in Tenochtitlan, a party of Spaniards from Vera Cruz had been attacked and killed in the province of Tepeyacac, an Aztec tributary. He seized on this as a pretext for retaliation, an opportunity to acquire tribute, and a starting-point

5 Cortés 1963:103; 1971:145; Díaz del Castillo 1908–16, 2:263; 1977, 1:407–8; López de Gómara 1964:231; 1965–66, 2:215–16.
6 Díaz del Castillo 1908–16, 2:259–60; 1977, 1:405.

for his renewed war with the Aztecs; although more importantly, this attack may have been undertaken to fulfil Cortés's pledge to the Tlaxcaltecs and to ensure their support for his war on Tenochtitlan. Cortés then asked for Tlaxcaltec assistance in punishing the towns of Tepeyacac, Quecholac and Tecamachalco.[7]

Spanish accounts claim that the Aztecs anticipated such an attack and sent troops throughout the region, but this is improbable and smacks of Spanish self-aggrandizement. While some forces may have been sent, it was still well before harvest so the Aztecs would not have been able to field large numbers of soldiers. Besides, Cortés's march on Tepeyacac began only a month after he fled from Tenochtitlan: given the turmoil there from Cuitlahua's succession, the loss of so many Aztec leaders, the beginning of the smallpox epidemic, and the Aztec belief that the Spaniards had fled in total defeat, it is unlikely any large-scale, sustained and coordinated offence would have, or could have, begun. Besides, such a strategy was inherently flawed. If they could have raised a large force, the Aztecs should have taken the offensive and marched against the Spaniards in Tlaxcallan and crushed them there. Reinforcing their tributaries would merely dilute Aztec forces since not enough could be sent to each town to ensure that an assault would be repulsed. Without significant forewarning of the Spaniards' target, such a defensive strategy was doomed.[8]

Around 1 August 1520, Cortés marched against Tepeyacac with 420 Spaniards, seventeen horses, six crossbowmen and 2,000 Tlaxcaltecs, but with no cannons or harquebuses, which highlighted the crucial importance of the horse in these battles. He took food for only one day, so a large support contingent was unnecessary. This also suggests great confidence that he would win quickly: it was true that the risk was minimal because the Spaniards were close enough to Tlaxcallan that supplies could be sent quickly or their forces could return. This was the rainy season when the men of Tepeyacac would be dispersed in agricultural pursuits and unprepared for war, but this was equally true of the Tlaxcaltecs and may well account for their low participation. The Mesoamerican tradition of flower wars may also have helped the Spanish attack. If the Spaniards were able to make an impressive show of strength, many towns may have capitulated and become allies of Cortés

7 Cortés 1963:103–4; 1971:144–5; Díaz del Castillo 1908–16, 2:263, 269; 1977, 1:407–8, 411–12; Oviedo y Valdés 1959, 4:74.
8 Díaz del Castillo 1908–16, 2:218–19, 273; 1977, 1:378, 414; López de Gómara 1964:238–9; 1965–66, 2:222–3; Sahagún 1989:103.

without military conquest. Both this and the season made for an easy campaign and a quick Spanish victory.[9]

Cortés camped three leagues from Tepeyacac and sent the town a message to surrender, which was rejected. Cortés then engaged Tepeyacac's army on a plain and, led by his horsemen, routed them with no Spanish deaths. Tepeyacac's rulers then pledged fealty to the Spaniards after which Cortés and his allies continued their conquest of the region, completely subduing it in a matter of weeks. Cortés recognized that these conquests were only as secure as his presence so he founded and fortified the town of La Villa de Segura de la Frontera at Tepeyacac. This settlement would secure Cortés's gains and serve as a base from which the Spaniards could reinforce their allies and retaliate against their enemies. Having done this, Cortés now controlled most of the major towns along the main route from Cholollan to Ahuilizapan, where the trail descended to the Gulf coast and Vera Cruz.[10]

While Cortés was pacifying the region, he received word that a resupply ship for Narváez had arrived from Cuba and had been captured. Its captain, Pedro Barba, was a friend of Cortés's, and he, thirteen soldiers and two horses were sent to Tepeyacac, followed eight days later by nine men, six crossbows and one horse from a second ship similarly taken.[11]

In the autumn of 1520, in an effort to block further Spanish expansion, Cuitlahua sent troops to Cuauhquecholan and Itzyocan, south of Cholollan straddling the main pass into Morelos and thence into the Valley of Mexico. However, Cortés sent a force of Spanish and Tlaxcaltec soldiers – thirteen horsemen, two hundred foot soldiers and thirty thousand Indian allies – to fight them, ostensibly at the secret request of those town's rulers. They passed near Huexotzinco, where Cortés was told that the kings were plotting against him, so he had them seized but later released. A Huexotzinca rebellion was possible, especially since a large force of Aztecs was now only a day's march away, but it is unlikely that this occurred. This seizure may have reflected Spanish anxiety over the reliability of their allies, but it is more likely that this was partial fulfilment of Cortés's agreement with the Tlaxcaltecs to give them control over

9 Aguilar 1963:157; 1977:94; Díaz del Castillo 1908–16, 2:269–70; 1977, 1:411–12; Ixtlilxochitl 1975–77, 2:238; Martyr d'Anghera 1970, 2:146; Muñoz Camargo 1966:236; 1984:262.

10 Cortés 1963:104–6; 1971:146–8; Díaz del Castillo 1908–16, 2:270–3; 1977, 1:412–14; Oviedo y Valdés 1959, 4:75.

11 Díaz del Castillo 1908–16, 2:274–7; 1977, 1:415–17.

that city. When the Spaniards neared Cuauhquecholan, the rulers met them and disclosed how the Aztecs were positioned and, in the ensuing battle, the Aztecs fled. However, they fell back to Itzyocan, reinforcing the Aztec troops there, but to little avail as the Spaniards defeated them. Cortés replaced the unrepentant rulers of both towns and the new kings pledged fealty to Cortés.[12]

Word then reached Cortés at Segura de la Frontera that another ship had reached Vera Cruz, which was soon followed by two more, and their companies added 145 men and nineteen horses to Cortés's forces. Attacks against Spaniards continued in many towns, however, and Cortés was engaged in fighting troops loyal to the Aztecs throughout the region.[13]

By this time, smallpox had swept throughout central Mexico, killing vast numbers of Indians. While Cortés's strength was growing, Tenochtitlan was again in political turmoil. When Cuitlahua died, Cuauhtemoc, son of King Ahuitzotl, became king of Tenochtitlan in February 1521. This inauguration followed Cuitlahua's death by over two months, during which both Tenochtitlan and the empire were without a ruler. Moreover, the crisis that Cuauhtemoc confronted gave him no time to consolidate his rule. In an effort to secure the loyalty of his vassals, Cuauhtemoc gave lavish gifts to some rulers and remitted the tribute of others, following a policy initiated by Cuitlahua. This, however, failed to have the desired effect and may even have been perceived as weakness. Without demonstrating his strength and broadening his political base throughout the empire, Cuauhtemoc's domestic support remained fragile and he was less able to act decisively at home, which may account for his failure to strike at the Spaniards in Tlaxcallan. Thus, the Aztecs faced the Spaniards with an able leader, but one who did not enjoy the unquestioned support of all of his tributaries.[14]

Because smallpox struck Cortés's allies as well as his enemies, this did not lessen his strength relative to Tenochtitlan as, proportionately, the same numbers died everywhere. It did strengthen Cortés politically, however. Not only was Tenochtitlan in disarray from two royal successions in eighty days, but also the

12 Cortés 1963:106–7, 109–11; 1971:149–55; Díaz del Castillo 1908–16, 2:278–80; 1977, 1:417–19; Oviedo y Valdés 1959, 4:77–80; Sahagún 1989:102.

13 Díaz del Castillo 1908–16, 2:282–9; 1977, 1:420–5.

14 Alvarado Tezozómoc 1975:163; Chimalpahin 1965:236; Códice Aubin 1980:86; Díaz del Castillo 1908–16, 2:273–4; 1977, 1:414–15; Ixtlilxochitl 1969: 11; 1975–77, 1:454, 2:236; López de Gómara 1964:239; 1965–66, 2:223; Martyr d'Anghera 1970, 2:149; Sahagún 1989:102–3.

kings of many other cities, including Tlaxcallan, contracted the disease and died. Cortés seized this opportunity and selected those loyal to him as their successors. Thus, while the plague weakened the Aztecs, it strengthened the Spaniards. Having secured himself politically and militarily, Cortés now turned his attention to his return to Tenochtitlan.[15]

15 Cortés 1963:118; 1971:165; Díaz del Castillo 1908–16, 2:290, 301; 1977, 1:425, 433.

8   THE RETURN TO TENOCHTITLAN

After Cortés fled Tenochtitlan, the Aztecs took no action against the badly mauled Spaniards, aside from sending a few reinforcements to allies near Tlaxcallan. In retrospect, a massive strike before the Spaniards could recuperate was perhaps the Aztecs' best option. But social and political circumstances made other courses of action more appealing to them. As we have seen, Tenochtitlan was in political turmoil as Cuitlahua became king, followed by Cuauhtemoc eighty days later, and neither king was able to consolidate his rule effectively. Smallpox raged through the city and region, killing multitudes, including many kings and nobles. Attention and manpower were diverted to repairing the destruction already caused in Tenochtitlan and the Aztecs may well have believed that the Spaniards would never return, at least until they began their depredations to the east, when it was too late.

Whatever effect this social disruption had on Aztec decision-making, there were also sound strategic reasons for adopting a defensive posture. The Aztecs could muster an enormous army in and around the Valley of Mexico, but logistical constraints kept them from dispatching all but a portion for any appreciable distance. Thus, the force they could send to Tlaxcallan may not have been large enough to defeat the Spaniards, who were reinforced by virtually the entire adult male population of the region. Besides, any troops dispatched to Tlaxcallan would inevitably include many of the king's noble supporters and their absence might weaken him politically during these turbulent times and perhaps even open the city to attack in the army's absence. Moreover, how far and how many forces could be sent depended on their logistical support which, in enemy territory, was very limited. But this constraint affected the Tlaxcaltecs as well as the Aztecs, so first Cuitlahua's, and then Cuauhtemoc's, decision to remain in the Valley of Mexico was prudent. There, the military situation was reversed: remaining in Tenochtitlan meant that the king had access to all his soldiers while forcing his enemies to bear the expense and manpower reductions involved in coming to him.

This decision also affected the Spaniards' tactical capabilities, especially their use of horses and formations. The Aztecs were painfully aware of how effective the Spaniards' defensive formations could be in open combat, so withdrawing to Tenochtitlan gave them several advantages. First, remaining in and around Tenochtitlan minimized Aztec logistical constraints and allowed them to assemble the largest feasible army, leaving the difficulties of mounting and supplying an army far from home to the Spanish forces. Second, the withdrawal allowed them to bring food into the city far more easily and cheaply than the Spaniards could supply themselves and their allies by land. Third, it also gave the Aztecs much greater mobility because the canoes enjoyed shorter interior lines of communication throughout the valley while the Spaniards would be forced to march around the valley along the shore. Fourth, the Aztecs could mobilize, concentrate and support troops by canoe at any point around the valley, leaving the Spaniards without a secure rear area and forcing them to defend everywhere at once. Fifth, with their great canoe fleets, the Aztecs would not be hemmed in by any land assault and could reinforce their own land forces, greatly complicating any Spanish attack. Sixth, horses would be of little use against the island city of Tenochtitlan, as any attack would have to move along the causeways where they had little room to manoeuvre and could more easily be hemmed in and defeated. Seventh, the Spaniards' ability to disrupt Aztec formations would be limited because of the depth of their lines on the causeways and the Aztecs could adopt effective countermeasures. And eighth, channelling the offensive along the causeways also minimized the number of allied troops that could support the Spaniards, greatly reducing this advantage. In sum, withdrawing to Tenochtitlan would minimize Cortés's main advantages and force him onto the offensive that would require greater risks, inevitably leading to higher Spanish losses.

Thus, the Aztec decision to await the Spaniards in the Valley of Mexico rather than attack them in Tlaxcallan offered the advantages of cheap and unseverable logistical support, the largest possible army, and unrestricted mobility and striking power anywhere in the valley, all balanced against the Spaniards' uncertain political support and diminishing logistical support. As events bore out, however, there were unanticipated complications for this strategy, but in the light of events to that point, the Aztec decision was sound.[1]

Cortés's forces were rested, more Spaniards had joined him from the coast, and his supply of horses, gunpowder and crossbows all increased, though they remained below pre-flight levels. Cortés had already begun the essential first phase of his return to Tenochtitlan, conquering Aztec tributaries east of the Valley of Mexico, securing their allegiance, generating logistical support, if not manpower, and guaranteeing the safety of the road to Vera Cruz. All this strengthened Cortés, but the actual conquest of Tenochtitlan demanded a fundamentally different strategy from the one he had employed previously.

During the first battle for Tenochtitlan, Cortés's forces had been trapped inside the city, cut off from outside support and assailed from all sides. As time and supplies ran out, he had been forced to act even though conditions were unfavourable and it had cost him dearly. Cortés's main strategic goal now was to reverse that situation, cut the Aztecs off from outside support, besiege their capital, and force them to fight under conditions dictated by the Spaniards.

Tenochtitlan was a large and powerful city, protected by its island location, and Cortés did not have enough men to march in and surround its army. Yet he could achieve essentially the same result by expanding the theatre of operations from the city itself to include the entire valley. He could not count on decisively defeating or allying with all the towns in the valley but he could still cut Tenochtitlan off if he could control the lake, and this he could accomplish by using superior European ships. Before he began his return to Tenochtitlan, Cortés ordered the construction of thirteen brigantines to begin, which he could do by virtue of his new, stronger alliance with Tlaxcallan. He also sent to Vera Cruz for the anchors, sails and rigging that he had stripped from his ships before they were scuttled, as well as equipment taken from subsequent arrivals. A thousand Indians carried the rigging to Tlaxcallan, accompanied by Spanish blacksmiths and, from a newly arrived ship, more harquebuses, powder, crossbows and other arms were transported to Tlaxcallan, accompanied by three horses and thirteen additional soldiers.[2]

The Tetzcoco region had suitable stands of timber and Cortés could have built his ships there, where they could be easily launched

1 Cortés 1963:112; 1971:156. Bernal Díaz del Castillo (1908–12, 2:109–10; 1977, 1:304) says that, during his first stay in Tenochtitlan, Cortés built two ships that were destroyed following Alvarado's massacre. If this were true, the Aztecs would surely have taken their capabilities into account in choosing a response to the Spanish threat, but they did not do so. This, and the fact that no other source mentions these ships, makes me doubt the truth of this claim.

2 Aguilar 1963:157; 1977:94; Cortés 1963:113, 116; 1971:157, 161; Díaz del Castillo 1908–16, 2:300, 302, 304; 1977, 1:432–5; Martyr d'Anghera 1970, 2:149–50; Muñoz Camargo 1966:237; Sahagún 1989:103–4.

into the lake. But this would also have revealed his plans to the Aztecs at a point when they still may have been able to take effective action against them. Moreover, the shipbuilders would have been subject to Aztec attacks throughout their lengthy construction, forcing Cortés to divert large numbers of Indian allies from offensive actions to defend the construction. By building ships in Tlaxcallan, the workers needed little defence, which freed most of the Tlaxcaltec soldiers for combat in the Valley of Mexico and greatly simplified Cortés's logistical problems as the labourers were fed at home. Thus, building the ships in Tlaxcallan was safer and cheaper, allowed the use of labourers who otherwise could not contribute to the war effort, and still permitted the Spaniards and their allies to begin the war before the ships were completed.

On 28 December 1520 Cortés had eight or nine cannons, forty horsemen and 550 Spanish soldiers, eighty of whom were crossbowmen or harquebusiers. With this force and ten thousand Tlaxcaltec soldiers, Cortés began his return march to the Valley of Mexico via Tetzmollocan. Before he left, the lords of Tlaxcallan allowed themselves to be baptized as they were now inextricably committed to the enterprise, their fate tied to Cortés's. The Spaniards could now take full advantage of their allies' presence. Now, any breach that Cortés's men opened in the enemies' lines could be exploited by his numerous allies and their sheer number kept the Spaniards from being encircled, as had been their fate previously. Late December was already within the central Mexican war season so Cortés could expect to meet considerable resistance, but the post-harvest period also guaranteed plentiful supplies and large allied forces. En route to Tenochtitlan, Cortés defeated an enemy force in a pass into the valley and reached Coatepec, near Tetzcoco, just two days after leaving Tlaxcallan. The next morning, nobles approached the Spaniards and invited them into Tetzcoco in peace.[3]

Tetzcoco's failure to oppose Cortés's entry was the legacy of years of political divisions. When the city's ruler, King Nezahualpilli, died in 1515, he left legitimate sons but no chosen successor. One, Tetlahuehuetzquiti, was not suited to rule, but others, including Coanacoch and Ixtlilxochitl, were. However, Moteuczoma put his nephew, Cacama, on the throne and Ixtlilxochitl fled to Metztitlan,

3 Aguilar 1963:158; 1977:95; Cortés 1963:118–20, 122; 1971:166, 168–70; Díaz del Castillo 1908–16, 4:1, 3–5; 1977, 1:436–9; Durán 1964:311; 1967, 2:562; Ixtlilxochitl 1969:11–12; 1975–77, 1:454–5; López de Gómara 1964:239, 244; 1965–66, 2:223–4, 228.

where he raised an army, returned, and conquered the area north of Tetzcoco, ultimately reaching an uneasy accommodation with Tenochtitlan. Although the region was divided, Cacama remained on the throne in Tetzcoco with Aztec support. However, he had opposed Moteuczoma's acquiescence to Cortés and was captured and subsequently killed during the flight from Tenochtitlan. Following the deaths of both Cacama and Moteuczoma, Tetzcoco was ruled by King Coanacoch, although the details of his accession are sketchy. He may have become king by Aztec imposition or through fratricide. But however Coanacoch reached the throne, Tetzcoco remained divided and Cortés's arrival shifted the balance of power against him, so he and his followers fled by canoe to Tenochtitlan.[4]

Following Coanacoch's flight, one of King Nezahualpilli's sons, Tecocol, became the new ruler as the head of the Spanish-backed faction. A willing Spanish ally who would not remain king for long without Cortés's support, Tecocol ordered his people to fortify the city and make arms, including cotton armour. As subsequent events would show, once the kings of outlying towns withdrew to Tenochtitlan, they were cut off and lost power. Whenever thrones were vacated, either by death or flight, new rulers took over but, despite Cortés's claims that he installed them, he lacked the knowledge or power to do so. Rather, existing contenders for the throne seized on Cortés's presence to shift the political balance toward their own faction in order to take power. Many of these new rulers doubtless lacked the complete support of their subjects, but they also lacked coordinated opposition. In the case of Tetzcoco, this alliance may have been engineered, at least in part, by Ixtlilxochitl, another of Nezahualpilli's sons, who had gone to Tlaxcallan and accompanied Cortés on his return to the Valley of Mexico. When Tecocol died 1 February 1521, he was succeeded by Ixtlilxochitl.[5]

Through these political manoeuvres, Tetzcoco, the second city of the empire, fell bloodlessly into Spanish hands, giving Cortés the ideal base for his attack and virtually eliminating any logistical limits on bringing additional troops from Tlaxcallan. The Spaniards were

4 Aguilar 1963:158; 1977:95; Alvarado Tezozómoc 1975:149; Cortés 1963:123; 1971:172; Díaz del Castillo 1908–16, 4:7–8; 1977, 1:440–1; Ixtlilxochitl 1969:12–13; 1975–77, 1:455, 2:241–2; López de Gómara 1964:245; 1965–66, 2:229; Oviedo y Valdés 1959, 4:89.

5 Díaz del Castillo 1908–16, 4:8–9; 1977, 1:441; Ixtlilxochitl 1969:12–15; 1975–77, 1:455–7, 2:390–1; Offner 1983:239–40.

lodged in royal palaces in Tetzcoco, as they were in all cities, friendly or hostile. This was a fortuitous conjunction of political symbolism and practicality, as these were the only quarters that were both defensible and large enough to house all of the Spaniards. Once Tetzcoco allied with Cortés, the kings of adjacent subordinate towns pledged their loyalty as well because they depended on support from Tetzcoco. Their own pro-Spanish factions were now significantly strengthened and their pledges of loyalty reflected this. In any event, this expanded Spanish domination of the area around Tetzcoco to the base of the Ixtapalapa Peninsula to the south.[6]

Long hostile to Tenochtitlan, the Chalca cities were subject to Aztec control from Ixtlapalapan but were probably Spanish allies, as Cortés knew. Leaving three to four thousand Indian allies and half the Spaniards in Tetzcoco, Cortés marched against Ixtlapalapan with the rest, supported by over seven thousand Tlaxcaltecs and twenty nobles from Tetzcoco. Two leagues from Ixtlapalapan, the Aztecs attacked the Spaniards from canoes and on land simultaneously, but Cortés forced them back to the city which, breaking through their lines, he entered and occupied. Whether this was a Spanish victory or an Aztec feint, Cortés's forces were now unknowingly in a vulnerable position. Much of Ixtlapalapan had been built out into the lake and, though protected by dykes, the city was actually below water level. But once Cortés's forces were quartered inside, the Aztecs broke the dykes and flooded the city. The violent flooding put Cortés's forces to flight and, though some drowned, most escaped to higher ground. All of the gunpowder was ruined, all their spoils were lost, and the Spaniards finally withdrew to Tetzcoco under constant attack by Aztecs who landed by canoe along the line of march. Isolated on a peninsula with only one avenue of advance or retreat, the Spaniards were exposed to constant assault by Aztec forces and Cortés's first major battle since re-entering the Valley of Mexico ended in defeat.[7]

Cortés reached Tetzcoco, but all was not well with his men. Several Spaniards from Narváez's party wanted to leave and allegedly plotted to assassinate Cortés. He seized the main conspirators but many important people were implicated and Cortés could not afford an open division among the Spaniards, as that

6 Cortés 1963:123–4; 1971:173–4; Díaz del Castillo 1908–16, 4:9; 1977, 1:442; López de Gómara 1964:245; 1965–66, 2:229.

7 Cortés 1963:125–6; 1971:174–5; Díaz del Castillo 1908–16, 4:10–13; 1977, 1:442–4; Ixtlilxochitl 1969:13; 1975–77, 1:456, 2:246; López de Gómara 1964:246–7; 1965–66, 2:230; Oviedo y Valdés 1959, 4:90–1.

would weaken him in the eyes of his Indian allies with potentially disastrous consequences. So he focused only on the leader, Antonio de Villafaña, one of Narváez's men, and hanged him rather than punishing the other conspirators, using Villafaña's execution to keep them in line. Despite continued unrest, Cortés controlled the divisions within his camp so the Aztecs faced an apparently unified opponent. The Spaniards, by contrast, did not. The Indians were divided by pre-existing antagonisms, by new ones that emerged with the arrival of the Spaniards, and frequently by political divisions within towns that hobbled their leaders' abilities to act decisively. Dividing the Aztecs was crucial to Cortés's success and throughout the campaign, he followed a carrot-and-stick policy of mercilessly attacking his enemies but forgiving the past transgressions of those who became his allies, greatly exacerbating existing divisions within and between cities. Had Narváez been able to march inland and establish an independent presence, the Aztecs or others may have been able to divide the Spaniards in a similar fashion. But Cortés kept Spanish divisions below the surface. Although many still wanted to return to Cuba, there were no Spanish attempts to negotiate a separate peace with the Aztecs: the dissidents wanted to change the agenda, not split it.[8]

Spanish political tactics had little effect if Indian kings had solid local support or if they were supported by Tenochtitlan and were close enough that Aztec influence was decisive. Otherwise, Spanish pressure frequently warped the local political hierarchy. Spanish support often proved crucial and some kings pledged allegiance to bolster their domestic power. If they resisted, Spanish and allied support was often enough to oust the king and enthrone more favourable challengers, although this was typically an Indian initiative rather than a Spanish stratagem. Such changes reinforced the allied towns' ties to the Spaniards, since these rulers now depended on continued support to retain their thrones; at the same time, the rapidly shifting political landscape diminished Aztec influence and complicated their efforts to maintain allies.

More towns, including Otompan, pledged loyalty to the Spaniards but others, such as the Chalca cities, that wanted to ally

8 Díaz del Castillo 1908–16, 4:88–91; 1977, 1:493–5; López de Gómara 1964:246; 1965–66, 2:229. The accounts differ on the timing of this aborted insurrection (Wagner 1944:336–7) and provide no basis for determining which of the various times is likeliest. However, I have placed it here, after the first attack on Ixtlapalapan, as the likeliest time, following a major military set-back. The other recorded times do not fall after similar incidents and, thus, seem less likely.

with Cortés could not because of the presence of Aztec troops. Cortés's concern for the Chalca area extended beyond his need for additional allies. This area was vital because it straddled the road to the Gulf coast which he had to keep open for more men and arms from Vera Cruz, which could have been funnelled to the north, and for food from both Chalco and Tlaxcallan, which could not. The Aztecs also recognized this and attacked the area repeatedly. Cortés dispatched Sandoval with fifteen to twenty horsemen, two hundred Spanish soldiers and all the Tlaxcaltecs to Chalco, but the Aztecs attacked the Tlaxcaltecs at the rear and inflicted heavy casualties before being driven off. In the main clash at Chalco, the Aztecs used long lances against the horses, but the battle took place on a level plain where the horses could be used to greatest effect and the Spaniards prevailed. Sandoval returned to Tetzcoco from Chalco with two sons of the king, who had recently died of smallpox. Cortés installed the elder as king of Chalco and the younger as the king of Tlalmanalco.[9]

Cortés then sent Aztec captives to Cuauhtemoc with a message of peace, as he did throughout the campaign, but this was spurned, as it was essentially a demand that the Aztecs surrender and become Spanish vassals. The Aztecs continued to mount raids by canoe against defecting lakeshore towns but these were suppressed by Spanish retaliation.[10]

When Cortés could fight his enemies on open terrain, he was generally successful, but his own successes gave him the same problem that had plagued the Aztecs earlier. So many towns on the eastern side of the lakes were allies that the Spaniards could not defend them all; dividing their forces among the many towns would leave none strong enough to repulse a determined Aztec assault. Therefore, Cortés kept his forces in Tetzcoco and dispatched them as needed, which typically meant the Spaniards responded after the damage was done, and might not respond at all when there were multiple calls for help. The allied cities were forced to become actively involved, providing intelligence about Aztec plans and armed defence of their homes. As long as the Aztecs could strike throughout the valley by canoe, further Spanish expansion only compounded Cortés's problems. Unless he could stop these attacks, the pro-Spanish rulers of allied towns would be in danger of

9 Cortés 1963:126–8; 1971:176–8; Díaz del Castillo 1908–16, 4:14, 16–21, 40; 1977, 1:445–9, 462; Ixtlilxochitl 1969:16; 1975–77, 1:458; López de Gómara 1964:248; 1965–66, 2:231; Oviedo y Valdés 1959, 4:91–3.
10 Díaz del Castillo 1908–16, 4:21–3; 1977, 1:449–51.

insurrection. Cortés could not defend all his allies by simply responding to Aztec initiatives: he had to take the offensive and strike directly at the source – Tenochtitlan.

To realize this objective, Cortés dispatched a force under Sandoval to Tlaxcallan to fetch the timber being cut for the ships. When he was almost there, he met a group of eight to ten thousand Tlaxcaltecs bringing the timbers toward Tetzcoco, guarded by an equal number of soldiers and accompanied by two thousand more carrying food. Sandoval joined them, guarding the front and sides while the Tlaxcaltecs guarded the rear. Marching north around the mountains and avoiding the still unsettled Chalca area, this party reached Tetzcoco around 1 February 1521, after four days' march, and construction of the brigantines began. On 3 February, Cortés marched north against Xaltocan, which had rejected his peace entreaties. Located in the lightly populated north, this area was not a major threat to the Spaniards. Xaltocan was well removed from the major area of operations, offered little danger to the Spaniards beyond small-scale canoe-borne sniping, and could easily have been bypassed and isolated had Cortés's purpose been primarily military. But Xaltocan was similar to Tenochtitlan in being built on an island, cut by canals, and connected to the mainland by a causeway. Xaltocan presented the same problems in miniature that Cortés would encounter in Tenochtitlan and since he had assembled a force two to four times larger than he had dispatched against any of the more significant and formidable cities in the southern portion of the valley, the assault was probably undertaken to test his forces and tactics.[11]

Xaltocan had been reinforced from Tenochtitlan and these troops attacked the Spanish forces from canoes in the canals. The lakeshore near Xaltocan was cut by creeks and canals, rendering the horses almost useless. Because the causeway into the town had been destroyed, the Spaniards could not enter, but the two sides exchanged fire. However, the Indians were unharmed because their canoes were armoured with thick wooden bulwarks. Frustrated, Cortés was about to withdraw when two Indians from Tepetezcoco, who were enemies of Xaltocan, told him that most of the causeway had not actually been destroyed; rather, the people of Xaltocan had

11 Cortés 1963:133–4; 1971:185–6; Díaz del Castillo 1908–16, 4:24, 27–8, 30–2; 1977, 1:451, 453–6; Durán 1964:310–11; 1967, 2:561–2; Ixtlilxochitl 1969:15–16; 1975–77, 1:457, 2:391; López de Gómara 1964:249–52; 1965–66, 2:232–5; Martyr d'Anghera 1970, 2:172–3; Muñoz Camargo 1966:237; Oviedo y Valdés 1959, 4:95–6, 98.

merely allowed more water in to cover it. On learning this, the Spaniards found the causeway, crossed into Xaltocan, and conquered the town.[12]

Recalling their disastrous experiences in Tenochtitlan, the victorious Spaniards were nevertheless afraid to remain in Xaltocan as long as the Aztecs controlled the water and thus left to camp on the mainland. This was not a major tactical success, given Cortés's overwhelming numerical superiority, but it did graphically demonstrate the effectiveness of water barriers and the Aztec control of the lakes that the Spaniards would have to overcome if they hoped to conquer Tenochtitlan. Cortés then marched from Xaltocan around the lakes to Cuauhtitlan, Tenanyocan and Azcapotzalco, all of which had been abandoned. None of these cities was large enough to defend itself against the Spaniards, so rather than mounting costly and ultimately futile resistance, their inhabitants withdrew to Tlacopan, concentrating their forces there. In the eastern valley, such towns often capitulated in the face of Spanish attack as they were beyond effective Aztec help and had closer ties to centres such as Tetzcoco. But in the west, the Aztecs were able to implement a coordinated strategy, pulling smaller populations into larger centres where they could defend themselves, limiting the number of places that Tenochtitlan had to defend, and complicating Cortés's situation by removing populations he could control through supportive rulers and then using these as a base of operations.[13]

Cortés was met by a large army and newly constructed barricades and ditches at Tlacopan, and his horses were able to break through and force the Aztecs to retreat only with great effort. The Spaniards entered, sacked and burned the city before Aztec reinforcements poured over the causeway from Tenochtitlan. Cortés attacked these as well and they were apparently forced back, but this was an Aztec stratagem to entice the Spaniards into a compromised position. Once they were fully on the causeway, the Aztecs turned and attacked while canoe-borne troops assailed them from both sides, squeezing the Spaniards on three sides. Exposed and vulnerable, Spanish cavalry and swordsmen could engage only those directly in front of them on the causeway. This Aztec tactic minimized the effects of Spanish weaponry and maximized the

12 Cortés 1963:134; 1971:187; Díaz del Castillo 1908–16, 4:32–4; 1977, 1:456–7; Ixtlilxochitl 1975–77, 2:247; López de Gómara 1964:252; 1965–66, 2:235.

13 Cortés 1963:134–5; 1971:187; Díaz del Castillo 1908–16, 4:34–5; 1977, 1:458–9; Ixtlilxochitl 1969:16; 1975–77, 1:457–8, 2:247; López de Gómara 1964:252; 1965–66, 2:235; Oviedo y Valdés 1959, 4:99.

effectiveness of their own, forcing Cortés into an immediate retreat, leaving several Spaniards dead and many wounded.[14]

Cortés remained under constant attack in Tlacopan for five or six days before withdrawing to Tetzcoco. Throughout the withdrawal, the Aztecs attacked the Spaniards' rear. The Spaniards were tired and it was much more difficult to maintain a solid front during a march than while attacking, which allowed the Aztecs to inflict greater damage. Moreover, the baggage and supplies were in the rear, offering an easier target aimed at the logistical weakness of Mesoamerican armies. This entire campaign lasted fifteen days, ending on 18 February 1521, when Cortés returned to Tetzcoco and, though it inflicted damage on the Aztecs, it did so at considerable cost in a series of battles that otherwise achieved little of permanent significance.[15]

Following his return, more rulers from nearby towns arrived to swear fealty but the Chalca cities remained under Aztec attack. Cortés's men were exhausted, so he sent Sandoval with a force of Spaniards, a few Tlaxcaltecs and a company of Tetzcocas, all of whom had remained in Tetzcoco and had not taken part in the northern campaign. Once in Chalco, Sandoval added local soldiers and attacked the Aztecs near Chimalhuacan, but the Aztecs fell back to some passes, where they were able to fend off the Spaniards. However, since they had merely withdrawn to the south, the Aztecs remained a threat to the Chalca cities once the Spaniards left. So Sandoval followed them to Huaxtepec where, thanks to the cavalry, they defeated the Aztecs again. He then marched to the fortified town of Yacapitztlan and after hard fighting – mostly by his Indian allies – Sandoval won again and finally returned to Tetzcoco. After the Spaniards withdrew, however, the Aztecs again attacked Chalco by canoe. But with aid from Huexotzinco, the Aztecs were repulsed without Spanish assistance.[16]

The Gulf coast road was still not secure, but more ships reached Vera Cruz on 24 February, landing men and arms that ultimately reached Cortés. However, if the Aztecs had severed this intermittent

14 Cortés 1963:134–6; 1971:187–8; Díaz del Castillo 1908–16, 4:35–7; 1977, 1:459–60; Ixtlilxochitl 1969:16; 1975–77, 1:458; López de Gómara 1964:252; 1965–66, 2:235; Sahagún 1975:81.
15 Cortés 1963:136; 1971:188–9; Díaz del Castillo 1908–16, 4:37–8; 1977, 1:460; Ixtlilxochitl 1969:16; 1975–77, 1:458; Oviedo y Valdés 1959, 4:100; Sahagún 1975:81.
16 Cortés 1963:136–8; 1971:189–91; Díaz del Castillo 1908–16, 4:38–41, 44–6, 49–53; 1977, 1:460–9; Ixtlilxochitl 1969:16–18; 1975–77, 1:458–9, 2:250; López de Gómara 1964:255; 1965–66, 2:237–8.

but sizeable flow of men and arms, Cortés's position would have significantly worsened, with all the political complications for both Spaniards and Indian allies. Simply repelling the Aztecs was not sufficient because they would pull back and wait for the Spaniards to leave. The Aztecs and their allies had to be eliminated from the adjacent areas, too. Thus, Cortés assembled a great force and on 5 April 1521 marched against the Aztecs at Yauhtepec, well to the south of the Chalca cities, which he reached on 11 April. There he assaulted two hilltop strongholds, but after two days, he was still unable to scale them in the face of thick fire, so he climbed an adjacent, undefended hill and fired his cannons and harquebuses into the Aztecs' positions until they surrendered. Cortés then marched on and conquered Cuauhnahuac on 13 April. This campaign secured the area south of the Valley of Mexico, reducing the fear of an attack from that direction. These conquests also effectively cut Tenochtitlan off from further support from the south by eliminating the conquered cities as a source and by cordoning off loyal towns farther south with a swath of Spanish-controlled territory. The next day, Cortés marched back toward the Valley of Mexico, reaching the city of Xochimilco on 16 April. This city, too, had been heavily fortified and Cuauhtemoc threw large forces against Cortés, keeping up the attack from canoes well into the night. At daybreak of the 18th, the Aztecs again attacked the Spaniards' encampment and Cortés's badly mauled troops were finally forced to withdraw.[17]

The next day, when more Aztec reinforcements arrived, Cortés began his retreat to Tetzcoco, going first to Coyohuacan while under constant attack. Coyohuacan was deserted and the Spaniards remained there a day before burning its main buildings and then marching toward Tlacopan, under constant attack. The Spaniards continued their march, passing the deserted cities of Azcapotzalco, Tenanyocan and Cuauhtitlan, retracing the same route they had taken during their earlier incursion, and reaching Tetzcoco on 22 April.[18]

Cortés claimed that this campaign had been for the purpose of learning the layout around Tenochtitlan in preparation for his brigantines but this seems unlikely since he had earlier stayed in

17 Cortés 1963:138–40, 142–4; 1971:191–4, 197–9; Díaz del Castillo 1908–16, 4:55–6, 58–79; 1977, 1:471–87; Ixtlilxochitl 1969:18–20; 1975–77, 1:459–60, 2:252; López de Gómara 1964:256–9; 1965–66, 2:238–42.
18 Cortés 1963:145–7; 1971:202–4; Díaz del Castillo 1908–16, 4:81–2, 85–6; 1977, 1:488–9, 491–2; Ixtlilxochitl 1969:20–1; 1975–77, 1:460, 2:252–4; López de Gómara 1964:261; 1965–66, 2:243.

Tenochtitlan for eight months and was surely familiar with the city and its environs. The incursion's more probable purpose was to assess the political and military climate of the area and to determine which towns would resist. And while their arms and horses had proven decisive outside the valley, when battles took place near the lakes where the Aztecs could use the great mobility of their canoes for attack and reinforcement, the Spaniards were consistently forced back. But this was about to change.[19]

19 Cortés 1963:146; 1971:202.

9   CONQUEST AND DEFEAT

Control of the lakes would be crucial to the conquest of Tenochtitlan. Cortés's ships had been under construction for several weeks and, although attacked repeatedly, the canoe-borne Aztecs were generally unsuccessful as the assembly site was situated half a league from the lakeshore. This fear of attack was probably why Cortés had all the timbers for the ships made in Tlaxcallan and then carried overland to Tetzcoco, rather than lack of materials or labourers in the Valley of Mexico. But the ships were now ready to be launched.

Twelve of the ships were 12.8 metres (42 feet) long and 2.4–2.7 metres (8–9 feet) abeam. They drew 0.6–0.8 metres (2 feet to 2 feet 6 inches) of water, had 1.2 metres (4 feet) of freeboard at the waist and 1.8–2.1 metres (6–7 feet) at the forecastle and the poop, were nearly flat-bottomed, and were about equally divided between one and two masts. The thirteenth, the flagship, was slightly larger at 14.6 metres (48 feet). In order to launch these ships from their landlocked construction site, Cortés ordered a canal built. Forty thousand Tetzcocas dug for seven weeks to construct a canal 3.7 metres (12 feet) wide and 3.7 metres (12 feet) deep; the ships were launched on 28 April 1521. This was toward the end of the dry season when the lakes were at their lowest, which must have greatly restricted the movement of Cortés's ships. Their flat-bottom design minimized this problem, but throughout the Conquest, the brigantines were concentrated in the deepest water in and around Tenochtitlan. The launching of the ships was to be coordinated with Cortés's main offensive so he also ordered other preparations. Each allied town in the valley was to make eight thousand copper arrowheads based on Spanish examples and, within eight days, more than fifty thousand excellent crossbow bolts were produced. Each crossbowman was also given two bow strings, the horses were all shod, and the lancers all practised, at which point Cortés sent requests to Tlaxcallan for twenty thousand warriors and to his allies within the valley to be ready to help.[1]

The Spaniards now had 86 horsemen, 700 foot soldiers and 118 crossbowmen and harquebusiers. From this number, Cortés selected crews for the thirteen ships, each holding twelve oarsmen (six to a side), twelve crossbowmen and harquebusiers, and a captain, for a total of twenty-five men per ship plus artillerymen, since each ship had a cannon mounted in the bow. Although seaborne guns are not as steady or accurate as land guns, placing them on ships – presumably in swivel mounts on the railings – gave these cannons great mobility, allowed them to adjust to changing circumstances and targets far more quickly than field cannons, and permitted vigorous pursuit if the enemy withdrew.[2]

The remaining land forces were divided into three armies. Pedro de Alvarado was given command of thirty horsemen, eighteen crossbowmen and harquebusiers, 150 Spanish foot soldiers and a force of twenty-five thousand Tlaxcaltecs and dispatched to Tlacopan. Cristóbal de Olid was placed in command of twenty crossbowmen and harquebusiers, 175 Spanish foot soldiers and a force of twenty thousand Indian allies and dispatched to Coyohuacan. Gonzalo de Sandoval commanded twenty-four horsemen, fourteen harquebusiers, thirteen crossbowmen, 150 Spanish foot soldiers and a force of more than thirty thousand Indian allies from Huexotzinco, Cholollan, and Chalco, and was dispatched to Ixtlapalapan. Although Spanish accounts generally minimize the contributions of their allies, the role of Indian leaders was crucial. In addition to the linguistic barriers, only native leaders could command their troops in battle and ensure their cooperation; although Indian allies reinforced the Spaniards, they necessarily operated as independent forces under their own leadership. However, their support was not unquestioned. The Tlaxcaltec forces were led by Xicotencatl but he was seized by Cortés, accused of rebellion and hanged in Tetzcoco, perhaps for conspiring with the Aztecs as alleged. Xicotencatl had always opposed the Tlaxcaltec alliance with the Spaniards and Cortés was doubtless aware of this, although he had not been in a position to challenge him earlier. But now that Tlaxcallan was irrevocably committed and Xicotencatl's position had been repudiated, he had

---

1 Aguilar 1963:158; 1977:95; Cortés 1963:149–50; 1971:206–8; Díaz del Castillo 1908–16, 4:91–3; 1977, 1:495–6; Gardiner 1959:125–6; Ixtlilxochitl 1969:14, 21; 1975–77, 1:456, 461; 2:255–6; López de Gómara 1964:262; 1965–66, 2:244; Martyr d'Anghera 1970, 2:173. For a fuller consideration of these reconstructions, see Gardiner 1959:130–2.

2 Cortés 1963:149; 1971:206–7; Díaz del Castillo 1908–16, 4:93–4; 1977, 1:497; Gardiner 1959:125; Sahagún 1989:104.

no significant domestic support and was vulnerable to the shifting political winds.[3]

The three cities targeted by Cortés were important, but they were by no means the only important cities nor even the largest. Their primary significance was locational: each controlled access to a major causeway linking them to Tenochtitlan. Severing these conduits would both stop the flow of men and materiel into Tenochtitlan and bottle up the Aztecs inside. The Spanish and allied armies left Tetzcoco on 22 May 1521, during the waning days of the city's smallpox epidemic. Alvarado and Olid marched north together around the lakes, passing through Cuauhtitlan, Tenanyocan and Azcapotzalco before reaching Tlacopan. From there, they marched to Chapoltepec, routed its defenders, and cut off the water to Tenochtitlan. As the most powerful city in Mesoamerica, Tenochtitlan had never had its economic lifelines threatened like this before. But the city was uniquely vulnerable.[4] Whatever else a city might be, it is a large population that cannot feed itself. Every city has to draw food in from outside to feed its populace and, defensively, this is its Achilles' heel. A landlocked city in Mesoamerica could draw in basic foodstuffs from a hinterland little more than a single day's journey. What food costs is not merely the expense of production plus a profit, but the cost of transportation as well and, as this meant the labour of an adult male for each 23 kilograms (50 pounds) carried, it was much higher in Mesoamerica than in Europe where draught animals and carts carried large loads at more reasonable rates. As a result, most cities in Mesoamerica were relatively small since their population could grow no larger than the number that could be reliably fed.

Tenochtitlan, however, was home to over 200,000 people, vastly more than any other Mesoamerican city: it owed its great size to its unique location in the middle of an interconnected series of lakes. These allowed Tenochtitlan to take advantage of the only truly efficient form of transportation available in Mesoamerica – canoes. Whereas a single porter could carry a 23 kilogram load, a single canoer could easily pole 920 kilograms (2,000 pounds) at the same

3 Aguilar 1963:156–8; 1977:93–5; Cortés 1963:150; 1971:208; Díaz del Castillo 1908–16, 4:99–101; 1977, 2:9–10; Durán 1964:309, 311–12; 1967, 2:559, 563; Ixtlilxochitl 1969:23; 1975–77, 1:462, 2:256; López de Gómara 1964:263–4; 1965–66, 2:246; Muñoz Camargo 1966:233; 1984:170, 259; Oviedo y Valdés 1959, 4:115; Sahagún 1989:101. Although Spanish accounts acknowledge very large allied Indian forces, native accounts put their numbers still higher. Ixtlilxochitl (1969:22–3; 1975–77, 1:461) puts it at an exaggerated 600,000 men.

4 For a fuller discussion of Tenochtitlan's political economy, see Hassig 1985.

speed. This meant that Tenochtitlan was in a vastly different situation from most other cities in Mesoamerica. Rather than drawing goods into the centre from a maximum radius of, say, 26 kilometres (16 miles), as would be the case for a landlocked city, Tenochtitlan could draw in food from a similar radius, not from the city centre, but from the entire lakeshore. The cost of overland shipment remained the same, but once foodstuffs reached the lakeshore, the cost of transport from there to Tenochtitlan via canoes was only 2.5 per cent for an equivalent distance overland, a negligible amount. Thus, the capital could afford to draw food in from a vastly larger hinterland than could landlocked cities.

Increasing the area on which Tenochtitlan could draw was, however, only a hypothetical solution to its food supply problem. Much of that land was already occupied by other cities, and many of these were allies or tributaries from whom more could not be easily extracted. To deal with that dilemma, Tenochtitlan turned to *chinampas*. *Chinampas* were artificial fields constructed in lakes which, in the Valley of Mexico, were only a couple of metres deep. To build a *chinampa*, stakes are driven into the lake bed to form an enclosure into which soil is dumped, primarily from the lake bottom. These excavations not only create deeper canals between the fields, but also yield very fertile soils. The end product is a series of artificial islands of exceptional fertility that do not require irrigation since they rise about half a metre above the lake level and the crop roots easily reach the water table. Because they are so low on the warm water, the *chinampas* are also not vulnerable to the frosts that strike the rest of the valley from September through May, so year-round cropping is possible, aided still further by the nightsoil shipped to the fields in canoes from Tenochtitlan.

Wide-scale *chinampa* construction in the Valley of Mexico was an Aztec innovation that began after the late 1450s. The southern two lakes were devoted to *chinampas*, were of relatively uniform size, and exhibit a regular layout indicative of state planning; this could have occurred only after the enemy town of Chalco on the southeastern lakeshore was conquered. Adding these 9,500 hectares (over 2.3 thousand acres) to the agricultural potential of the Valley of Mexico went a long way toward supplying most of Tenochtitlan's needs, but not all. Still more food was required by the growing capital, and this could come only from the lands of their allies.

Tenochtitlan could not directly compel its allies to send more food since it depended on them for soldiers and other political support. But it did manipulate the economy of central Mexico to achieve this end. Each city produced much of its own needs, including textiles, ceramics and stone tools, which it then sold to its own dependent communities in return for agricultural products. They were thus relatively self-sufficient economic systems: neither needed to buy most of the products from Tenochtitlan nor needed to sell them agricultural produce.

Tenochtitlan did not intervene in this system directly, but it did harness its tribute system to alter the economies of neighbouring cities to suit its own needs. Tenochtitlan received an enormous amount of finished materials as tribute from its dependencies, such as gold jewellery and cotton mantles. Part was redistributed among the nobles, but much of this tribute was sold through the market. Because tribute goods were essentially free – beyond the costs of war – they could be sold at or below their cost of production. No producer could compete with this politically subsidized trade and the inhabitants of nearby cities were effectively forced out of the trade. Neighbouring towns could not compete against Tenochtitlan in the sale of manufactured goods received in tribute and these crafts declined. The sole area in which they could compete was agriculture, since not even Tenochtitlan could afford to import food from great distances. Thus, during the decades of Aztec dominance, manufacturing in the other cities of the Valley of Mexico declined while their agricultural production increased. By dominating the market in manufactured goods, the Aztecs effectively forced their nearby allies away from self-sufficient economies and toward an integrated valley-wide economy in which they acted as the agricultural hinterland of Tenochtitlan's industrial and commercial core.

Despite its enormous population, especially for Mesoamerica, Tenochtitlan managed to secure a reliable agricultural hinterland. To the extent they could, the Aztecs had insured themselves against famine, but these measures were responses to ecological reversals, not to war. Most of Tenochtitlan's foodstuffs – whether from their own *chinampas*, purchased in trade, or secured as tribute – remained outside the city proper. Tenochtitlan lacked sufficient storage facilities to maintain its own warehouses and most food entered the city only as needed. Sieges were rare and shortlived in Mesoamerica and, as large as it was, no one in Mesoamerica could threaten Tenochtitlan with one. But the Spaniards cut Tenochtitlan off in an entirely unexpected way from food supplies that were otherwise available and plentiful. The same was at least partly true of its water supply. Although Tenochtitlan was an island city, the lake was brackish and all drinking water had to be brought in. Much of it came in by canoe, but a significant portion flowed into the city from the springs at Chapoltepec along an aqueduct built by King Ahuitzotl in 1499. Cutting this flow was a major, though not decisive, blow to the Aztecs; it signalled the initiation of Cortés's strategy of starving out the defenders rather than defeating them solely on the battlefield.[5]

Having struck the first blow against the flow of subsistence goods into the capital, the two Spanish captains returned to Tlacopan and tried to march across the causeway to Tenochtitlan. Any battle on the causeways would nominally favour the defenders because its width restricted the number of soldiers who could actually engage in combat, greatly prolonging the fight and working against the side with the poorer logistical support, which was usually the attacker. In this case, however, normal Mesoamerican conditions did not apply entirely. Relatively few Spaniards attacked each causeway, but a greater proportion of their most effective troops were actively involved and they used superior weapons. Thus, restricting the fighting to several long corridors was not as disadvantageous to the Spaniards as it normally would have been, but it did mean they bore the brunt of the combat and could not employ their allies as effectively as in open combat. However, fighting on the causeways did reverse the normal defensive advantage and presented the Spaniards with a limited front of massed troops who were ideal targets for their fire. Cannons could kill and disrupt the Aztec front, but because of their relatively slow rates of fire, most of the fighting was hand to hand, pitting the steel swords, pikes and armour of the Spaniards against the wood and obsidian swords, spears and cotton armour of the Aztecs.

Despite a clear one-to-one technological superiority, the Spaniards were continually threatened by the sheer mass of Aztec defenders. The danger of being trapped and killed by the crush of Aztec soldiers was constant, so the Spaniards stressed mobility. This allowed them to use their weapons to greatest advantage, probably by repeatedly advancing for hand-to-hand combat and falling back while the cannons, harquebuses and crossbows were fired to disrupt the Aztecs. Moreover, the Aztecs could not attack the rear because it was protected by large numbers of Indian allies, allowing the Spaniards to concentrate on their front. The Aztecs tried to fight

5 Aguilar 1963:158; 1977:95; Cortés 1963:151; 1971:209; Díaz del Castillo 1908–16, 4:103–5; 1977, 2:11–13; Hassig 1981; Ixtlilxochitl 1969:26; 1975–77, 1:463, 2:258; Sahagún 1975:82–4.

their own way but were forced to adjust their tactics in response to Spanish weaponry. Spanish cannons were particularly devastating because they could kill from a distance that Aztec weapons could not reach. But the Aztecs soon learned that the cannons could fire only in a straight line so they began to dodge from side to side instead of marching in straight lines, and they ducked when the cannons were about to fire rather than remaining erect. Moreover, if a cannon fired from far enough away that the Aztecs could dodge the shot, it was also too far away for the Spanish forces to exploit the breach it caused; instead, the Aztecs had enough time to reform and meet any assault. However, their counter-measures were limited by the causeways that funnelled them in masses into their Spanish foes, so the Aztecs responded by building barricades which offered protection from crossbow and harquebus fire, although cannons could demolish them after a few shots.[6]

The Aztecs were most effective with their naval assault. Canoe-borne soldiers attacked the Spaniards on the causeways, firing arrows, darts and slingstones into their flanks while thick wooden planks protected their own warriors from all but cannon fire. The Spaniards returned fire with their crossbows, harquebuses and cannons, when they could be spared from their frontal assault. But these fired slowly and the canoes did not offer densely packed targets and remained beyond the reach of Spanish swords and pikes. Thus, the Spaniards faced enemies on three sides, two of which were beyond effective retaliation. The situation was sufficiently bad that the Spaniards quickly limited the use of horses on the causeways, since their mobility was severely restricted anyway. The initial Spanish assault was forced back with heavy losses and Olid took his army and marched south to Coyohuacan and set up camp. The forces of Olid and Alvarado had been repulsed when they were together; now that they had separated, neither force was in a position to take the offensive and both remained in their respective camps, fighting only to ward off Aztec attacks.[7]

Meanwhile, Sandoval began his march on 30 May 1521, going south through mostly friendly territory until he reached Ixtlapalapan. He attacked and burned the city and most of its defenders fled in canoes. At the same time, Cortés launched his fleet and sailed to Tepepolco, a fortified island near Tenochtitlan. Cortés landed 150 men and captured the island but, alerted by smoke signals from its

6 Ixtlilxochitl 1969:29; 1975–77, 1:464–5; Sahagún 1975:86, 114.
7 Cortés 1963:151; 1971:210; Díaz del Castillo 1908–16, 4:105–8; 1977, 2:13–14; Ixtlilxochitl 1969:26; 1975–77, 1:463; Sahagún 1975:84, 86.

hilltop, a large force of Aztec canoes counter-attacked. Cortés's small force was no match for the approaching Aztecs and he abandoned the island to meet them at sea, where he had the advantage of Spanish ships. In the first naval engagement, the brigantines proved convincingly superior, sailing through and overturning the canoes which then fled into canals that were too narrow for Cortés's ships to follow. He next sailed his fleet toward Coyohuacan, where Olid's forces were under attack. Landing thirty men and three cannons, Cortés seized the small site of Xoloco on the Ixtlapalapan causeway and camped there for the night. The next day he reached Coyohuacan, helped drive off the attacking canoes, and made a breach in the causeway so his ships could pass through and defend both sides. This breach was made by Indian labourers, whose role is nevertheless virtually ignored in the Spanish accounts despite the fact that more of the success of the siege of Tenochtitlan was owed to engineering on a massive scale by tens of thousands of allied Indian labourers than to combat.[8]

Once the breach was made, Cortés's brigantines passed through, accompanied by thousands of allied canoes; once inside, they quickly destroyed or dispersed the Aztec fleet. After the deployment of Cortés's ships along these causeways, Sandoval's forces marched in relative safety from Ixtlapalapan to Mexicatzinco where a causeway ran to Coyohuacan. But the Aztecs responded by sending a fleet of canoes to sever the causeway and prevent the two forces from linking up. As the causeway to Mexicatzinco was being destroyed, Cortés sailed to reinforce Sandoval. Keeping ships on both sides of the causeways was essential because the Aztecs would concentrate their canoes on the side opposite the brigantines. Thus positioned, they could freely fire at the Spaniards on the causeways so Cortés had to place ships on both sides: this kept the canoes at bay but tied up twice as many ships as would otherwise have been necessary. Nevertheless, this allowed the Spanish forces to move, albeit with great difficulty, and Sandoval's army fought its way across the causeway to join Olid at Coyohuacan on 31 May 1521.[9]

It is not clear why Sandoval moved from the Ixtapalapa Peninsula to Coyohuacan. If he had destroyed the peninsula as an

8 Aguilar 1963:159; 1977:96; Cortés 1963:152–5; 1971:211–15; Díaz del Castillo 1908–16, 4:108–11; 1977, 2:14–16; Ixtlilxochitl 1969:26–7, 30–3; 1975–77, 1:463–4, 466, 2:257, 260; López de Gómara 1964:266–9, 271; 1965–66, 2:248–50, 252; Oviedo y Valdés 1959, 4:118–19; Sahagún 1975:85, 87.

9 Díaz del Castillo 1908–16, 4:112–16; 1977, 2:17; Ixtlilxochitl 1969:24, 27–8; 1975–77, 1:464–5; López de Gómara 1964:269; 1965–66, 2:250; Sahagún 1989:109.

enemy base, he could then have supported other Spanish operations, but because he had mostly stayed in his own camp until the brigantines arrived and there were subsequent hostilities in the area, Sandoval's movement probably indicates a failure of Spanish strategy. Unsupported, his army was too small for major offensive actions, which was also the case with Alvarado and Olid. Sandoval had to join Olid's forces or at least move onto the causeways where, with the help of the brigantines, he could limit the areas of engagement and minimize his disadvantages. Sandoval and Olid both took the base of their respective causeways from Ixtlapalapan and Coyohuacan and marched to the juncture, where they merged into a single causeway to Tenochtitlan. After the Spaniards had reached that point, only one force could be used effectively on the narrow causeway. Thus, Sandoval's army was pulled back and sent to Tepeyacac to capture the still open northern causeway.

The Spanish ships greatly complicated Cuauhtemoc's planning. Aztec defensive efforts had been concentrated along the narrow fronts where causeways ran but now the Spaniards could land forces virtually anywhere around the Valley of Mexico. In actuality, the Spaniards' ability to do this was quite limited since each ship held few men and none could carry horses, but this threat forced the Aztecs to prepare for defence everywhere, diluting their efforts on the active fronts. But the ships' greatest importance was perhaps their ability to bring artillery into range of many areas of Tenochtitlan not previously threatened.

In response to these Spanish initiatives, the Aztecs built traps for both men and ships. The relatively shallow lakes allowed the Spaniards to wade across breaches between segments of the causeway in many places, enabling the Aztecs to dig pits in the lake bottom that could not be seen from above, and Spaniards who fell into them could drown or be more easily captured by canoes. A similar approach was used against the ships. The Aztecs placed sharpened stakes in the lake floor to impale the ships, especially near the water traps in case the Spanish fleet came to aid the floundering soldiers. Protected by ships on either side of the causeway, Spanish forces advanced along the causeways. But they could control only their immediate areas and were unable to consolidate their gains. As soon as they moved, Aztec forces reoccupied abandoned positions, deepened and widened the breaches, and built even stronger defences.[10]

10 Cortés 1963:155, 159; 1971:215, 219–20; Díaz del Castillo 1908–16, 4:117; 1977, 2:18; Durán 1964:313; 1967, 2:565; Sahagún 1989:110.

The Spaniards' initial strategy had been to attack along the causeways during the day and withdraw to the relative security of their camps at night. But since the Aztecs reoccupied the areas thus abandoned, the Spaniards spent much of their time and resources retaking the same places day after day. The Spaniards could not afford this costly and wasteful practice and soon changed tactics. Instead of withdrawing for the night, they would advance along the causeways until they reached a wide place and set up camp there. Moreover, the Spaniards began posting guards at heavily defended barricades and bridges to prevent the Aztecs from rebuilding and reoccupying them. Although this complicated Aztec efforts, it did not completely frustrate them. Nevertheless, with these changes, the Spaniards began making more progress along the causeways. Logistics became increasingly important to both sides as the campaign wore on. The Spaniards were accompanied by large numbers of Indian women who ground maize and prepared food, and these became targets of Aztec attacks. Although these attacks generally failed, they forced the Spaniards to divert resources to protect their camps. But it was Tenochtitlan that was particularly vulnerable logistically: famine was taking hold in the city.[11]

The Spaniards had already cut the aqueduct from Chapoltepec and their occupation of the main causeways cut off the shipment of food and water into the city by foot. Moreover, the brigantines kept canoe traffic to a minimum during the day. Just as the few hundred Spanish soldiers served as shock troops for their tens of thousands of Indian allies, the brigantines typically sailed in twos or threes and played a similar role for the thousands of allied war canoes. Without the support and screening of allied canoes, the brigantines could break up Aztec fleets but could not exploit their gains and risked being overcome by swarms of Aztec canoes when they could not outrun them. With sails, oars and favourable winds, the brigantines were faster than the Indian canoes, but so many tried to reach Tenochtitlan that a blockade was hopeless without the help of allied canoes. The perimeter of Tenochtitlan offered at least 24 kilometres (15 miles) of shoreline where canoes could land and the causeways doubled or tripled that perimeter. The few brigantines launched at night or diverted from combat during the day could not intercept the thousands of canoes plying the lakes. Patrolling farther from the city and causeways greatly increased both the distance each brigantine was responsible for and the likelihood that canoes would

11 Díaz del Castillo 1908–16, 4:119–21, 133–4; 1977, 2:19–20, 28–9.

slip through. Sailing closer minimized patrol distances and maximized the likelihood of interdicting blockade runners but it also increased the ships' vulnerability to attack and to stakes hidden in the water. Moreover, Aztec canoes could cross areas too shallow for the brigantines to follow. Thus, large fleets of allied canoes played a crucial role in this effort and, without them, the Spaniards' blockade of Tenochtitlan would have failed.[12]

Cortés kept two of his brigantines on patrol at night to interdict supply-laden canoes, even though darkness increased the risks of navigating in the shallow and trap-strewn lakes and reduced the number of ships available for military support during the day. They succeeded in stopping some canoes from reaching Tenochtitlan but, in response, the Aztecs set up an ambush. Hiding thirty of their largest war canoes among the reeds growing in the lake, the Aztecs dispatched two or three supply canoes as a lure. When the brigantines spotted them, they gave chase and the canoes fled past the hidden war canoes. The Aztecs had driven sharpened stakes into the lake bottom along the route they expected the Spanish ships to follow and, when they did, the Aztec canoes attacked en masse. Trapped between the attacking canoes and the stakes, all the Spaniards were wounded, one captain was killed, and his ship was captured. The Aztecs had already learned to be wary of the brigantines, which reduced their combat effectiveness, and the Spaniards on the brigantines were now learning equivalent lessons. However, the Spaniards ultimately prevailed in the naval struggle. When the Aztecs tried this ploy again, Cortés was prepared, having learned of the plan from some Indian captives. As before, canoes lured the Spanish ships past forty hidden Aztec canoes. But the Spaniards reversed the Aztec ploy and pretended to flee when attacked, drawing the Aztecs with them past the place where Cortés had stationed six brigantines. These counter-attacked and destroyed the canoes, putting an end to that Aztec ploy. Despite this naval success, ships could harass and contain, but they could not win the struggle for Tenochtitlan. They played a vital role, especially in reducing the Aztecs to starvation, but the war was ultimately won by the land forces.[13]

The struggle for the causeways continued. However, anyone who charged ahead of the rest or was otherwise separated was easily

---

12 Ixtlilxochitl 1969:24, 27; 1975–77, 1:462, 464; López de Gómara 1964:280; 1965–66, 2:261.

13 Díaz del Castillo 1908–16, 4:122–4, 130–2; 1977, 2:21–2, 26–8; López de Gómara 1964:273; 1965–66, 2:255. Contra Gardiner (1959) who claims the pivotal role for the naval battle.

captured, so the Spaniards were forced to move only as units. Although they were prevailing on the causeways, the Spaniards would often pursue the Aztecs across breaks in the causeways, only to have them turn and push the Spaniards back, pinning them against the open breach where they were unable to manoeuvre. After a few such set-backs, Cortés ordered his forces not to advance unless the breaches were filled in first. The Aztecs were left with little choice except to continue building barricades and widening breaches, as well as implanting stakes to hinder the movement of the brigantines.[14]

Tenochtitlan was not alone in opposing the Spaniards: there were many loyal towns in the Valley of Mexico, but their support shifted with the tide of battle. The people of Xochimilco, Cuitlahuac, Mizquic, Colhuacan, Mexicatzinco and Ixtlapalapan all responded to Cuauhtemoc's call for help and brought their canoes to support the Aztecs, but the Xochimilcas and Cuitlahuacas turned on the Aztecs, taking advantage of the situation to loot. In response, the Aztecs attacked the Xochimilcas and Cuitlahuacas, killed many and took others captive. The prisoners were then taken before Cuauhtemoc and Mayehua, king of Cuitlahuac, who were both in Tenochtitlan, and each sacrificed four of the rebellious leaders. Mayehua's rule may well have been contested within his city because he had fled to Tenochtitlan, and Aztec control over towns that they no longer dominated directly was slipping badly. Foot soldiers bore the brunt of combat on the causeways because the many breaches and barricades thwarted the horses and rendered them virtually useless. But as the Spaniards advanced and the breaches were filled, Alvarado ordered his cavalry brought forward. The horses should have excelled in leading the advance on the causeways, but the Aztecs attacked from all four sides simultaneously and they were helpless against fire from the canoes.[15]

The best defence that the Aztecs could have adopted against the cavalry was a formation so closely packed that the horses could not charge through it. But this would have required extensive retraining for which the Aztecs had no time; even if they had, such close formations would have been even more vulnerable to Spanish firepower. Thus, while the Aztecs could not mount an organizational defence, they could, and did, adopt technological defences. These

14 Cortés 1963:169–70; 1971:238; Díaz del Castillo 1908–16, 4:124; 1977, 2:22; Sahagún 1975:87.
15 Díaz del Castillo 1908–16, 4:125; 1977, 2:22–3; Ixtlilxochitl 1969:34; 1975–77, 1:468; Sahagún 1975:95–6; 1989:115–16.

included the use of extra-long lances to spear the horses before they reached the front lines. They also shifted from combat in open areas that favoured horses to confrontations in broken terrain where horses could not charge, and they achieved the same effect in Tenochtitlan by placing barricades and boulders in open plazas. And as a last resort, Aztec soldiers escaped the horses by jumping into the canals where they could not follow.[16]

Although the Aztecs failed to come up with a completely effective response to the Spanish tactics, they adopted a combination of responses that kept the Spaniards off balance. Surrounding the enemy was a standard Aztec tactic that was at least partly successful against the Spaniards. Guns and cavalry ensured that the Spaniards could break through virtually any Aztec line but these could not be brought to bear everywhere simultaneously. So even if the Spaniards broke through, the Aztecs could salvage something from the encounter by attacking their withdrawing and frequently disorderly rear elements. The Aztecs also made astute use of feigned withdrawals and ambushes, often drawing the overconfident Spaniards forward before cutting them off and counter-attacking. Once caught in such presses, many Spaniards jumped or fell off the causeways, often into hidden pits or the waiting hands of Aztecs in canoes. The Aztecs often found themselves in similar situations but, for them, jumping into the water offered safety. So despite the Spaniards' overall progress, these Aztec successes made the Spaniards more cautious and greatly slowed their march into Tenochtitlan.[17]

The effectiveness with which the Indian allies had supported the Spaniards in open areas was largely absent in the causeway battles. Here, these allies became liabilities if the Aztecs attacked from all directions, because when the Spaniards were forced to withdraw under fire, they were hindered by the great press of their own allies. To remedy this problem, Cortés allegedly ordered them off the causeways. Although battles had limited fronts, fighting without Indian support was still suicidal. Doing so would allow the Spaniards to bring their weapons to bear in all directions, give them greater mobility, and thus minimize the effectiveness of such Aztec traps, but this was an unlikely scenario. With the Spaniards divided into at least three armies, manning thirteen ships, standing guard at night at their base camps, and recuperating from wounds, they could

16 Cortés 1963:112; 1971:156.
17 Díaz del Castillo 1908–16, 4:126; 1977, 2:23–4; Sahagún 1975:98–103.

not have launched an unaided attack, even on the causeways. Therefore, any allies ordered off the causeways were doubtless those engaged in filling breaches, not the indispensable combat troops.[18]

Spanish victories were not limited to the battlefield. Each success reverberated throughout the Valley of Mexico as towns previously allied with Tenochtitlan shifted their loyalty to the Spaniards. This was particularly true of towns in the southern portion of the valley, including Ixtlapalapan, Huitzilopochco, Colhuacan and Mizquic. The Spaniards claimed that these towns provided little real support, which suggests that they may have been positioning themselves politically in the event of a victory by Cortés, but the townspeople did intercept supplies bound for Tenochtitlan, provide labourers, and bring food for the Spaniards. Whether or not the allegiance of these lakeshore towns was wholehearted – and it was probably encouraged by the presence of Spanish ships – it did reduce active support for the Aztecs. The Aztecs were being slowly but inexorably pushed back along the causeways and they recognized that they had to take the offensive or they were doomed. Throughout the campaign, the Aztecs had attacked the Spaniards' camps but now Cuauhtemoc ordered a simultaneous night attack from land and water on all three Spanish camps. Night attacks were difficult to coordinate and control, but the Aztecs knew precisely where the Spanish camps were. Moreover, they also knew that the brigantines were less useful at night. The attacks were carried out on two successive nights; although a number of Spaniards were killed, the Aztecs ultimately failed to dislodge them.[19]

Even though they were generally victorious, the Spaniards could not sustain open combat, especially if they could not use their horses. Even if they killed many Aztecs for each Spaniard lost – twenty-five to one was the ratio claimed before their flight from Tenochtitlan – they would ultimately lose a war of attrition. Instead, they customarily adopted a defensive posture when attacked and took the offensive only when it favoured them. For example, they took the offensive on the causeways where they could minimize the effects of the Aztecs' vast numerical superiority and maximize the effectiveness of their own weapons and tactics but they maintained defensive postures around their camps. When Cortés was attacked, he remained in his camp and fought a defensive battle, conserving

18 Díaz del Castillo 1908–16, 4:129–30; 1977, 2:25–6.
19 Aguilar 1963:159; 1977:96; Díaz del Castillo 1908–16, 4:132–3, 135; 1977, 2:28–30; Ixtlilxochitl 1969:35, 37–8; 1975–77, 1:469–70; López de Gómara 1964:277; 1965–66, 2:258; Oviedo y Valdés 1959, 4:127.

his men, maximizing the effects of his weapons, and forcing the Aztecs to fight where they could not bring their superior numbers to bear. This forced the Aztecs to take the most chances and, consequently, to suffer more casualties.[20]

Cuauhtemoc then decided to concentrate all his forces against a single camp and for this purpose chose Alvarado's at Tlacopan. A larger force might succeed against Spanish firepower through the sheer crush of numbers but Cuauhtemoc decided to attack at dawn, which was typical in Mesoamerican warfare: sunrise provided a means of coordinating widely dispersed assaults without clocks or other readily available artificial timepieces and allowed the maximum amount of daylight for fighting. Whether or not Cuauhtemoc was forced into a daylight attack by the complexity of commanding and coordinating so large a force, the timing also helped the Spaniards, allowing them to use their brigantines effectively and to repulse the Aztecs.[21]

The campaign continued as before, although the Spaniards did not enjoy complete success. During an assault on 30 June 1521, the Aztecs feigned a withdrawal and Cortés pursued them, neglecting to fill a breach before he crossed, something that was easier to do now that fewer allies accompanied these assaults. The Aztecs sent their war canoes into the breach and then turned and attacked, catching the Spaniards between the two forces. Cortés was wounded in the leg and was seized and being dragged off by several Aztecs but he was rescued by his men, although sixty-eight other Spaniards were captured alive and eight horses were killed. More Spaniards were captured than killed in this battle because they had been surrounded and cut off. In a battle between opposing fronts, taking captives was much harder. Steel armour also made it difficult to kill the Spaniards except by wounds to the neck and head, so taking them alive was often easier than killing them outright. But perhaps even more important, taking captives alive fit Mesoamerican traditions of rewarding these exploits.[22]

Ten of these Spanish captives were taken to the Great Temple and sacrificed. Their severed heads were then sent to the battlefront and thrown at the Spaniards, which must have demoralized them.

20 Oviedo y Valdés 1959, 4:64.
21 Díaz del Castillo 1908–16, 4:135–6; 1977, 2:30.
22 Aguilar 1963:159; 1977:96; Díaz del Castillo 1908–16, 4:140–1, 168; 1977, 2:33, 53; Durán 1964:313–15; 1967, 2:565–6; Ixtlilxochitl 1969:39–41; 1975–77, 1:472–3; López de Gómara 1964:281–2; 1965–66, 2:262–3; Oviedo y Valdés 1959, 4:133; Sahagún 1975:104; 1989:121.

After the Spaniards withdrew to their camps for the night, they could hear the drums from the Great Temple and see the other captured Spaniards being made to dance in front of the image of the Aztec god Huitzilopochtli before their hearts were cut out. Aside from its religious significance, the Spaniards were sacrificed for psychological impact, both on Cortés's forces and on the Aztecs' allies. The sacrificed Spaniards were flayed and their faces – beards attached – were tanned and sent to allied towns as tokens of Aztec success, as proof of Spanish mortality, and in order to solicit assistance and to warn against betraying the alliance.[23]

Buoyed by this success, the Aztecs attacked each of the Spanish camps throughout the next four days. The loss of so many Spaniards following the assault on his camps was a major set-back for Cortés. The tide of battle had seemingly turned against him and, ever sensitive to the political situation, his Indian allies began defecting. Most of the soldiers from Tlaxcallan, Cholollan, Huexotzinco, Tetzcoco, Chalco and Tlalmanalco returned to their homes, leaving only token forces with the Spaniards. But Ixtlilxochitl stayed, advising Cortés to continue interdicting the supplies for Tenochtitlan, which he did because the brigantines still controlled the lakes. After the main assault on his camps, Cortés returned to the offensive but, with reduced allied support, it slowed enormously. The Spaniards' situation improved, however, when they discovered a way to break the stakes the Aztecs had planted in the lake bed without impaling their ships. Now they could sail relatively unimpeded and, with the help of the brigantines, the Spaniards repulsed the attacks that continued for the next two weeks.[24]

As it became clear that the Aztecs had failed to destroy the Spaniards completely, allied troops began to return from Tetzcoco, Tlaxcallan, Huexotzinco and Cholollan to re-ally with the Spaniards. Díaz del Castillo says that the Spaniards' allies left because the god, Huitzilopochtli, had told them that the Spaniards would now be defeated; when this failed to happen, they returned. Such claims may actually have been made, but the allied withdrawal from and subsequent rejoining of the battle reflects the same pattern of support based on the changing tide of battle and on the perception of power that permeated Mesoamerican political alliances. Now the Spanish forces again advanced on the city and Cortés sent another

23 Cortés 1963:171–2; 1971:241–2; Díaz del Castillo 1908–16, 4:141, 143–5, 149–51; 1977, 2:34–6, 39–41; Ixtlilxochitl 1969:42; 1975–77, 1:472–3; López de Gómara 1964:281–2; 1965–66, 2:262–3; Oviedo y Valdés 1959, 4:133.
24 Díaz del Castillo 1908–16, 4:152–8, 160–1; 1977, 2:41–5, 47.

entreaty for peace to Cuauhtemoc, which also went unanswered. The Spanish forces had moved close enough to Tenochtitlan to reach and destroy a spring that the Aztecs used for drinking water, even though it was brackish. The Aztecs, in turn, dug a new well and arranged for the Xochimilcas to bring water into the capital by canoe at night. In response to Cortés's peace demand, the Aztecs renewed their attacks, forcing the Spaniards off the causeways and into their camps where they were again besieged for six or seven days.[25]

Throughout the siege, the Aztecs received little help from tributary cities beyond the Valley of Mexico. Part of this may have been general hostility toward Aztec domination, but this is unlikely in towns whose kings owed their rule to Aztec support. One reason for the lack of support is that the Spanish invasion had created hostile zones that separated these towns from the Valley of Mexico. Another reason few allied cities sent help to Tenochtitlan was because doing so would strip them of their armies and leave them vulnerable to Spanish attack. But as a result of Aztec successes and apparent Spanish vulnerability, trouble erupted in some of the outlying areas. Cortés received word from Cuauhnahuac, one of his allied towns, that they were under attack by troops from Malinalco, an Aztec ally. The direct military consequences of this clash would have been minimal for the Spaniards, regardless of who won, even if the Malinalcas then marched against Cortés, as they would increase Aztec forces but not otherwise shift the strategic balance. However, the political effects of this attack were potentially enormous.[26]

The Spaniards were being battered but Cortés could not permit an Aztec victory against towns loyal to him, even if they were beyond the Valley of Mexico and not directly involved in the war, because the snowball effect could rapidly strip him of his allies if they felt that his protection was inadequate. Accordingly, Cortés dispatched eighty foot soldiers, ten horsemen and Indian allies under the command of Andrés de Tápia; this force met the Malinalcas between their city and Cuauhnahuac, routed them, and returned to the Valley of Mexico ten days later. Two days after that, Cortés learned that the Matlatzincas in the Valley of Tolocan to the west were also marching against the Spaniards. Cortés again sent eighteen horsemen, a hundred foot soldiers and a large force of Indian allies under the command of Sandoval to meet them. On the second day

25 Díaz del Castillo 1908–16, 4:161, 163, 167–8; 1977, 2:47–9, 51–2.
26 Cortés 1963:172; 1971:242; Ixtlilxochitl 1969:42; 1975–77, 1:473; López de Gómara 1964:282–3; 1965–66, 2:263; Oviedo y Valdés 1959, 4:134–5.

of the march, Sandoval found the Matlatzincas on a plain and routed and pursued them to Matlatzinco, which he sacked and burned. This was the only attempt by a town outside the Valley of Mexico to come to Tenochtitlan's assistance. The Matlatzincas were located near the Tarascan empire and relied on the Aztecs to resist any incursions. Moreover, the Matlatzinca rulers had played a very active part in the expansion of the Aztec empire and had close political and kin ties to the Aztecs. Nevertheless, the Spaniards did not strike at all the Aztec towns beyond the Valley of Mexico because it would have diverted crucial resources from their main target, Tenochtitlan.[27]

The Aztecs renewed their attacks but now, with fewer troops in reserve, they could no longer reopen the canals as quickly as the Spaniards filled them. Both sides were being worn down and hunger gripped the city as the Aztecs ran low on food and water. The lake supplied some food, but this practice could only continue surreptitiously because the brigantines and allied canoes targeted anyone whom they caught fishing. Although Aztec combat losses could not be replaced, the Spaniards were also losing men; their gunpowder was almost exhausted by mid-July when more Spanish ships reached Vera Cruz with fresh supplies of gunpowder, crossbows and Spanish soldiers that quickly made their way to Tenochtitlan.[28]

When the Spaniards finally reached Tenochtitlan itself, the Aztecs once more changed their tactics. Now, instead of facing Spanish gunfire only with vulnerable formations, they attacked the Spaniards' flanks from the buildings lining the streets, regaining the edge that their canoes had provided earlier. In response, Cortés ordered all of his allies to send their farmers to the city with their tools to raze the buildings on both sides of his advance, using the rubble to fill the breaches in the causeways and provide a more easily traversable, continuous surface. This was a major shift: breaches in the causeways had previously been filled by allied

27 Cortés 1963:172–5; 1971:242–5; Hassig 1988:184–5, 190; Ixtlilxochitl 1969:42–3; 1975–77, 1:473–4; López de Gómara 1964:283–4; 1965–66, 2:263–5; Oviedo y Valdés 1959, 4:135–6. Díaz del Castillo's (1908–16, 3:168–70; 1977, 2:53) account reverses the sequence and commanders of these events, but largely agrees with Cortés, López de Gómara and Ixtlilxochitl otherwise. I have followed the latter version because it was recorded shortly after the events in question, in contrast to Díaz del Castillo's gap of several decades.

28 Cortés 1963:176, 178–80; 1971:247, 250–3; Díaz del Castillo 1908–16, 4:171–2; 1977, 2:55; Ixtlilxochitl 1969:45; 1975–77, 1:475; López de Gómara 1964:285, 293; 1965–66, 2:266; Sahagún 1975:104–5; 1989:120.

soldiers, but this much larger operation now used ordinary labourers, freeing soldiers for combat once they were inside Tenochtitlan and more could be used effectively.[29]

When Cortés finally entered Tenochtitlan to stay, the Aztecs withdrew to Tlatelolco. This area was presumably safer because Spanish troops had been more successful in advancing from the south into the city, but the move may also have been influenced by Spanish naval operations. The Spaniards used their ships to fire into Aztec positions and to land small parties of soldiers which greatly complicated Aztec defensive planning. But because Tlatelolco's causeways were still intact, the brigantines were less of a threat there. Nevertheless, the Spanish advance continued, reaching the great market of Tlatelolco around 1 August 1521. Spanish horsemen entered the marketplace unexpectedly and, exploiting the element of surprise, rode down and lanced many Aztecs. The Aztecs resisted and, though forced back, fought the Spaniards from the roofs of the adjacent houses. They could not stand up against the cavalry charges but they would sally forth to fight and, when pushed back, they retreated to the houses. Once inside the houses, they smashed holes in the rear walls and escaped and it was too dangerous for the Spaniards to follow. But this was only a holding action and did not signify a successful defence against Spanish attack. But Spanish tactics were not always successful either.[30]

Although Spanish cavalry was devastating on open plains, its role was greatly restricted in urban combat. The mobility of the horsemen was limited on the causeways and they were attacked from the sides with virtual impunity in the city streets. But once the Spaniards entered large plazas, horses were again formidable weapons. To counter this, the Aztec defenders scattered stones and boulders throughout the plazas to prevent the horses from galloping, and concentrated on attacking the Spaniards as they withdrew. The Spaniards, in response, turned the Indian tactic of feigned withdrawal and ambush against the Aztecs themselves until they stopped attacking the withdrawing forces altogether.[31]

Meanwhile, on behalf of the allied forces, Ixtlilxochitl captured his brother, Coanacoch, who was leading the loyalist Tetzcocas. With their leader now in Cortés's hands, those Tetzcocas who were

29 Aguilar 1963:159; 1977:96; Cortés 1963:176–7; 1971:248; Ixtlilxochitl 1969: 43–4; 1975–77, 1:474.
30 Díaz del Castillo 1908–16, 4:172; 1977, 2:55; Sahagún 1975:105, 107–8; 1989:112–14, 123–4.
31 Cortés 1963:177; 1971:249; Díaz del Castillo 1908–16, 4:172–3; 1977, 2:55–6.

fighting on the Aztec side shifted to Ixtlilxochitl's side in a major set-back for Cuauhtemoc. Within four days, all three Spanish armies had advanced to the Tlatelolco marketplace and they now controlled seven-eighths of the city. Their increased control also allowed the Spaniards to move freely between their camps, greatly easing their efforts to coordinate the offensive.[32]

The supply of gunpowder was again very low so when one soldier volunteered to build a catapult to bombard Cuauhtemoc's quarters, Cortés ordered him to proceed. After four days of construction, the completed catapult was taken to the marketplace and fired, but it was a failure because the stones rose no higher than the catapult itself. Even though it failed, this incident illustrates the continued reliance that Cortés placed on heavy artillery and its ability to strike at a distance, safe from Aztec retaliation. Hand-to-hand fighting continued, but now that the battle was inside the city, more soldiers were involved, including allied forces, who fought independently. The Indian allies had been a major asset when they supported Spanish-led assaults, but it was a different story when they faced Aztec troops alone. Without Spanish arms to break up Aztec formations, the Tlaxcaltecs and Tetzcocas met the Aztecs on equal terms and were soundly defeated. During these clashes, the Aztecs could maintain their formations and fight conventionally and without peer. Even in the final days of the battle for Tenochtitlan, when they were exhausted and hungry and their best soldiers were already dead or wounded, the Aztecs were still able to cut off and kill many enemy Indians when they attacked without Spanish support. The Aztecs' conventional superiority was so striking that the Spaniards sometimes disguised themselves as Indians and marched in the middle of their allies in order to entice the Aztecs into attacking what appeared to be an Indian force unsupported by Spanish arms. If the Aztecs did attack, the Spaniards would fire their weapons before the Aztecs realized what was happening.[33]

Throughout the Conquest, the Aztecs captured and used Spanish weapons. But cannons and, presumably, harquebuses were destroyed rather than used when they fell into Aztec hands because they lacked powder and could not master their complexity, having no similar weapons of their own. For instance, when the Spaniards first entered

32 Cortés 1963:181–2; 1971:253–5; Díaz del Castillo 1908–16, 4:173–4; 1977, 2:56; Ixtlilxochitl 1969:46–7; 1975–77, 1:475; López de Gómara 1964:285, 293; 1965–66, 2:266, 273.

33 Cortés 1963:183; 1971:256–7; Díaz del Castillo 1908–16, 4:178–9; 1977, 2:59; López de Gómara 1964:288; 1965–66, 2:268; Sahagún 1975:114–16.

Tenochtitlan's central plaza, they placed a cannon atop the gladiatorial sacrifice stone and fired at the Aztecs in the courtyard. But the Spaniards fled when counter-attacked, leaving the cannon behind. The Aztecs seized the abandoned cannon and dropped it into the lake where it could not be recovered. The Aztecs did use crossbows against the Spaniards at one point, but their shots went wide, either because they were not skilled with this weapon or, more likely, because the crossbows were fired under duress by captured Spaniards and their poor performance was deliberate. Where there were direct analogies to native arms, however, the Aztecs were quick to master captured Spanish weapons, especially swords. Some were mounted on long poles like lances and scythes but others were used as swords by elite warriors. However, too few steel swords were captured to have a decisive effect on any of the battles.[34]

In early August 1521, Cuauhtemoc finally requested a meeting with Cortés, and negotiations began, during which the Aztecs ate lavishly in an effort to convince the Spaniards that their food was plentiful. There was a lull in the fighting for several days as negotiations continued, but Cuauhtemoc always sent nobles instead of appearing himself and Cortés finally resumed his attack. In a last-ditch effort to inspire the defenders, Cuauhtemoc dressed an elite warrior in King Ahuitzotl's attire to lead the attack. But despite initial success, the effort ultimately failed; on 13 August, the Spaniards easily broke through the last Aztec defences. Even though the Aztecs had exhausted all their weapons, resistance continued and Cortés ordered the brigantines to sail among the houses. He also ordered a general search for Cuauhtemoc so he could be captured alive. After the final land assault, the Aztecs surrendered.[35]

The eventual outcome of the battle for Tenochtitlan had been apparent to the Aztecs for some time and their leaders had discussed what they should offer the Spaniards in tribute and how they should surrender. However, accounts of the final surrender differ in Spanish

34 Durán 1964:313, 315; 1967, 2:565, 567; Ixtlilxochitl 1969:31–2; 1975–77, 1:466–7; López de Gómara 1964:290; 1965–66, 2:270; Sahagún 1975:87–9, 116; 1989:110–12.
35 Acosta 1954: 242; 1970–73, 2:523; Cortés 1963:185–9; 1971:260–4, Díaz del Castillo 1908–16, 4:177; 1977, 2:58–9; Ixtlilxochitl 1969:48–51; 1975–77, 1:477–8; Sahagún 1975:117. Sahagún (1989:131) says that this warrior was dressed as the god, Huitzilopochtli, but this is almost surely a later rationalization of these events. His earlier version said that it was Ahuitzotl's attire and this was based on a translation of an Aztec-language account. The earlier version is more compelling, not simply because it came from the Aztecs themselves, but also in the great detail with which the garb was described.

and Indian versions. According to Spanish accounts, once the city was lost, Cuauhtemoc fled with a fleet of fifty canoes and Sandoval ordered the brigantines to pursue. The ship commanded by García Holguin overtook Cuauhtemoc's canoe, which stopped after being threatened with cannon fire, and the king surrendered and asked to be taken to Cortés. Also captured with Cuauhtemoc were his wife and about thirty nobles, including the king of Tlacopan. Aztec accounts claim that Cuauhtemoc and his advisers had already decided to surrender and were en route to do so when Holguin seized their canoe, which seems a likelier sequence of events. The city was defeated and in Spanish hands and there was no place for Cuauhtemoc to go, nor was there any purpose in his going anywhere. In any case, Tenochtitlan was in ruins and Cuauhtemoc was taken prisoner after the three-month siege.[36]

Despite the surrender, the Spaniards' allies continued to attack the Aztecs, killing thousands and stealing their property. The massacre in Tenochtitlan continued for four days. It was an odd event, not for what it says about Mesoamerican warfare, but for what it suggests about Cortés's control. In Mesoamerica, defeat did not necessarily mean sacking the vanquished. Rather, victory was conceived as a gradient: the more effort required to subdue the enemy, the greater their punishment would be. Consequently, a town was usually sacked only if it resisted to the end. Thus, the fate that befell Tenochtitlan was not atypical of defeat in Mesoamerica generally: it had resisted to the end and sacking the city and massacring its inhabitants were well within normal expectations. But this was not necessarily the accepted chain of events for European warfare. Under the prevailing conventions of martial conduct, inhabitants of surrendered towns were not supposed to be abused. Nevertheless, this ideal was not achieved often. What the sacking and massacre of Tenochtitlan meant, then, is problematic. From a Spanish perspective, Cortés's inaction can be interpreted as rewarding his Indian allies before asserting control. From an Indian perspective, however, these acts were the logical culmination of a determined, though ultimately unsuccessful, resistance. Which interpretation is correct is uncertain, but it definitely casts doubts on the degree and extent of Cortés's control. If the massacre occurred

36 Acosta 1954:242; 1970–73, 2:523; Aguilar 1963:160; 1977:97; Chimalpahin 1965:236–7; Cortés 1963:189; 1971:264–5; Díaz del Castillo 1908–16, 4:179–81, 183; 1977, 2:60–2; Ixtlilxochitl 1969:52; 1975–77, 1:478–9; López de Gómara 1964:291–2; 1965–66, 2:271–2; Muñoz Camargo 1984:213; Oviedo y Valdés 1959, 4:151; Sahagún 1975:119–20; 1989:134–5.

in keeping with Mesoamerican military practice, it suggests that the Indian allies, not the Spaniards, were in control. The alternative explanation, that Cortés orchestrated the massacre, shows the Spaniards in no better light because, although sackings and massacres were common in Europe, they typically grew from the commanders' inability to control their troops. Thus, either interpretation of the massacre in Tenochtitlan suggests that Cortés lacked the power to maintain control over his allies.[37]

By now, Tenochtitlan was filled with the dead, although most died of starvation rather than combat. With Cortés's permission, the survivors marched out of the city for the next three days, after which he ordered the aqueduct repaired and the dead removed and buried. Cortés had defeated the Aztecs with a surviving force of nine hundred Spaniards, eighty horses, sixteen pieces of artillery and thirteen brigantines. But the pivotal role had been played by his two hundred thousand Indian allies, even though they went virtually unacknowledged and certainly unrewarded.[38]

37 Hale 1985:179–208; Hassig 1988:112.
38 Aguilar 1963:160; 1977:98; Díaz del Castillo 1908–16, 4:185, 187, 193; 1977, 2:64–5, 69; Durán 1964:312; 1967, 2:564; López de Gómara 1964:291, 293; 1965–66, 2:271–3; Sahagún 1975:85; 1989:110, 135–7.

10 AFTERMATH

The conquest of Mexico was not the victory of a Spanish juggernaut. It was a campaign fought in fits and starts and was very much a learning experience for both sides. All participants regarded the others as something different from what they really were: the Spaniards saw the Indians as inferior and easily defeated, while the Indians viewed the Spaniards as perhaps supernatural and powerful, if not invincible. Although these perceptions changed with harsh experience, they patterned the behaviour of both sides, leading to miscalculations that profoundly affected the meeting of Old and New Worlds.

The Spanish arrival presented groups such as the Cempohualtecs and Tlaxcaltecs with new political opportunities that they ultimately seized. Both Indians and Spaniards sought alliances in their own fashion. The Indians frequently gave the Spaniards the daughters of kings and nobles in efforts to link the two sides through elite marriages. But the Spaniards failed to recognize the significance of these acts and accepted the women largely as concubines. For their part, the Spaniards claimed to seek alliances through religious conversion, but both these claims and their actions were primarily motivated by political purposes, to justify the war.

The Spaniards did not vigorously pursue religious conversions. Combatants on both sides prayed to their gods, but meaningful conversion in the sense that Roman Catholic religious doctrine was transmitted, understood and believed, almost surely did not occur during the Conquest period. Whatever conversion effects did occur would have satisfied both the Spaniards' legal and religious obligations, but Christianity was still culturally impenetrable to the Indians and true comprehension was not what the conquistadors sought. Rather, public conversions were political statements and occurred only after an alliance had been established and the Indians could no longer back out. This happened at Cempohuallan after the attack on the Aztecs for which the Indians would be blamed, and at Tlaxcallan after the Spaniards had fled Tenochtitlan, renegotiated their alliance, and promised the Tlaxcaltecs vassalage over adjacent city-states.

Despite its superficiality, the Christianization of Indian rulers was the price of Spanish assistance and meant a breach in traditional patterns of authority. Conversion prized rulers away from the local priesthood and made them dependent on Spanish support because, unaided, the rulers could not withstand the internal opposition that their conversions generated. Public conversion did not signal an actual change in belief, but rather a political alliance from which there was no escape. Thus, there was a pattern of apparent conversion of allied rulers to Christianity. Conversion would alienate the native priesthood and at least some of the populace, but it nevertheless occurred when the loss of internal support was offset by the power and political support gained from the Spaniards. By contrast, religious conversions did not take place in Tenochtitlan, not because the Aztecs were more devout, but because they were at the political apex in Mesoamerica. They did not need Spanish support to maintain their position and were thus not compelled to undergo public conversion. Only the Aztecs did not need Spanish power to advance their political position in the existing power structure of Mesoamerica, which is why only they rejected even the superficial trappings of Christianity.

Thus, neither a Spanish religious imperative nor an Aztec loss of faith explains the success of the Conquest. The fate of both Aztecs and Spaniards was tied to their political situations and both had little choice but to follow the courses they selected. The Aztecs could resist or lose their empire; the Spaniards could conquer Meso-america, be killed by the Aztecs or be tried for treason in Cuba. The main protagonists were on a collision course: while both sides chose that course, neither saw the consequences clearly. Circumstances and events forced decisions on them, but the costs and consequences were beyond their anticipation.

Cortés unquestionably brought new and effective military technologies to the confrontation. Steel swords, metal armour, harquebuses, crossbows, cannons, horses and ships all gave the Spaniards a great technological advantage. The Aztecs successfully altered their tactics and countered some of these innovations but they could not counter them all. Instead, the Aztecs' main advantage lay in the size, skill and organization of their military. Although the casualties would have been high, early in the Conquest the massive Aztec armies could have crushed the Spaniards through numbers alone, despite the technological imbalance.

What made the conquest of Mexico possible was not the Spaniards' military might, which was always modest, but the assistance of tens and even hundreds of thousands of Indian allies – labourers, porters, cooks and especially soldiers. The Spaniards were so few that it was not their technology alone that was important, but the way it was coupled with Indian forces. Spanish arms could disrupt opposing formations in a way that native arms could not, but victories were typically won by large numbers of allied troops who could exploit these breaches. The Spaniards' most serious threat was the way they could convert relatively unimportant groups into a significant offensive force. This was a world-shattering alteration of the political landscape, but the Aztecs did nothing about it, either because they failed to recognize it in time or, perhaps, because of ineffective political leadership and tributary control problems. The self-serving conquistador accounts notwithstanding, the Conquest was not simply a matter of Spanish brains versus Indian brawn.

Spanish technology was important, but the key to the success of the Conquest was acquiring native allies who magnified the impact of those arms. Doing this required a thorough understanding of the political organization of Mesoamerican states and empires, the nature of rule and patterns of royal succession, and the individuals and factions involved. Cortés had some grasp of the situation, but not the detailed knowledge or understanding necessary to determine which faction to attack and which to support: only the Indians had this knowledge. The political manipulations that funnelled men and materiel to the Spaniards were engineered by the Indians in the furtherance of their own factional interests. The Tlaxcaltecs could have destroyed the Spaniards, either in their initial clashes or after their flight from Tenochtitlan, and some factions wanted to do so. But the Tlaxcaltec leaders saw the advantages of an alliance, given their own imperilled position *vis-à-vis* the Aztecs, and *chose* to ally with Cortés. The Conquest was not primarily a conflict between Mexico and Spain, but between the Aztecs and the various Mesoamerican groups supporting Cortés. The clash was centred on issues internal to Mesoamerica; Cortés neither represented the forces of Spain nor had formal Spanish backing. Instead, he fought on his own behalf in hope of eventual Spanish royal support and legitimation.

The Aztecs fought a Mesoamerican war and lost. They chose to defend their capital on the assumption that they would gain a defensive military advantage and the stringent logistical constraints on Mesoamerican warfare would work in their favour. However, technological innovations and, more importantly, political shifts stripped the Aztecs of these advantages. But if the conquest of Mexico was an Indian victory over Indians rather than a Spanish victory over Indians, why did all of the Indians fare so poorly thereafter? The answer can be largely found in the different goals pursued by the Indians and the Spaniards.

Cortés conquered Tenochtitlan, not the entire Aztec empire. Most Aztec allies did not participate: some were neutralized by the Spaniards or cordoned off from the main theatre of operations, but most did not fight because the Aztec empire was not a tightly integrated political entity that could command participation from its parts. Nevertheless, the fall of Tenochtitlan did signal changes for its tributaries. When a Mesoamerican empire fell, its constituent cities continued as before except that they were now independent or they had new overlords. Much the same would have been expected when the Aztecs fell, and certainly their defeat meant that former tributaries were freed. But it also left them vulnerable: as a result, they were separated and easily defeated in the subsequent Spanish pacification operations, although much of this was accomplished with the help of Tlaxcaltec soldiers.

The Spaniards' encounter with the Indians was not simply culture contact in which beneficial innovations were freely adopted or merged with the existing cultures. It was a conquest, signalled by military defeat and greatly affecting the cultural realm. The conquered Mesoamericans' very notions about the nature of the world were not merely questioned, but suppressed, subordinated or destroyed, and alien cultural ideas were imposed, at least superficially, even if they were not internalized. Victory left the Spaniards with the political and economic power to impose their culture whereas defeat left the Aztecs and the rest of Mesoamerica with little alternative but to adapt: they had lost the power to maintain their own culture at anything above the local level.

But most of Cortés's Indian allies were primarily concerned with local conditions. Their burdens were eased by the overthrow of the Aztecs and they thus benefited. However tumultuous an event, the overthrow was seen as relatively minor by the Indians, as this type of political restructuring was common and normally signalled a change in the hierarchy rather than in the system itself. The situation of most former tributaries improved significantly after the Conquest: they now kept goods previously owed as tribute to Tenochtitlan, they had access to European goods, and they enjoyed Spanish protection from Aztec retaliation. These benefits, however, were short term.

The Conquest meant very different things to the Spaniards from what it did to the Indians. To the Indians who allied with Cortés, it meant the removal of an enemy and/or tributary lord, which benefited them. The Indian allies used the situation to improve their immediate circumstances by removing the Aztec threat. They foresaw only what they could: an overthrow similar to others in Mesoamerica that shifted the existing situation in ways more favourable to themselves.

The Spaniards, by contrast, saw the Conquest as a means of bringing all of the Indians under their rule. The Spaniards had a longer-term view based on their experiences in Europe; to them, the Conquest meant the removal of the only significant competing Mesoamerican power, which left the Indians fully exposed to the expansion of Spanish control. The Indians could only have assumed the continuation of a hegemonic imperial system, which is what they had known, and could not have anticipated the territorial one that the Spaniards were to impose. The Spaniards focused on what was to become the national level – the control of all groups in Mesoamerica, the imposition of centralized rule, and the collection of tribute on a massive scale. For the Spaniards, this was one more step in their imperial success, but for the Indians, it was a world-shattering event, although this was not immediately clear to all of them.

The Tlaxcaltecs aided the Spaniards in the continued conquest of other areas in Mesoamerica, presumably because they thought it was to their advantage. But these conquered areas felt no particular allegiance to Tlaxcallan, so the Tlaxcaltecs conquered areas that the Spaniards then controlled and used against them. Tlaxcallan emerged from the Conquest as a power, but did not parlay that into a ruling position in Mesoamerica. One reason that they failed to do so was that they were poorly positioned, both geographically and socially. The Tlaxcaltecs lacked the overarching power that enabled the Aztecs to dominate large areas and the Spaniards were unchallengeable after they established reliable allies elsewhere, as with Tetzcoco. The Spaniards supported groups favourable to themselves and played them off against each another. Moreover, the Spaniards had no interest in increasing the Tlaxcaltecs' power after the Conquest, as they were doubtlessly seen as the main potential competitors.

Part of Tlaxcallan's inaction may have been caused by the

Spaniards' failure to comply with the terms of their pre-Conquest agreement. Cortés had promised Tlaxcallan control over Huexotzinco, Cholollan and other cities, which had been its allies previously. But making them tributaries would have given Tlaxcallan a substantial empire in the east, one that would have dominated all communication with the Gulf coast. The Spaniards failed to aid in the subjugation of these cities and the Tlaxcaltecs could not do so alone. Thus, although they remained strong in their own territory, the Tlaxcaltecs were not a significant threat elsewhere and the Spaniards faced no major challengers. Nevertheless, the Spaniards feared an Indian rebellion. In the early years after the Conquest, armed Spaniards were ordered to Tenochtitlan, now renamed Mexico City, to repel an imagined threat, and the social, religious, political and economic life of the Indians was allowed to continue as before. Spanish priests did not reach New Spain, as Mexico was now called, until June 1524, three years after the Conquest; only after more colonists with additional arms arrived in Mexico did the Spaniards subdue all the other groups and truly consolidate their control. It was not until 1525, well after the arrival of the first priests, that the Spaniards struck directly at native society and began destroying Indian temples, books and images of gods; and by that time, it was too late for an Indian rebellion to succeed.[1]

Mexico was not conquered from abroad but from within. The Spaniards were important and quickly took full credit even when they served only as the most visible, if not the most crucial, element. The Aztecs did not lose their faith, they lost a war. And it was a war fought overwhelmingly by other Indians, taking full advantage of the Spanish presence, but exploiting their own unique inside understanding of Mesoamerican political dynamics that Cortés could never master. The war was more of a coup or, at most, a rebellion, than a conquest. Conquest came later, after the battles, as the Spaniards usurped the victory for which their Indian allies had fought and died.

1 Barnadas 1984:519.

11 CONSEQUENCE AND CONCLUSION

The Conquest had major consequences for the indigenous societies of Mexico, now colonized as New Spain, many of which are still felt to the present day. Some of these changes were deliberate and had consequences that could be reasonably well anticipated, as in the areas of religion and political organization. Other changes were deliberate but had unexpected consequences, as with the introduction of Old World animals and with alterations in the indigenous economy; still others were unintentional, such as depopulation and changes in social organization.

The indigenous practice that the Spaniards sought most to overturn was religion. Although conversion activity may have been grounded in honestly held religious convictions, it also had a political purpose. Only by following through on the religious conversion of the Indians could Spain justify its actions according to its own laws as well as in the eyes of the Church, whose approval was ultimately needed for political legitimacy. Thus, an important result of religious conversion was to shore up the colonial regime politically, but it also had the effect of simultaneously undercutting Indian rule. As the native religious hierarchy crumbled, so too did a crucial support for the native social structure and for its political regime.

During the initial first years of nervous coexistence, native religion was uneasily tolerated, but once the Spaniards grew strong enough to enforce their will, they suppressed native religious practices as completely as they could. Temples and idols were destroyed, along with the other main outward manifestations of polytheistic native religion: within a single generation, the indigenous priesthood was virtually extinct. Private beliefs were harder to eradicate, but public observances largely ceased or continued under the guise of acceptable Christian rituals. In the early 1530s, Bishop Zumarraga began an ecclesiastical inquisition in Mexico in an attempt to eradicate native beliefs. A number of Indians were tried and convicted of heresy and burned at the stake, among them several prominent political leaders. However, this penalty applied only to Indians who had converted to Christianity and then lapsed once again into "paganism". The Indians immediately grasped the idea that if they never converted they could not be tried for heresy, and the public burnings caused an almost immediate cessation of conversions. In the face of this monumental failure, it was decreed that the Indians were not subject to the inquisition at all, and conversions resumed, with the attention of the inquisition being reserved for Protestants, Jews and backsliding and heretical catholics of European ancestry. Many of the native conversions were peaceful, however, especially after the eradication of native priests, and the Church, especially the Franciscan, Dominican and Augustinian orders, played a prominent religious role, constructing churches in virtually every significant Indian town during the sixteenth century, and also played a major political role in native affairs. Nevertheless, many native beliefs bore striking similarities to those of the Roman Catholic Church and inevitably permeated orthodox beliefs, resulting ultimately in a highly syncretic religion.[1]

The Spaniards were less intent on completely restructuring native political life, although they did cause drastic changes, initially at the highest levels, but these soon permeated even the lowest levels of indigenous society. The threat of an Indian rebellion was constantly in the Spaniards' minds, especially during the first half of the sixteenth century. The effectiveness of Indian soldiers and arms was unquestioned, and the Spaniards employed them as late as the 1540s against hostile Indians elsewhere. Although no Indian rebellion materialized in central Mexico, the continuation of indigenous states and empires was a threat to Spanish control and they were quickly destroyed. This left the town (*cabecera*) and its dependencies (*sujetos*) to be governed by native rulers as the highest remaining level of political organization among the Indians.[2]

Native rulers governed legitimately under indigenous political notions of rule, as the Spaniards also acknowledged. However, the Spaniards soon labelled native rulers *caciques*, a term imported from the Indies, and this inappropriate application led to considerable confusion. Unlike a *tlatoani* (native ruler), which had a definite social meaning in Aztec society, *cacique* did not, and many

1 Braden 1930:149, 170; Ennis 1977:64–5; Gibson 1964:98–135; 1966:78–9; Greenleaf 1969:7–8; Lea 1922:210; Schwaller 1978:5, 52–3. For an example of this syncretism a full century after the Conquest, see Ruiz de Alarcón (1984).
2 Códice Osuna 1976: fol. 8–470.

illegitimate pretenders made their way to power, undermining the position and privileges of the traditional elites. By the mid-sixteenth century, Indian towns had largely adopted Spanish political forms, including town councils, councilmen, judges and other officials. In many places, an elected Indian governor who served a fixed term eventually replaced the *caciques*, who then declined in importance, often retaining only vestigial rights and privileges. Governance at a regional or national level increasingly lay solely in Spanish hands. Despite the presence of Indian officials, control even at the town level was increasingly exercised by Spanish clergy or landowners who permitted the Indians to operate only within prescribed limits.[3]

Spanish-induced changes were not limited to religion and politics, of course, but the Spaniards did not seek to effect the changes in many other aspects of Indian life that their presence nevertheless caused. The initial Spanish intention was to leave the native economic system largely intact and merely tap it for goods and labour, as had Indian rulers. Thus the native tribute system was immediately reoriented to supply the new Spanish overlords as well. But all aspects of native life were affected by one of the most devastating, though unintentional, changes of Spanish contact – depopulation.

When Cortés first landed in 1519, central Mexico (which extends from the desert north of Mexico City to the Isthmus of Tehuantepec) held an estimated 25.2 million people. Eighty years later, at the end of the sixteenth century, the population had dropped by 95 per cent, to just over 1 million. Some of these losses were occasioned by warfare, but the vast bulk were the result of Old World diseases to which the Indians had no immunities. Many epidemics followed the Spaniards' arrival, notably smallpox in 1520–21, followed by major outbreaks of typhus in 1545–48 and 1576–81. Numerous other diseases, including measles, influenza and mumps, also swept through Mexico, and the lowlands, where the anopheles mosquito lived, were savaged by malaria as well.[4]

Massive depopulation affected virtually all Indian institutions and practices. Notable among these were residence patterns.

3 Gibson 1964:167, 180; 1984:388–95; Wasserstrom 1983:11–21.

4 Cook and Borah 1971:9–10; Gibson 1964:448–9. I am using the estimates of Cook and Borah (1971:80–2), despite various voiced objections (e.g. Bath 1978; Zambardino 1980), because they are the most thoroughly analysed and I regard them as the reasonable high estimates. If these are not acceptable, Sanders (in Denevan 1976a:291) holds what I regard as the reasonable low estimate, roughly half that of Cook and Borah. Whatever the starting figures, however, there is general agreement on the late-sixteenth-century numbers.

Prehispanically, residence was apparently extended, with households including husband and wife, children, parents and various collateral relatives. But after the massive depopulation, many households reverted to nuclear families of just husband, wife and offspring. The population loss was so severe that many towns were no longer viable and twice in the sixteenth century, particularly in the 1590s, the remaining Indians were forcibly gathered into fewer, larger towns where they could be more effectively controlled. Just as residence patterns were changed by the demographic collapse, so too was the broader native social system. Whereas preconquest native communities had an upper noble, or ruling, class, lower nobles, commoners and serfs, as well as slaves, there was marked social compaction after the Conquest. The Spaniards lumped all nobles into a single class (*principales*) that nevertheless tended to dominate political offices, and everyone else now occupied a single commoner class (*macehuales*), until the rights and privileges of the *principales* were so eroded that a meaningful distinction no longer existed in the seventeenth century.[5]

The drastic population decline affected all aspects of life in New Spain, and nowhere was this more apparent than in the economic realm. Except in the somewhat nebulous case of rebellion, slavery had been outlawed. But labour, not land, was the real cornerstone of wealth in the New World, and this was ensured through the *encomienda*, which was a grant by the king not of land ownership *per se*, but rather the right to the labour of the Indians on that land. Obligatory labour was not an alien concept in Mesoamerica – political dependants often paid their rulers in both goods and services – and the Spanish imposition of the *encomienda* labour obligation was added to the existing political obligations of the commoners and exercised through native rulers who increasingly served as middlemen between the Indian commoners and their Spanish masters.[6]

The indigenous tribute system proved satisfactory for the Spaniards at first, but its effectiveness declined. Following the smallpox epidemic during the Conquest, approximately 40 per cent of Mesoamerica's population died. This was not, however, spread equally across the population. Most who died were infants, children, the aged and the infirm, which left an unusual population profile. The largest percentage of those who survived were adults, so even

5 Gibson 1964:36; 1984:393–4; Lockhart and Schwartz 1983:116–17.
6 Gibson 1964:58–97; 1966:48–67; Hassig 1985:178–9.

though the total population was now significantly smaller, it was, in fact, healthier in economic terms. Not only were many lands vacated through death so that the remaining Indians could abandon more marginal areas, but also those who remained were healthy adults and were therefore more productive. Whereas a preconquest married man may have been supporting a relatively large number of dependants, this same man now had far fewer mouths to feed, thanks to the massive number of deaths caused by smallpox. As a result, much of what an Indian man could produce could be siphoned off as surplus, and it was this that funded the early Spanish fortunes.

Because it was based on a demographic aberration, this economic prosperity was not destined to last. Those who survived the epidemic had children at a normal rate. But since adults of child-bearing age made up such a large percentage of the epidemic survivors, they reproduced in extraordinarily large numbers for the population as a whole. As a result, within fifteen years, there were vastly more dependants than before, both a large number of new children and a growing number of adults who had now grown older and were less economically productive themselves. Thus, by the early 1540s, the native population was probably as large or larger than it was immediately after the Conquest, but it was not an economically healthy population. Because so many of the Indians were young or old, the ratio between the number of economically productive adults and their dependants was significantly worse. The adults doubtless worked just as hard as before, but they had so many more mouths to feed that less and less of what they produced could be supplied as surplus.[7]

Population changes were not, however, the only factors affecting the economy of New Spain. In addition to diseases, the Spaniards also introduced new plants, such as wheat, lettuce and numerous fruits. Some of these provided significant additions to the native agricultural complex, but wheat and sugar cane had the greatest impact which was largely negative for the Indians. Wheat offered no nutritional advantage over native staples, such as maize, but it was the traditional bread crop of Spain and the Spaniards began its cultivation almost immediately. This was both a cultural preference and a major social marker: Spaniards ate wheat, Indians ate maize. However, wheat required both irrigation for multiple crops and twice as much labour as maize for comparable caloric yields. Thus,

7 Hassig 1985:180–5.

when the Spaniards took land out of maize cultivation and planted wheat, it was a net loss in agricultural productivity. Sugar cane introduced via the Indies also played a significant role in New Spain. Cultivated and then processed, sugar cane promised great financial returns when shipped back to sweet-poor Europe. But again, this required irrigation and intensive cultivation, so while sugar-cane was a major cash-crop export for the Spaniards, it also took much of the best lands out of subsistence cultivation.[8]

Even more important than the new crops were the many animals introduced into New Spain. Among these were horses, cattle, donkeys, sheep, goats, pigs and chickens, all of which affected native society. The larger animals offered, for the first time, a more efficient means of transportation than had hitherto been available in Mesoamerica, although they did not become widespread or available to Indians on a general basis until late in the century. But even in Spanish hands, these draught animals had an enormous impact on the political economy of New Spain, as food could now be brought into cities from unprecedented distances. Cities that had previously not competed with each other for foodstuffs now did so, and Mexico City was especially predatory. Using its formidable political power as the capital of New Spain, Mexico City poached on the agricultural produce of other cities, often mandating its importation as a matter of law. The net effect was to drive many Indian farmers off the land altogether, since they were now required to transport and sell their produce at prices far below market levels, effectively subsidizing life in the capital at the expense of people living elsewhere.[9]

Some European animals added to the food supply, however, and still others, such as sheep, provided new materials for clothing, augmenting the indigenous cotton. The chicken was perhaps the most useful animal introduced, at least initially, since it was added without disrupting the native plant and animal complex. But many of the other animals, especially horses, cattle, sheep and goats, ended up competing with Indians for land. This competition would doubtless have been controlled had the Indians been allowed to incorporate the animals however it best suited their needs. But most of the larger animals were owned by Spaniards and were allowed to graze freely, often in the agricultural fields of the Indians. In

8 Florescano 1965:571; Moreno Toscano 1965:640.
9 Bejarano 1889–1916, 9:619; Cuevas 1975:249; Florescano 1965:597; García Pimentel 1897:74; Guthrie 1941:38; Hassig 1985:242–4; Lee 1947:653; Recopilación 1973: 4-10-11.

addition to the direct destruction of crops, the introduction of large numbers of domesticated animals led to massive overgrazing that destroyed much of the ground cover. The impact of this was felt particularly in the Valley of Mexico; where large-scale timbering was also going on largely as a result of the reconstruction of Mexico City. These twin plagues of deforestation and ground-cover destruction led to massive runoffs of the summer rains: less water was now held in the plants and soil and the runoff swept much of the valley's topsoil into the lakes, raising their bottoms and flooding the nearby cities. To remedy this, the Spaniards embarked on a plan to drain the lakes in the expectation that this would alleviate the problem and also open vast new tracts of fertile land for farming and grazing. Work began toward the end of the sixteenth century, but draining the lakes undermined the canoe-based transportation system that had fed the capital. Now, much costlier mule trains and ox carts had to be used, leading to higher prices, and the drained areas became alkali flats from which noxious clouds of dust blew during the windy season to plague the city. [10]

In 1575, New Spain began to enter a depression that was to last almost a century, and which was the result of Spanish miscalculation, mismanagement and studied lack of concern for the long-term consequences of their actions. The first Spaniards enjoyed unprecedented prosperity as a result of the favourable demographic profile that was destined not to last. The number of Indian labourers inexorably declined, but a fall-off in production was only one part of the problem. New Spain was bound together economically by vast numbers of human porters. In comparison to Old World technologies, this was a very inefficient means of moving products overland and their rapid replacement wagons and mules would seem logical. But that meant major capital investments, not only in wagons and draught animals, but in constructing roads suitable for their use, since Indian roads frequently were inadequate. However, from the perspective of the Spaniards, they could coerce Indian labour or use porters as part of their tribute obligations at little or no cost. So despite its inefficiency, the porter system continued to dominate trade and the movement of goods to market in New Spain.[11]

Mexico's rapid depopulation inevitably doomed this labour-intensive form of transport, and there was nothing the Spaniards

10 Bejarano 1889–1916, 1:79–80; Chevalier 1970:98; Matesanz 1965:539–43; Moreno Toscano 1965:644.
11 Hassig 1985:187–219.

could do about it. In addition, the Spaniards failed to use their labourers to construct roads suitable for mule trains and ox carts during the early years when there were still enough Indians to do so. The demographic collapse, and all of its consequences, was either unforeseen by the Spaniards, or was perceived as being too far in the future. Faced with a choice of using their labourers to ends that might prove beneficial in the long run or employing them to generate immediate wealth, the Spaniards chose short-term gains. Toward the end of the century, there were no longer enough Indians to serve as porters and keep the economy of New Spain alive, nor had adequate roads been built on a European model. Mules and wagons were available and could have provided adequate transportation, at least in theory, but without suitable roads, they were slow and very costly. Most consumers could not bear this added expense and production reverted to locally needed and consumed products. Only such luxuries as silver were still exported from throughout New Spain. It was now too expensive for most other goods to be shipped great distances, and New Spain's economy declined as the country broke into a series of balkanized regions between which there was little exchange.[12]

By the end of the sixteenth century, the Indians, though still a majority, were but a fraction of their previous numbers. The political system was in the hands of Spaniards and the Indians enjoyed only local control. Their economy was enormously transformed by the introduction of new plants and animals, by the alteration of their marketing system, and by new values that elevated such goods as gold and silver while undermining the traditional value of other items, such as feathers and mineral pigments. Their religion was in tatters and they now worshipped in Catholic churches, although they retained many of their own beliefs and practices in new guises. Their intellectual traditions were destroyed. Native writing systems were replaced by the Latin alphabet and indigenous books were destroyed as the works of the devil. Their vigesimal (base-20) counting system was replaced by the European decimal system and the native calendar was quickly replaced by the European, on both religious and economic principles, since such matters as labour demands and markets were now determined according to the European system.

Those who fought on the Spaniards' side during the Conquest,

12 Bakewell 1971:226, 231, 235; Borah 1951; Hassig 1985:259–61; TePaske and Klein 1981:123–9, 134.

especially the Tlaxcaltecs, had their own reasons for doing so. Each group or faction had acted in what they felt to be their own best interests in deciding whether or not to ally with the Spaniards. But none could have knowingly sought the fate that would ultimately befall them, so it is doubtful that any of the Indians who allied with the Spaniards foresaw the world-shattering changes the Conquest would bring. Within a few short decades, most of what comprised the Indian world was gone, swept away by disease, war, religious zealotry and Spanish political and economic control. The Tlaxcaltecs and others were in a difficult political position when they allied with the Spaniards, but they would never have participated in their own cultural destruction merely to ensure the physical destruction of their enemies. Indian participation in the Conquest was self-interested but short-sighted, and their immediate gains were quickly swept away by the unstoppable tide of Spanish domination.

SHORT CHRONOLOGY OF THE CONQUEST

1492	Columbus reaches the New World
1502	King Ahuitzotl dies and Moteuczoma Xocoyotl becomes the ninth Aztec king
1515	King Nezahualpilli of Tetzcoco dies and is succeeded by Cacama

1517
8 February	Córdoba sails from Cuba
Late February	Córdoba reaches Yucatan
29 March	Córdoba reaches Campeche
20 April	Córdoba returns to Cuba

1518
3 May	Grijalva reaches Cozumel
31 May	Grijalva reaches Laguna de Términos
11 June	Grijalva reaches Coatzacualco
15 November	Grijalva returns to Cuba

1519
10 February	Cortés sails for Yucatan
21 April	Cortés reaches San Juan de Ulua
12 May	Aztecs decamp, abandoning Cortés
3 June	Cortés reaches Cempohuallan
Mid June	Cortés leaves Cempohuallan on his march inland
26 July	Cortés dispatches a ship to Spain
2 September	Cortés fights first battle with Tlaxcaltecs
23 September	Cortés enters city of Tlaxcallan
10 October	Cortés leaves Tlaxcallan for Cholollan
c. 25 October	Cortés leaves Cholollan for Tenochtitlan
8 November	Cortés enters Tenochtitlan
14 November	Cortés seizes Moteuczoma

1520
| 20 April | Narváez lands at San Juan de Ulua |

Feast of Toxcatl	Alvarado massacres the Aztec nobles
c. 27 May	Cortés reaches Narváez's camp at Cempohuallan
c. 28 May	Cortés attacks and defeats Narváez
24 June	Cortés reaches Tenochtitlan
29 June	Moteuczoma killed
30 June	Cortés and the Spaniards flee Tenochtitlan
11 July	Cortés and the Spaniards reach City of Tlaxcallan
1 August	Cortés marches against Tepeyacac
16 September	Cuitlahua becomes the tenth Aztec king
Mid October	Smallpox epidemic begins in Tenochtitlan
Early December	Smallpox epidemic ends in Tenochtitlan
4 December	King Cuitlahua dies of smallpox
28 December	Cortés begins his return to Tenochtitlan

1521

February	Cuauhtemoc becomes the eleventh Aztec king
3 February	Cortés marches on Xaltocan
18 February	Cortés returns to Tetzcoco
5 April	Cortés begins march against Yauhtepec
11 April	Cortés reaches Yauhtepec
13 April	Cortés conquers Cuauhnahuac
16 April	Cortés reaches Xochimilco
18 April	Cortés is forced to withdraw from Xochimilco
22 April	Cortés returns to Tetzcoco
28 April	Cortés launches his brigantines
22 May	Alvarado, Olid and Sandoval are dispatched with three armies to begin the battle for Tenochtitlan
31 May	Sandoval and Olid link up at Coyohuacan
30 June	Sixty-eight Spaniards are captured in battle and sacrificed
Mid-July	Fresh munitions arrive from Vera Cruz
1 August	Spaniards reach the great market in Tlatelolco
13 August	Cuauhtemoc is captured and the Aztecs surrender

BRIEF SKETCHES OF THE PARTICIPANTS

ACAMAPICHTLI ("Reed-fist") A noble from Colhuacan, he was chosen as the Aztecs' first king, ruling from 1372 to 1391.

AGUILAR, GERÓNIMO DE (1489?–1531?) Settled in Santo Domingo, lost in a shipwreck in 1511 and washed ashore in Yucatan where he was held by the Maya until he was rescued by Cortés in 1519.

AHUITZOTL ("Otter") The son of Moteuczoma Ilhuicamina, he was the eighth Aztec king, ruling from 1486 to 1502.

ALFONSO IX (1171–1230) King of León from 1188 to 1230.

ALVARADO, PEDRO DE (1485–1541) A member of both Grijalva's and Cortés's expeditions to Mexico, he led the Toxcatl massacre in Tenochtitlan, commanded one of Cortés's three armies, and was dubbed Tonatiuh, the Aztec sun god, because of his blond hair.

ANONYMOUS CONQUISTADOR An anonymous member of the Conquest of Mexico, known only through his chronicle of that event.

AVILA, ALONZO DE Conquistador who came to Mexico with Cortés, he led the land forces during the battle at Potonchan.

AXAYACATL ("Water-mask") The son of Moteuczoma Ilhuicamina, he was the sixth Aztec king, ruling from 1468 to 1481.

BARBA, PEDRO Captain of a ship sent to resupply Narváez, he arrived late and was captured. He then joined his friend, Cortés, in the conquest of Mexico.

CACAMA ("Secondary-ear-of-maize") He became king of Tetzcoco in 1515 on the death of his father, Nezahualpilli, with the help of his uncle, Moteuczoma Xocoyotl. After Moteuczoma collaborated with the Spaniards, he plotted against him but was taken prisoner and died in 1520 during Cortés's flight from Tenochtitlan.

CHARLES V (1500–58) Holy Roman Emperor under that name from 1519 to 1556 and king of Spain as Charles I from 1516 to 1556.

CHIMALPOPOCA ("He-smokes-like-a-shield") The son of Huitzilihuitl, he was the third Aztec king, ruling from 1417 to 1427, when he was assassinated, allegedly by Maxtla.

COANACOCH ("Serpent-earpendant") A son of Nezahualpilli, he became king of Tetzcoco in 1520 after the death of Cacama. When Cortés returned to Tetzcoco, Coanacoch fled to Tenochtitlan and led loyalist Tetzcocas against the Spaniards until he was captured by his brother, Ixtlilxochitl.

COCOZCA ("Necklaces") A son of Nezahualpilli, he was placed on the throne of Tetzcoco in 1520 with Spanish backing after the imprisonment of Cacama. He was apparently assassinated by his brother, Coanacoch, after the Spaniards fled Tenochtitlan.

COLUMBUS, CHRISTOPHER (1451–1506) Italian Cristoforo Colombo; Spanish Cristóbal Colón. A Genoese sailor who discovered the New World on behalf of Spain, leading four separate voyages there in 1492–93, 1493–96, 1498–1500 and 1502–04.

CÓRDOBA, FRANCISCO HERNÁNDEZ DE Led Governor Velásquez's first expedition of exploration and discovered Yucatan. He died in Cuba in 1517 from wounds sustained at Chanpoton during the expedition.

CORTÉS, HERNAN (1485?–1547) Born in Medellín, he emigrated to Hispaniola in 1504 and led the third expedition to Mexico, culminating in its conquest.

CUAUHTEMOC ("He-descends-like-an-eagle") The son of Ahuitzotl, he was the eleventh and final Aztec king. He ruled from 1520 until Tenochtitlan was conquered by Cortés, and was killed by the Spaniards in 1525.

CUITLAHUA ("Excrement-owner") The son of Axayacatl, he was the king of Ixtapalapan before succeeding his brother, Moteuczoma Xocoyotl, to become the tenth Aztec king. He ruled for only eighty days in 1520 before dying of smallpox.

DÍAZ DEL CASTILLO, BERNAL (1495–1583) Born in Medina del Campo, he emigrated to the New World in 1514 and was a member of the Mexican expeditions of Córdoba, Grijalva and Cortés.

DUERO, ANDRÉS DE Secretary to Governor Velásquez of Cuba and a secret partner with, and advocate for, Cortés to lead the third expedition to Mexico.

DURÁN, DIEGO (1537?–88) Born in Seville, he emigrated to New Spain in 1542, became a Dominican in 1556, and chronicled Aztec religion and history.

ESCALANTE, JUAN DE Conquistador with Cortés's expedition who was left in charge of the Spanish garrison at Vera Cruz when Cortés marched to Tenochtitlan.

GRIJALVA, JUAN DE (1480?–1527) Born in Cuéllar and accompanied his uncle, Diego Velásquez de Cuéllar, on the conquest of Cuba in 1511. In 1518 he led the second expedition to Mexico.

GUERRERO, GONZALO Lost in a shipwreck, presumably in 1511 with Gerónimo de Aguilar, he washed ashore in Yucatan, where he was held by the Maya. He married and rose to high position in Maya society and refused to return to Spanish society when Cortés landed in Yucatan in 1519.

HOLGUÍN, GARCÍA Conquistador in command of one of the brigantines in the Valley of Mexico who captured Cuauhtemoc.

HUITZILIHUITL ('Hummingbird-feather') The son of Acamapichtli, he was the second Aztec king, ruling from 1391 to 1417.

ITZCOATL ('Obsidian-serpent') The son of Acamapichtli and uncle of Chimalpopoca, he was the fourth Aztec king, ruling from 1427 to 1440.

IXTLILXOCHITL ('Black-eyed-flower') A son of Nezahualpill who rebelled against the imposition of Cacama on the throne of Tetzcoco. He raised an army and took control of the northern part of Tetzcocan territory. He later allied with Cortés, became king of Tetzcoco after Tecocol died, and was a pivotal leader in the conquest of Tenochtitlan.

JULIANILLO A Maya Indian captured during Córdoba's expedition to Mexico, baptized and taken to Cuba to learn Spanish but he died before he could serve as translator in subsequent expeditions.

LARES, AMADOR DE The king's accountant in Cuba and a secret partner with, and advocate for, Cortés to lead the third expedition to Mexico.

MALINCHE (probably Malinalli, 'Grass'; baptized as Marina) One of twenty women given to Cortés by the Maya after their defeat at Potonchan. Speaking both Yucatec Maya and Nahuatl, she (along with the Maya-speaking Aguilar) served as a vital linguistic link between Cortés and the Aztecs. She was also the mother of Cortés's son, Martín.

MAXTLA ('Breechcloth') Son of Tetzotzomoc, he assassinated his brother and seized the throne of the Tepanec empire on the death of his father. He was defeated by the Aztecs under Itzcoatl in 1428.

MAYEHUA ('Glove') King of Cuitlahuac, he fled to Tenochtitlan and fought on the Aztec side during the Spanish seige.

MELCHOREJO A Maya Indian captured during Córdoba's expedition to Mexico, baptized and taken to Cuba to learn Spanish so he could serve as translator in subsequent expeditions. He escaped from Cortés's men at Potonchan and returned to the Maya.

MOTEUCZOMA ILHUICAMINA ('He-frowned-like-a-lord He-pierces-the-sky-with-an-arrow') The son of Huitzilihuitl, he was the fifth Aztec king, ruling from 1440 to 1468.

MOTEUCZOMA XOCOYOTL ('He-frowned-like-a-lord The-younger') The son of Axayacatl, he was the ninth Aztec king, ruling from 1502 to 1520 when he was killed while held hostage by the Spaniards.

NARVÁEZ, PÁNFILO DE (1480?–1528) He was placed in command of a large fleet by Governor Velásquez and ordered to capture and return Cortés to Cuba. He landed on the Veracruz coast on 20 April 1520 but was defeated and captured by Cortés on 28 May 1520.

NEZAHUALPILLI ('Fasted-noble') King of Tetzcoco from 1472 to 1515.

OLID, CRISTÓBAL DE Conquistador who commanded one of Cortés's three armies during the seige of Tenochtitlan.

SANDOVAL, GONZALO DE Conquistador who commanded one of Cortés's three armies during the seige of Tenochtitlan.

SANTIAGO St James, who was credited with appearing to lead Spanish forces in battle both in the reconquest of Spain and in the conquest of Mexico.

TECOCOL ('Someone's-anger') Son of Nezahualpilli who became king after the flight of Coanacoch. A Spanish ally, he died around 1 February 1521.

TENTLIL ('Black-at-the-lips') The Aztec governor of the Totonac area, he resided at Cuetlachtlan and was the first Aztec official to greet Cortés when he landed on the Veracruz coast.

TETLAHUEHUETZQUITI ('He-causes-people-to-laugh-at-things') Son of Nezahualpilli, he was not considered fit to rule when his father died in 1515.

TETZOTZOMOC ('Fractured-stone') Ruler of the Tepanec empire from 1367 until his death in 1426.

TIZOC ('He-has-bled-people') The son of Moteuczoma Ilhuicamina, he was the seventh Aztec king, ruling from 1481 to 1486 when he was assassinated after five years of neglectful leadership.

VELÁSQUEZ DE CUÉLLAR, DIEGO (1465–1524) He accompanied Columbus on his second voyage to the New World in 1493 and conquered Cuba in 1511–14, becoming its first governor. He authorized the first voyages to Mexico by Córdoba in 1517, Grijalva in 1518, and Cortés in 1519, as well as an unsuccessful punitive expedition led by Pánfilo de Narváez in 1520 to capture Cortés.

VILLAFAÑA, ANTONIO DE Conquistador who reached Mexico with Narváez's expedition. He joined in the conquest of Mexico and later led a conspiracy against Cortés, but it was discovered and he was hanged.

XICOTENCATL ('Person-from-Xicotenco [Place-at-the-edge-of-bumble-bees]') A Tlaxcaltec general who resisted Cortés's entry into Tlaxcallan. Always opposed to the Spaniards, even after Tlaxcallan's alliance with them, he was later hanged in Tetzcoco by Cortés for allegedly conspiring with the Aztecs against him.

ZUMARRAGA, JUAN DE (1468–1548) A Spanish Franciscan, he became the first Bishop of Mexico in 1528.

GLOSSARY

arroba A Spanish unit of measure, equal to approximately 11.5 kilograms (25 pounds 6 ounces).

atlatl A spearthrower, used to throw small spears or 'darts'.

brigantine A small, swift, typically square-masted ship.

cabecera A politically dominant town governed by its own local ruler.

cacique A Taino word meaning ruler, brought from the Indies by the Spaniards and applied to native rulers in Mexico.

calpolli An incompletely understood Aztec organizational unit that, among other things, denoted neighbourhoods or barrios.

caravel An imprecisely defined type of sea-going sailing ship, typically carrying two masts.

chinampas Artificial gardens built in the lake by constructing dirt-filled enclosures. These were known as the floating gardens because they appeared to float on the surface of the water.

culebrina A heavy early field cannon capable of firing projectiles of up to 11 kilograms (24 pounds).

encomienda A political grant of rights to labour of the Indians living within a specified area.

falconet A light cannon, typically swivel mounted on a ship's rail, and, at this time, breechloading.

harquebus A smoothbore matchlock gun similar to, but smaller than, the later musket.

harquebusier A soldier armed with an harquebus.

hidalgo A lesser noble, but the term was used somewhat

indiscriminately during the Conquest era to refer to nobles, gentlemen or merely some degree of gentility.

league   A Spanish unit of linear measure; at least two different leagues were in use in colonial Mexico, a statute league of 4.19 kilometres (2.6 miles) and a common league of 5.5 kilometres (3.4 miles), although in practice, the league often served as a rather vague denotation of distance, with 5 leagues commonly being used for a day's journey, emphasizing travel time rather than actual linear distance.

macehual   A member of the indigenous commoner class, spelled *macehualli* prehispanically but *macehual* after the Conquest.

macuahuitl   An Aztec wooden broadsword inset with obsidian blades.

principal   A post-Conquest term used to denote a member of the indigenous noble class, collapsing pre-Conquest distinctions.

Reconquista   The reconquest of Spain from the Moors, ending in 1492 with the conquest of Granada.

requerimiento   A Spanish legal statement to be read before battle and absolving the conquistadors of responsibility. It demanded that the Indians recognize the authority of the Church, pope and king.

sujeto   A dependent community, governed from a *cabecera*.

tepoztopilli   A wooden spear inset with obsidian blades and used as a staff weapon like a halberd.

tercio   A 1536 Spanish military innovation in which soldiers were organized into 250-man companies and which emphasized the infantry.

tlameme   A human porter used to carry burdens in Mesoamerica.

tlatoani   A pre-Conquest indigenous Mesoamerican king or ruler.

xiquipilli   A count of 8,000; also used to refer to a basic Aztec army of 8,000 men.

xochiyaoyotl   Flower war; commonly regarded as ritual combat, but actually part of an extended confrontation with powerful opponents in which they could be engaged while continuing conquests elsewhere.

ADDITIONAL RECOMMENDED READING

For first-hand accounts by the Spanish conquistadors, see:

CORTÉS, HERNÁN
1971 *Letters from Mexico*. Anthony Pagden, trans. New York: Grossman Publishers.

DE FUENTES, PATRICIA
1963 *The Conquistadors: First-Person Accounts of the Conquest of Mexico*. New York: Orion Press.

DÍAZ DEL CASTILLO, BERNAL
1908–16 *The True History of the Conquest of New Spain*. Alfred Percival Maudslay, trans. 5 vols, London: Hakluyt Society (or any of a number of abridged versions currently available).

For Aztec accounts of the Conquest, see:

SAHAGÚN, BERNARDINO DE
1975 *Florentine Codex: General History of the Things of New Spain. Book 12 – The Conquest of Mexico*. Salt Lake City: University of Utah Press.
1978 *The War of Conquest: How It Was Waged Here in Mexico: The Aztecs' Own Story*. Salt Lake City: University of Utah Press.

For an account of Cortés's life, see:

MADARIAGA, SALVADOR DE
1969 *Hernán Cortés: Conqueror of Mexico*. Garden City, NY: Anchor Books.

For a detailed, though somewhat dated, analysis of the accounts of exploration and Conquest of Mexico, see:

WAGNER, HENRY R.
1942 *The Discovery of Yucatan by Francisco Hernández de Córdoba*. Berkeley, CA: Cortes Society.
1942 *The Discovery of New Spain in 1518 by Juan de Grijalva*. Berkeley, CA: Cortes Society.
1944 *The Rise of Fernando Cortés*. Berkeley, CA: Cortes Society.

For the Aztecs and their military situation, see:
HASSIG, ROSS
1985 *Trade, Tribute, and Transportation: The Sixteenth-Century Political Economy of the Valley of Mexico.* Norman: University of Oklahoma Press.
1988 *Aztec Warfare: Political Expansion and Imperial Control.* Norman: University of Oklahoma Press.
1992 *War and Society in Ancient Mesoamerica.* Berkeley and Los Angeles: University of California Press.

For an account of the Aztec situation after the Conquest, see:
GIBSON, CHARLES
1964 *The Aztecs Under Spanish Rule: A History of the Indians of the Valley of Mexico, 1519–1810.* Stanford, CA: Stanford University Press.

For the Spanish military situation, see:
MARTÍNEZ, RAFAEL BAÑÓN, AND THOMAS M. BARKER, eds
1988 *Armed Forces and Society in Spain Past and Present.* Boulder, CO: Social Science Monographs.

For a general overview of the European military situation, see:
JONES, ARCHER
1987 *The Art of War in the Western World.* Urbana: University of Illinois Press.

BIBLIOGRAPHY

Acosta, José de, 1954 *Obras*. Madrid: Ediciones Atlas.

Acosta, Joseph de, 1970–73 *The Natural and Moral History of the Indies*. 2 vols, New York: Burt Franklin.

Acuña, René, ed., 1982–87 *Relaciones geográficas del siglo XVI*. Mexico City: Universidad Nacional Autónoma de México.

Aguilar, Francisco de, 1963 'The Chronicle of Fray Francisco de Aguilar'. In De Fuentes 1963.

Aguilar, Francisco de, 1977 *Relación breve de la conquista de la Nueva España*. Mexico City: Universidad Nacional Autónoma de México.

Alfonso el Sabio, 1972 *Las Siete Partidas del Rey Don Alfonso el Sabio*. 3 vols, Madrid: Ediciones Atlas.

Alvarado Tezozómoc, 1975 *Crónica mexicáyotl*. Mexico City: Universidad Nacional Autónoma de México.

Anales de Cuauhtitlan, 1975 'Anales de Cuauhtitlan'. In *Códice de Chimalpopoca* 1975.

Andrews, J. Richard, 1975 *Introduction to Classical Nahuatl*. Austin: University of Texas Press.

Arnold, J. Barto, III, 1978 'Archaeology'. In Arnold and Weddle 1978.

Arnold, J. Barto, III, and Robert Weddle, 1978 *The Nautical Archaeology of Padre Island: The Spanish Shipwrecks of 1554*. New York: Academic Press.

Bakewell, P. J., 1971 *Silver Mining and Society in Colonial Mexico, Zacatecas, 1546–1700*. Cambridge: Cambridge University Press.

Barnadas, Josep M., 1984 'The Catholic church in colonial Spanish America'. In Bethell 1984a.

Bath, B. H. Slicher van, 1978 'The Calculation of the Population of New Spain, especially for the period before 1570'. *Boletín de Estudios Latinoamericanos y del Caribe* 24:67–95.

Baxby, Derrick, 1981 *Jenner's Smallpox Vaccine: The Riddle of Vaccinia Virus and its Origin*. London: Heinemann Educational.

Behbehani, Abbas M., 1988 *The Smallpox Story in Words and Pictures*. Kansas City: University of Kansas Medical Center.

Bejarano, Ignacio, comp., 1889–1916 *Actas de cabildo de la Ciudad de México*. 54 vols, Mexico City.

Bethell, Leslie, ed., 1984a *The Cambridge History of Latin America, Volume 1, Colonial Latin America*. Cambridge: Cambridge University Press.

Bethell, Leslie, ed., 1984b *The Cambridge History of Latin America, Volume 2, Colonial Latin America*. Cambridge: Cambridge University Press.

Biblioteca, 1870–75 *Biblioteca histórica de la Iberia*. 20 vols, Mexico City: I. Escalante.

Borah, Woodrow, 1951 'New Spain's Century of Depression'. *Ibero-Americana* 35.

Boyd-Bowman, Peter, 1973 *Patterns of Spanish Emigration to the New World (1493–1580)*. Buffalo: Council on International Studies, State University of New York.

Braden, Charles S., 1930 *Religious Aspects of the Conquest of Mexico*. Durham, NC: Duke University Press.

Brereton, J. M., 1976 *The Horse in War*. Newton Abbot, Devon: David & Charles.

Brundage, Burr Cartwright, 1972 *A Rain of Darts: The Mexica Aztecs*. Austin: University of Texas Press.

Burne, Alfred H., 1955 *The Crecy War: A Military History of the Hundred Years War from 1337 to the Peace of Bretigny, 1360*. New York: Oxford University Press.

Calnek, Edward E., 1976 'The Internal Structure of Tenochtitlan'. In Wolf 1976.

Calnek, Edward E., 1978 'The Internal Structure of Cities in America: Pre-Columbian Cities; The Case of Tenochtitlan'. In Schaedel, Hardoy and Kinzer 1978.

Carrasco, Davíd, 1982 *Quetzalcoatl and the Irony of Empire: Myths and Prophecies in the Aztec Tradition*. Chicago: University of Chicago Press.

Carrasco Pizana, Pedro, 1950 *Los Otomíes: Cultura e historia prehispánicas de los pueblos mesoamericanos de habla otomiana*. Mexico City: Universidad Nacional Autónoma de México.

Castro, Américo, 1971 *The Spaniards: An Introduction to their History*. Berkeley and Los Angeles: University of California Press.

Chardon, Roland, 1980a 'The Elusive Spanish League: A Problem of Measurement in Sixteenth-Century New Spain'. *Hispanic American Historical Review* 60:294–302.

Chardon, Roland, 1980b 'The Linear League in North America'. *Annals of the Association of American Geographers* 70:129–53.

Chardon, Roland, 1980c 'A Quantitative Determination of a Second Linear League Used in New Spain'. *Professional Geographer* 32:462–6.

Chaunu, Huguette, and Pierre Chaunu, 1955–59 *Séville et l'Atlantique (1504–1650)*. 8 vols, Paris.

Chaunu, Pierre, 1979 *European Expansion in the Later Middle Ages*. New York: North-Holland.

Chavero, Alfredo, 1964 'Lienzo de Tlaxcala'. *Artes de Mexico* 51/52.

Chevalier, Francois, 1970 *Land and Society in Colonial Mexico: The Great Hacienda*. Berkeley and Los Angeles: University of California Press.

Chiappelli, Fredi, ed., 1976 *First Images of America: The Impact of the New World on the Old.* 2 vols, Berkeley and Los Angeles: University of California Press.

Chimalpahin Cuauhtlehuanitzin, San Antón Muñón, 1965 *Relaciones originales de Chalco Amaquemecan.* Mexico City: Universidad Nacional Autónoma de México.

Cipolla, Carlo M., 1965 *Guns, Sails, and Empires: Technological Innovation and the Early Phases of European Expansion 1400–1700.* New York: Minerva Press.

Cipolla, Carlo M., ed., 1974 *The Fontana Economic History of Europe: Vol. 2. The Sixteenth and Seventeenth Centuries.* Glasgow: Collins/Fontana Books.

Códice Aubin, 1980 *Códice Aubin.* Mexico City: Editorial Innovación.

Códice Chimalpopoca, 1975 *Códice Chimalpopoca: Anales de Cuauhtitlan y Leyenda de los Soles.* Mexico City: Universidad Nacional Autónoma de México.

Códice Osuna, 1976 *Pintura del Gobernador, Alcaldes y Regidores de México: 'Códice Osuna'.* 2 vols, Madrid: Ministerio de Educación y Ciencia Dirección General de Archivos y Bibliotecas.

Collis, Maurice, 1972 *Cortés and Montezuma.* London: Faber & Faber.

Colón, Hernando, 1984 *Vida del Almirante Cristóbal Colón.* Mexico City: Fondo de Cultura Económica.

Conquistador Anónimo, 1941 *Relación de algunas cosas de la Nueva España.* Mexico City: Editorial América.

Conquistador Anónimo, 1963 'The Chronicle of the Anonymous Conquistador'. In De Fuentes 1963.

Contamine, Philippe, 1984 *War in the Middle Ages.* Oxford: Basil Blackwell.

Conway, G. R. G., 1953 *La Noche Triste. Documentos: Segura de la Frontera en Nueva España, año de MDXX.* Mexico City: Antiguo Librería Robredo de José Porrúa e hijos.

Cook, Sherburne F., and Woodrow Borah, 1971 *Essays in Population History: Mexico and the Caribbean. Volume One.* Berkeley and Los Angeles: University of California Press.

Cortés, Hernán, 1963 *Cartas y documentos.* Mexico City: Porrúa.

Cortés, Hernán, 1971 *Letters from Mexico.* Anthony Pagden, trans. New York: Grossman Publishers.

Crosby, Alfred W., Jr, 1973 *The Columbian Exchange: Biological and Cultural Consequences of 1492.* Westport, CT: Greenwood Press.

Cuevas, P. Mariano, 1975 *Documentos inéditos del siglo XVI para la historia de México.* Mexico City: Porrúa.

Davies, Nigel, 1974 *The Aztecs: A History.* New York: G. P. Putnam's Sons.

Davis, Tenney L., 1943 *The Chemistry of Powder and Explosives.* Los Angeles: Angriff Press.

De Fuentes, Patricia, ed., 1963 *The Conquistadors: First-Person Accounts of the Conquest of Mexico.* New York: Orion Press.

Demanda, 1971 'Demanda de Ceballos en nombre de Pánfilo de Narváez contra Hernando Cortés y sus compañeros'. In García Icazbalceta 1971.

Denevan, William M., ed., 1976a *The Native Population of the Americas in 1492.* Madison: University of Wisconsin Press.

Denevan, William M., 1976b 'Mexico: Introduction'. In Denevan 1976a.

Díaz, Juan, 1942 'Itinerario'. In Wagner 1942b.

Díaz, Juan, 1950 'Itinerario de Juan de Grijalva'. In Yáñez 1950.

Díaz del Castillo, Bernal, 1908–16 *The True History of the Conquest of New Spain.* Alfred Percival Maudslay, trans. 5 vols, London: Hakluyt Society.

Díaz del Castillo, Bernal, 1977 *Historia verdadera de la conquista de la Nueva España.* 2 vols, Mexico City: Porrúa.

Durán, Diego, 1964 *The Aztecs: The History of the Indies of New Spain.* Doris Heyden and Fernando Horcasitas, trans. New York: Orion Press.

Durán, Diego, 1967 *Historia de las Indias de Nueva España e islas de la Tierra Firme.* 2 vols, Mexico City: Porrúa.

Durán, Diego, 1971 *Book of the Gods and Rites and The Ancient Calendar.* Fernando Horcasitas and Doris Heyden, trans. Norman: University of Oklahoma Press.

Elliott, J. H., 1966 *Imperial Spain, 1469–1716.* New York: Mentor Books.

Elliott, J.H., 1984a 'Settlement in America'. In Bethell 1984a.

Elliott, J.H., 1984b 'The Spanish Conquest and settlement of America'. In Bethell 1984a.

Ennis, Arthur, 1977 'The Conflict between the Regular and Secular Clergy'. In Greenleaf 1977.

Fenner, F., D. A. Henderson, I. Arita, Z. Jezek, and I. D. Ladnyi, 1988 *Smallpox and its Eradication.* Geneva: World Health Organization.

Finer, Samuel E., 1975 'State- and Nation-Building in Europe: The Role of the Military'. In Tilly 1975.

Florescano, Enrique, 1965 'El abasto y la legislación de granos en el siglo XVI'. *Historia Mexicana* 14:567–630.

Foley, Vernard, George Palmer and Werner Soedel, 1985 'The Crossbow'. *Scientific American* 252:1:104–10.

García Icazbalceta, Joaquin, 1971 *Colección de documentos para la historica de México.* 2 vols, Mexico City: Porrúa.

García Pimental, Luis, 1897 *Descripción del arzobispado de México hecha en 1570 y otros documentos.* Mexico City: José Joaquin Terrazas.

Gardiner, C. Harvey, 1959 *Naval Power in the Conquest of Mexico.* Austin: University of Texas Press.

Gheyn, Jacob de, 1986 *The Exercise of Armes: A Seventeenth Century Military Manual.* David J. Blackmore, ed. London: Greenhill Books. Originally published 1607.

Gibson, Charles, 1964 *The Aztecs under Spanish Rule: A History of the Indians of the Valley of Mexico, 1519–1810.* Stanford, CA: Stanford University Press.

Gibson, Charles, 1966 *Spain in America.* New York: Harper Torchbooks.

Gibson, Charles, 1975 'Writings on Colonial Mexico'. *Hispanic American Historical Review* 55:287–323.

Gibson, Charles, 1984 'Indian Societies under Spanish Rule'. In Bethell 1984b.

Greenleaf, Richard E., 1969 *The Mexican Inquisition of the Sixteenth Century*. Albuquerque University of New Mexico Press.

Guthrie, Chester L., 1941 'A Seventeenth Century "Ever-Normal Granary"'. *Agricultural History* 15:37–43.

Hale, J. R., 1985 *War and Society in Renaissance Europe, 1450–1620*. New York: St Martin's Press.

Hamilton, Edward P., 1990 *Adventure in the Wilderness: The American Journals of Louis Antoine de Bougainville, 1756–1760*. Norman: University of Texas Press.

Hardoy, Jorge E., 1973 *Pre-Columbian Cities*. New York: Walker.

Haring, Clarence Henry, 1918 *Trade and Navigation between Spain and the Indies in the Time of the Hapsburgs*. Cambridge, MA: Harvard University Press.

Hassig, Ross, 1981 'The Famine of One Rabbit: Ecological Causes and Social Consequences of a Pre-Columbian Calamity'. *Journal of Anthropological Research* 37:171–81.

Hassig, Ross, 1985 *Trade, Tribute, and Transportation: The Sixteenth-Century Political Economy of the Valley of Mexico*. Norman: University of Oklahoma Press.

Hassig, Ross, 1988 *Aztec Warfare: Imperial Expansion and Political Control*. Norman: University of Oklahoma Press.

Hassig, Ross, 1992 *War and Society in Ancient Mesoamerica*. Berkeley and Los Angeles: University of California Press.

Hopkins, Donald R., 1983 *Princes and Peasants: Smallpox in History*. Chicago: University of Chicago Press.

Información, 1870–75 'Información recibida en Mexico y Puebla. El ano de 1565. A solicitud del gobernado y cabildo de naturales de Tlaxcala, sobre los servicios que prestaron los Tlaxcaltecas a Hernan Cortes en el conquista de Mexico, siendo los testigos algunas de los mismos conquistadores'. In Biblioteca 1870–75.

Innes, Hammond, 1969 *The Conquistadors*. New York: Alfred A. Knopf.

Ixtlilxochitl, Fernando de Alva, 1969 *Ally of Cortes: Account 13: Of the Coming of the Spaniards and the Beginning of the Evangelical Law*. Douglass K. Ballentine, trans. El Paso: Texas Western Press.

Ixtlilxochitl, Fernando de Alva, 1975–77 *Obras Completas*. 2 vols, Mexico City: Universidad Autónoma Nacional de México.

Johnson, William Weber, 1987 *Cortés: Conquering the New World*. New York: Paragon House.

Jones, Archer, 1987 *The Art of War in the Western World*. Urbana: University of Illinois Press.

Joralemon, Donald, 1982 'New World Population and the Case of Disease'. *Journal of Anthropological Research* 38:108–27.

Kirkpatrick, F. A., 1967 *The Spanish Conquistadores*. Cleveland, OH: Meridian Books.

Lea, Henry Charles, 1922 *The Inquisition in the Spanish Dependencies*. New York: Macmillan.

Lee, Raymond L., 1947 'Grain Legislation in Colonial Mexico, 1575–1585'. *Hispanic American Historical Review* 27:647–60.

Leon-Portilla, Miguel, 1966 *The Broken Spears: The Aztec Account of the Conquest of Mexico*. Boston, MA: Beacon Press.

Lockhart, James, 1972 *The Men of Cajamarca: A Social and Biographical Study of the First Conquerors of Peru*. Austin: University of Texas Press.

Lockhart, James and Stuart B. Schwartz, 1983 *Early Latin America: A History of Colonial Spanish America and Brazil*. New York: Cambridge University Press.

López de Gómara, Francisco, 1964 *Cortés: The Life of the Conqueror*. Lesley Byrd Simpson, trans. Berkeley and Los Angeles: University of California Press.

López de Gómara, Francisco 1965–66 *Historia general de las Indias*. 2 vols, Barcelona: Obras Maestras.

McHenry, J. Patrick, 1962 *A Short History of Mexico*. Garden City, NY: Doubleday.

MacKay, Angus, 1977 *Spain in the Middle Ages: From Frontier to Empire, 1000–1500*. New York: St Martin's Press.

MacLachlan, Colin M., 1988 *Spain's Empire in the New World: The Role of Ideas in Institutional and Social Change*. Berkeley and Los Angeles: University of California Press.

MacLachlan, Colin M., and Jaime E. Rodríguez O., 1980 *The Forging of the Cosmic Race*. Berkeley and Los Angeles: University of California Press.

McNeill, William H., 1977 *Plagues and Peoples*. Garden City, NY: Anchor Books.

Madariaga, Salvador de, 1969 *Hernán Cortés: Conqueror of Mexico*. Garden City, NY: Anchor Books.

Martínez, Rafael Bañón, and Thomas M. Barker, eds., 1988 *Armed Forces and Society in Spain Past and Present*. Boulder, CO: Social Science Monographs.

Martyr d'Anghera, Peter, 1970 *De Orbe Novo: The Eight Decades of Peter Martyr D'Anghera*. 2 vols, New York: Burt Franklin.

Matesanz, José, 1965 'Introducción de la ganadería en Nueva España 1521–1535'. *Historia Mexicana* 14:533–66.

Merriman, Roger Bigelow, 1962 *The Rise of the Spanish Empire in the Old World and in the New*. 4 vols, New York: Cooper Square.

Miller, Robert Ryal, 1985 *Mexico: A History*. Norman: University of Oklahoma Press.

Mols, Roger, 1974 'Population in Europe 1500–1700'. In Cipolla 1974.

Moreno Toscano, Alejandra, 1965 'Tres problemas en la geografía de maíz 1600–1624'. *Historia Mexicana* 14:631–55.

Moreno Toscano, Alejandra, 1981 'El Siglo de la conquista'. In *Historia General de México*. 2 vols, Mexico City: El Colegio de México.

Mörner, Magnus, 1976 'Spanish Migration to the New World prior to 1810: A Report on the State of Research'. In Chiappelli 1976, II.

Muñoz Camargo, Diego, 1966 *Historia de Tlaxcala*. Guadalajara: Edmundo Aviña Levy.

Muñoz Camargo, Diego, 1981 *Descripción de la ciudad y provincia de Tlaxcala de las Indias y del mar océano para el buen gobierno y ennoblecimiento dellas*. Mexico City: Universidad Nacional Autónoma de México.

Muñoz Camargo, Diego, 1984 'Descripción de la ciudad y provincia de Tlaxcala'. In Acuña 1982–87.

Myers, Henry A., 1982 *Medieval Kingship*. Chicago: Nelson-Hall.

O'Callaghan, Joseph F., 1975 *A History of Medieval Spain*. Ithaca, NY: Cornell University Press.

Offner, Jerome A., 1983 *Law and Politics in Aztec Texcoco*. Cambridge: Cambridge University Press.

Oviedo y Valdés, Gonzalo Fernández de, 1942 'Fernández de Oviedo's Account'. In Wagner 1942b.

Oviedo y Valdés, Gonzalo Fernández de, 1959 *Historia general y natural de las Indias*. 5 vols, Madrid: Ediciones Atlas.

Padden, R. C., 1967 *The Hummingbird and the Hawk: Conquest and Sovereignty in the Valley of Mexico, 1503–1541*. New York: Harper Colophon Books.

Pagden, Anthony, 1990 *Spanish Imperialism and the Political Imagination: Studies in European and Spanish-American Social and Political Theory 1513–1830*. New Haven, CT: Yale University Press.

Parkes, Henry Bamford, 1969 *A History of Mexico*. Boston MA: Houghton Mifflin.

Parry, J.H., 1966 *The Spanish Seaborne Empire*. New York: Alfred A. Knopf.

Parry, J.H., 1981a *The Age of Reconnaissance*. Berkeley and Los Angeles: University of California Press.

Parry, J.H., 1981b *The Discovery of the Sea*. Berkeley and Los Angeles: University of California Press.

Parry, J. H., and P. M. Sherlock, 1971 *A Short History of the West Indies*. New York: St Martin's Press.

Payne-Gallwey, Ralph, 1986 *The Crossbow: Mediaeval and Modern, Military and Sporting; Its Construction, History and Management*. London: Holland Press.

Pope, Dudley, 1965 *Guns: From the Invention of Gunpowder to the 20th Century*. New York: Delacorte Press.

Pope, Saxton T., 1923 'A Study of Bows and Arrows'. *University of California Publications in American Archaeology and Ethnology* 13:9:329–414.

Powers, James F., 1988 *A Society Organized for War: The Iberian*

Municipal Militias in the Central Middle Ages, 1000–1284. Berkeley and Los Angeles: University of California Press.

Quatrefages, René, 1988 'The Military System of the Spanish Hapsburgs'. In Martínez and Barker 1988.

Ramsey, John Fraser, 1973 *Spain: The Rise of the First World Power*. University: University of Alabama Press.

Recopilación, 1973 *Recopilación de leyes de los reynos de las Indias*. 4 vols, Madrid: Ediciones Cultura Hispánica.

Rees, Peter William, 1971 'Route Inertia and Route Competition: An Historical Geography of Transportation between Mexico City and Vera Cruz'. Ph.D. diss., University of California – Berkeley.

Ricketts, Thomas Francis, and John Beuzeville Byles, 1966 *The Diagnosis of Smallpox*. 2 vols, Washington, DC: US Department of Health, Education, and Welfare, Public Health Service [Reprint of 1908 London edition].

Rodgers, William Ledyard, 1939 *Naval Warfare under Oars, 4th to 16th Centuries: A Study of Strategy, Tactics and Ship Design*. Annapolis, MD: United States Naval Institute.

Rosenblat, Angel, 1954 *La Población Indígena y el Mestizaje en América*. 2 vols, Buenos Aires: Editorial Nova.

Rosenblat, Angel, 1976 'The Population of Hispaniola at the Time of Columbus'. In Denevan 1976a.

Rowdon, Maurice, 1974 *The Spanish Terror: Spanish Imperialism in the Sixteenth Century*. London: Constable.

Ruiz de Alarcón, Hernando, 1984 *Treatise on the Heathen Superstitions and Customs that Today Live among the Indians Native to this New Spain 1629*. Translated and edited by J. Richard Andrews and Ross Hassig. Norman: University of Oklahoma Press.

Sahagún, Bernardino de, 1975 *Florentine Codex: General History of the Things of New Spain. Book 12 – The Conquest of Mexico*. Salt Lake City: University of Utah Press.

Sahagún, Bernardino de, 1978 *The War of Conquest: How it was Waged Here in Mexico: The Aztecs' Own Story*. Salt Lake City: University of Utah Press.

Sahagún, Bernardino de, 1981 *Florentine Codex: General History of the Things of New Spain. Book 2 – The Ceremonies*. Salt Lake City: University of Utah Press.

Sahagún, Bernardino de, 1989 *Conquest of New Spain: 1585 Revision*. Salt Lake City: University of Utah Press.

Salas, Alberto Mario, 1950 *Las Armas de la Conquista*. Buenos Aires: Emecé Editores.

Sanders, William T., 1970 'The Population of the Teotihuacan Valley, the Basin of Mexico and the Central Mexican Symbiotic Region in the Sixteenth Century'. In Sanders, Kovar, Charlton and Diehl 1970.

Sanders, William T., Anton Kovar, Thomas Charlton, and Richard A. Diehl, 1970 *The Natural Environment, Contemporary Occupation and 16th Century Population of the Valley. The Teotihuacan Valley Project*.

Final Report. Vol. 1. Occasional Papers in Anthropology, no. 3. Department of Anthropology, Pennsylvania State University.

Sanders, William T., Jeffrey R. Parsons and Robert S. Santley, 1979 *The Basin of Mexico: Ecological Processes in the Evolution of a Civilization.* New York: Academic Press.

Sauer, Carl Ortwin, 1966 *The Early Spanish Main.* Berkeley and Los Angeles: University of California Press.

Schaedel, Richard P., Jorge E. Hardoy and Nora Scott Kinzer, eds, 1978 *Urbanization in the Americas from its Beginnings to the Present.* The Hague: Mouton Publishers.

Schwaller, John Frederick, 1978 'The Secular Clergy in Sixteenth-Century Mexico'. Ph.D. diss., Indiana University.

Stone, George Cameron, 1961 *A Glossary of the Construction, Decoration and Use of Arms and Armor in All Countries and in All Times.* New York: Jack Brussel.

Tapia, Andrés de, 1950 'Relación de Andrés de Tapia'. In Yáñez 1950.

Tapia, Andrés de, 1963 'The Chronicle of Andrés de Tapia'. In De Fuentes 1963.

Tarassuk, Leonid, and Claude Blair, 1982 *The Complete Encyclopedia of Arms and Weapons.* New York: Simon & Schuster.

TePaske, John J., and Herbert S. Klein, 1981 The 'Seventeenth-Century Crisis in New Spain: Myth or Reality?' *Past and Present* 90:116–35.

Tilly, Charles, ed., 1975 *The Formation of National States in Western Europe.* Princeton, NJ: Princeton University Press.

Todorov, Tzvetan, 1984 *The Conquest of America: The Question of the Other.* New York: Harper & Row.

Vaillant, George C., 1966 *Aztecs of Mexico: Origin, Rise, and Fall of the Aztec Nation.* Baltimore, MD: Penguin.

Vigon, Jorge, 1947 *Historia de la artillería Española*, vol. 1. Madrid: Instituto Jeronimo Zurita.

Wagner, Henry R., 1942a *The Discovery of Yucatan by Francisco Hernández de Córdoba.* Berkeley, CA: Cortes Society.

Wagner, Henry R., ed., 1942b *The Discovery of New Spain in 1518 by Juan de Grijalva.* Berkeley, CA: Cortes Society.

Wagner, Henry R., 1944 *The Rise of Fernando Cortés.* Berkeley, CA: Cortes Society.

Wasserstrom, Robert, 1983 *Class and Society in Central Chiapas.* Berkeley and Los Angeles: University of California Press.

White, Jon Manchip, 1971 *Cortés and the Downfall of the Aztec Empire.* New York: St Martin's Press.

Wilson, Samuel M., 1990 *Hispaniola: Caribbean Chiefdoms in the Age of Columbus.* Tuscaloosa: University of Alabama Press.

Wolf, Eric R., ed., 1970 *Sons of the Shaking Earth.* Chicago: University of Chicago Press.

Wolf, Eric R., ed., 1976 *The Valley of Mexico*. Albuquerque: University of New Mexico Press.

Wright, L. P., 1969 'The Military Orders in Sixteenth and Seventeenth Century Spanish Society: The Institutional Embodiment of a Historical Tradition'. *Past and Present* 43:34–70.

Yáñez, Agustín, ed., 1950 *Crónicas de la conquista de México*. Mexico City: Ediciones de la Universidad Nacional Autónoma.

Zambardino, Rudolph A., 1980 'Mexico's Population in the Sixteenth Century: Demographic Anomaly or Mathematical Illusion?' *Journal of Interdisciplinary History* 11:1–27.

MAPS

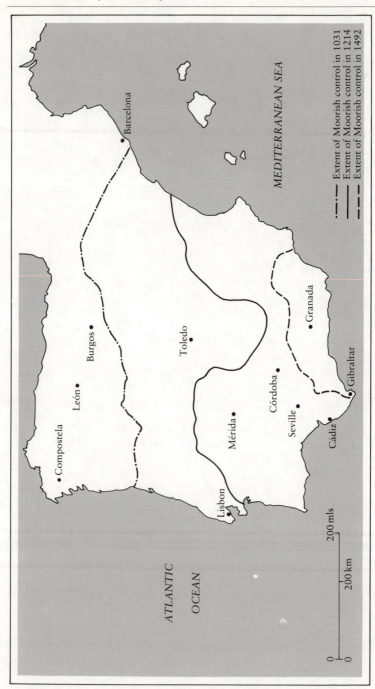

1. Spain and the *Reconquista*

ATLANTIC OCEAN

MEDITERRANEAN SEA

Compostela

León

Burgos

Barcelona

Toledo

Mérida

Córdoba

Seville

Lisbon

Granada

Gibraltar

Cádiz

Extent of Moorish control in 1031
Extent of Moorish control in 1214
Extent of Moorish control in 1492

0

0

200 mls

200 km

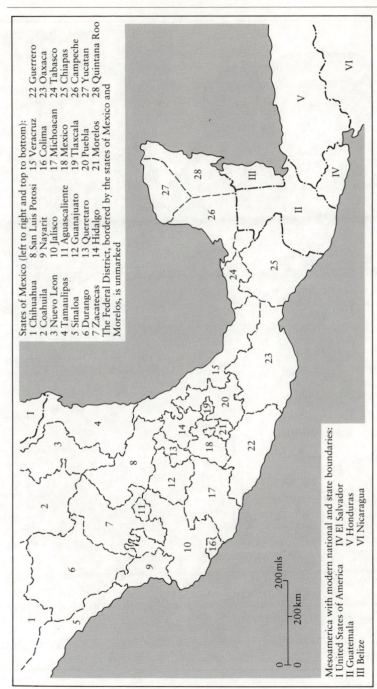

States of Mexico (left to right and top to bottom):
1 Chihuahua	8 San Luis Potosi	15 Veracruz	22 Guerrero
2 Coahuila	9 Nayarit	16 Colima	23 Oaxaca
3 Nuevo Leon	10 Jalisco	17 Michoacan	24 Tabasco
4 Tamaulipas	11 Aguascaliente	18 Mexico	25 Chiapas
5 Sinaloa	12 Guanajuato	19 Tlaxcala	26 Campeche
6 Durango	13 Queretaro	20 Puebla	27 Yucatan
7 Zacatecas	14 Hidalgo	21 Morelos	28 Quintana Roo

The Federal District, bordered by the states of Mexico and Morelos, is unmarked

Mesoamerica with modern national and state boundaries:
I United States of America	IV El Salvador
II Guatemala	V Honduras
III Belize	VI Nicaragua

200mls
200km

2. Mesoamerica with modern state boundaries   (After Hassig; 1992)

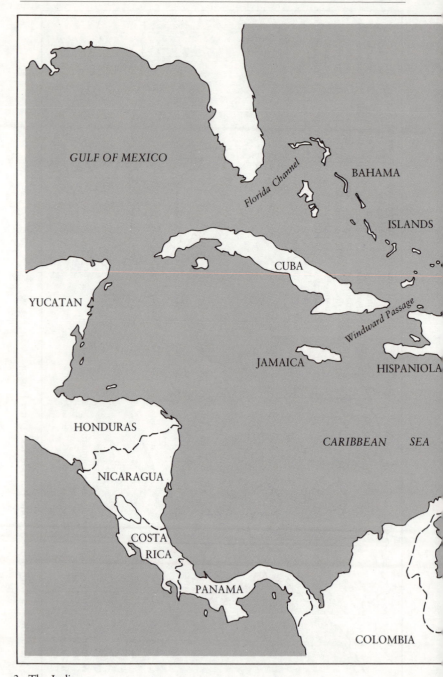

3. The Indies

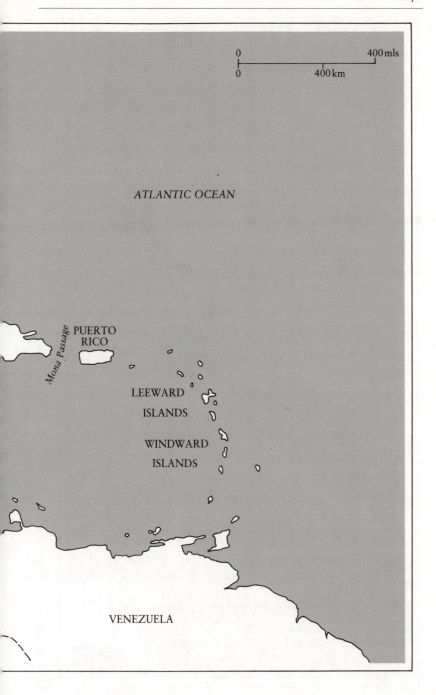

ATLANTIC OCEAN

Mona Passage

PUERTO
RICO

LEEWARD
ISLANDS

WINDWARD
ISLANDS

VENEZUELA

0
0

400 mls
400 km

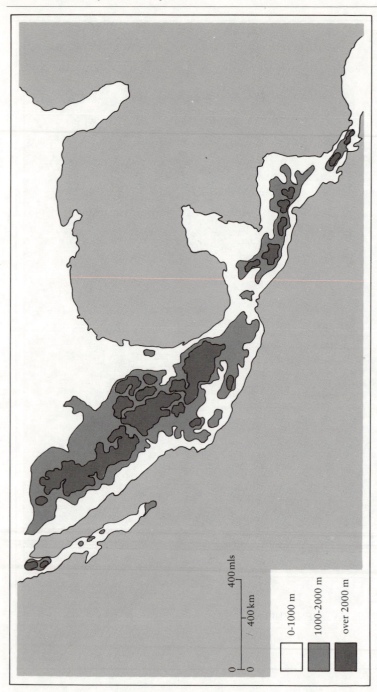

4. Mesoamerica, showing the major altitude divisions (After Hassig; 1992)

400 mls

400 km

0-1000 m

1000-2000 m

over 2000 m

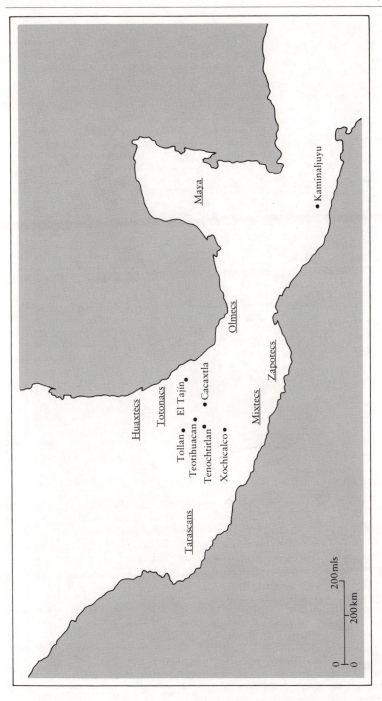

5. Precolumbian Mesoamerica

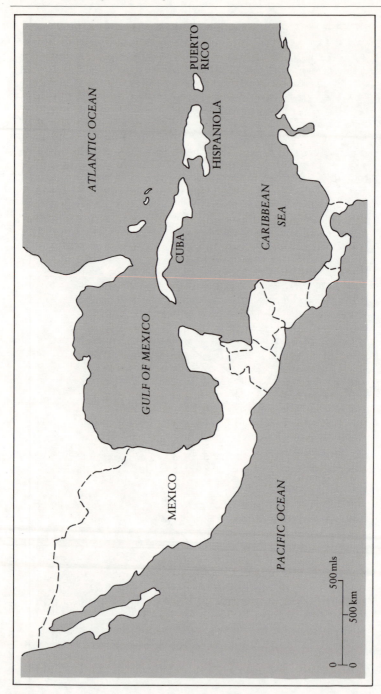

6. The Indies, the Caribbean and the coast of Mexico

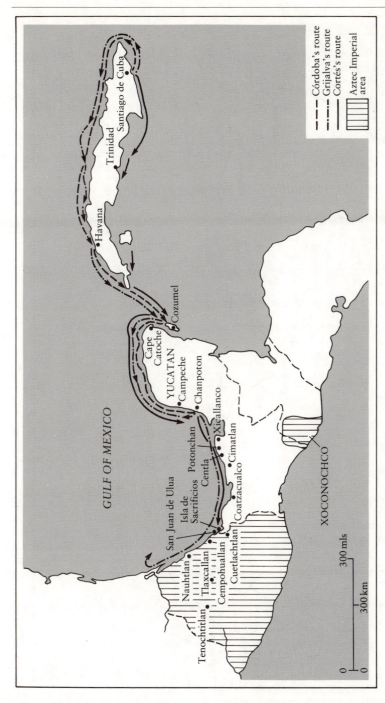

7. Yucatan and the Gulf coast of Mexico, showing Córdoba's, Grijalva's and Cortés's journeys

189

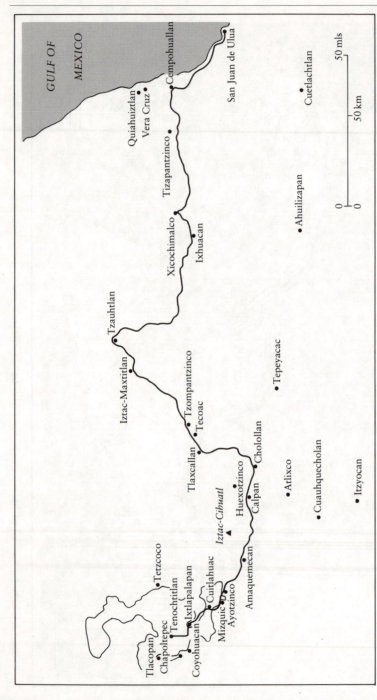

8. Cortés's route from Vera Cruz to Tenochtitlan

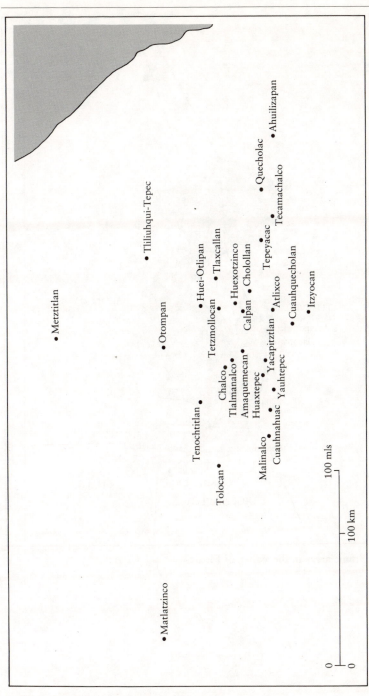

9. Central Mexico

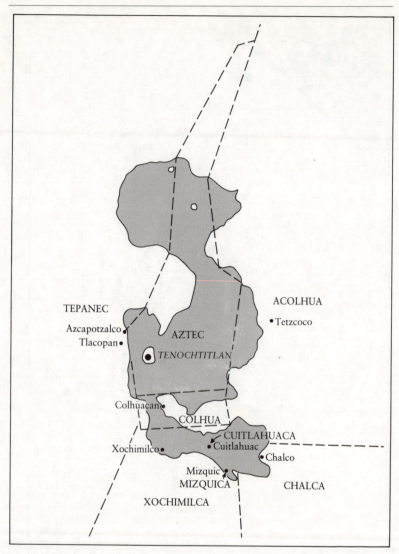

10. Ethnic areas in the Valley of Mexico

11. The Valley of Mexico

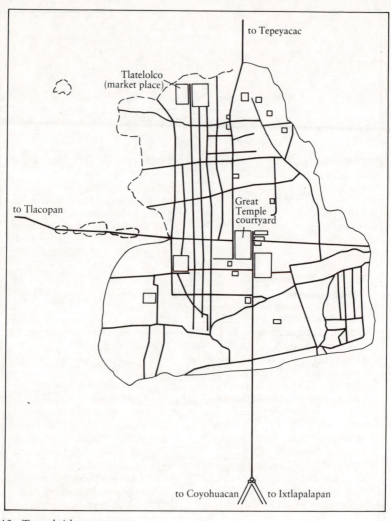

to Tepeyacac

Tlatelolco
(market place)

to Tlacopan

Great
Temple
courtyard

to Coyohuacan   to Ixtlapalapan

12. Tenochtitlan

INDEX

captives, Spanish, 48, 135
caravels, 41, 166
Caribbean: area, 47; exploration
of, 13, 46; Indians, 9, 37; sea,
12, 46; trade, 12
Caribs, 10–11
Castile, 6, 10, 46
casualties: Aztec, 140, 143; Maya,
38, 51; ratio, 134; Spaniards,
37, 40, 50–1, 65, 67–9, 71, 87,
96, 100, 103, 118, 131, 134–5;
Tlaxcaltec, 65, 71
catapult, 140
causeways: battles on, 117, 126–7,
131–4, 137; breached, 128–9,
132, 138; bridges over, 93, 95;
Coyohuacan, 95, 128–9;
Cuitlahuac, 82; destroyed, 128;
for supplies, 123; horses on,
127, 132, 139; Mexicatzinco,
128; Ixtlapalapan, 82, 95,
128–9; repaired, 132; Spanish
allies ordered off, 133–4;
Tenochtitlan, 83, 87, 123;
Tepeyacac, 95, 129; Tlacopan,
95, 126; Tlatelolco, 139;
Xaltocan, 116–17
cavalry: in Europe, 7–9; Spaniards,
50, 58, 72, 97–8, 117, 132–3,
139
Cempohuallan (Zempoala), 60, 61;
Cortés at, 57; ruler of, 57–8,
60–1; *see also* Cempohualtecs;
Totonacs
Cempohualtecs, 58, 64, 79; allied
with Cortés, 60, 144;
messengers, 64, 71; *see also*
Cempohuallan; Totonacs
cenotes, 39
Centla (Cintla), 50
Chalca: cities, 76, 82, 83; allied
with Cortés, 96, 113–15; area,
115–16; canoe attack on, 118;
threatened by Aztecs, 118;
people, 86
Chalco, 81; allied with Cortés, 122,
136; Aztec attacks, 115; Aztec
conquest of, 124; defence of,
115; king of, 115; Sandoval at,
115, 118

Chanpoton: Córdoba at, 40;
Cortés at, 48; Grijalva at, 43–4
Chapoltepec (Chapultepec), 123;
aqueduct from, 126, 130
Chardon, Roland, 55 n.6
Charles V, 55, 62, 161
chiefdom, 9
Chimalhuacan, 81, 118
Chimalpopoca, 21, 162
chinampas, 124–5, 166
Cholollan (Cholula), 64, 78–81,
84; allied with Aztecs, 78, 80–1,
100; allied with Cortés, 122,
136; allied with Tlaxcallan, 34,
78, 80–1; as Tlaxcaltec
tributary, 100, 149; factions, 81;
king killed, 80–1; road through,
81, 105; Tlaxcaltec hostility
towards, 78–80
Chololtecs, 78
Cimatlan, 41
cities: abandoned, 117; economic
systems, 125; in New World, 36
Citlaltepec, 97
clubs, 15–16, 37; *see also* maces
Coanacoch, 111–12, 162;
captured, 139
Coatepec, 111
Coatzacualco (Coatzacoalcos), 43
Cocozca, 89, 162
Colhuacan (Culhuacan), 132, 134
colonies: Caribbean, 12–13;
Mexico, 149–50; New World,
11, 13; Spain, 6; Teotihuacan,
17–18; Toltec, 20
Columbus, Christopher, 10–12, 37,
162
combat range, 16, 24
Compostela, 5
conquest, legal justification, 10, 36
Cook, Sherburne, 11 n.14, 152 n.4
Córdoba, 6
Córdoba, Francisco Hernández de,
36–41, 43, 162
Cortés, Hernan, 162; account, 138
n.27; Amaquemecan, 81; and
political intrigue in Cuba, 45;
alliances, 103; appointed leader
by Vera Cruz city council, 55–6;
appointed leader by Velásquez,

governor: Aztec, 22, 53, 82; Indian
colonial, 152
Granada, 6
Grijalva, Juan de, 41–4, 48, 53,
163; dressed by Indians, 43, 43
n.18
Grijalva River, 43, 48
Guatemala, 14, 17, 20
Guatemala City, 17
Guerrero, Gonzalo, 48, 163
gunpowder: composition, 65;
exhausted, 79, 95, 138, 140;
low, 140; resupplied, 103, 109,
138; ruined, 113
guns, 36; effectiveness, 133; in
Europe, 8; *see also* harquebus;
matchlock; musket

Haiti, 10, 11 n.14
harquebus, 8, 145, 166; against
barricades, 127; captured and
destroyed, 140; effectiveness,
37–8, 52, 65, 72, 98, 126;
length of use, 38; number, 47,
92, 111, 122; range, 38, 68, 98;
rate of fire, 38, 42, 69;
reloading, 38 n.6, 67; resupply,
110; ships, 122; size, 38; *see also*
guns; matchlock; musket
harquebusiers, 8–9, 60, 100, 166
Hassig, Ross, 14 n.1, 15, 15 n.2
Havana, 12; Cortés sailed for, 46
hegemonic empire, 22–3, 33, 54,
76, 148; *see also* empires
helmets: Aztec, 25; Spanish, 53
hidalgo, 46, 166
Hispaniola, 10–13
Holguín, García, 142, 163
Honduras, 10, 14
horses: and lances, 50–1;
armoured, 98; as domesticated
animals, 155; Aztecs adapt to,
133, 139; brought from Cuba,
46–7; eaten, 97; effectiveness,
50–1, 98, 115, 120; in
Tenochtitlan, 139; landed in
Mexico, 49; neutralized, 109,
116–17, 127, 132–3, 139;
numbers, 47, 49, 58, 60, 62,
67–9, 71, 90, 92, 100, 105–6,

109–11, 122, 143; on
causeways, 127, 132; shipped,
47; speed, 50, 71; with lancers,
50; wounded or killed, 65, 67–9,
71, 96, 99, 135
Huaxtec area, 20
Huaxtecs, 33
Huaxtepec, 118
Huei-Otlipan (Hueyotlipan),
99–100
Huexotzinco (Huejotzingo), 72, 78,
81; allied to Tlaxcallan, 34, 71,
78, 96; as Tlaxcaltec tributary,
100, 149; dissension, 71; rulers
of, 100, 105; Spanish allies, 122,
136; suspect loyalties, 100, 105;
ties to Chalco, 82, 118
Huitzilihuitl, 163
Huitzilopochco, 134
Huitzilopochtli, 91, 136, 141 n.35

Iberia, 5–7
idols: destroyed, 61
Indies: colonization, 11–12; crops,
11; depopulation, 12; indigenous
economic organization, 11;
population, 10, 11 n.14;
precontact history, 10–11;
precontact political organization,
11, 11 n.14; Spanish population,
12–13; war, 9
infantry: and horses, 71; in Europe,
7–9; Spaniards, 50
inquisition, 150–1
intelligence: Aztec, 53, 63; Spanish,
115
Isla de Sacrificios, 43
Itzcoatl, 21–2, 163
Itzyocan (Izucar), 105–6
Ixhuacan, 64
Ixtlilxochitl, 163; captured
Coanacoch, 139; contender for
throne, 111–12; Spanish ally,
112, 136, 140
Ixtlilxochitl, Fernando de Alva, 138
n.27
Ixtlapalapan (Ixtapalapa), 113;
Cortés at, 82, 113–14, 114 n.8;
conspired against Aztecs, 89;
flooded, 113; king of, 94; razed,